Drama and Education

Drama and Education provides a practical, comprehensive guide to drama as a tool for teaching and learning. It is among the first practical drama and performance textbooks that address brain-based, neuroscientific research, making the argument that creativity is necessary in our lives, that embodied learning is natural and essential, and that contextual learning helps us find our place in society in relationship to other peoples and cultures. As well as a historical and theoretical overview of the field, it provides rationale and techniques for several specific methodologies: linear drama, process-oriented drama, drama for social justice, and performance art.

Each approach is supplemented with sample lesson plans, activities, ideas for differentiation, and extensive bibliographies. The topics are discussed from five key angles:

- Historical and theoretical foundations
- Curricular applications
- Practical toolkits for a range of classrooms and learning environments
- Different strategies for lesson plans
- Extension options for longer workshops.

Alongside these core methods, the integration of other innovative forms—from performance art to Theatre of the Oppressed—into drama-based learning is explored, as well as the pragmatic concerns such as assessment, planning, and advocacy for arts learning and arts education partnerships. *Drama and Education* is the comprehensive textbook for teachers and students on Applied Theatre and Theatre and Education courses.

Manon van de Water is the Vilas-Phipps Distinguished Achievement Professor at the University of Wisconsin-Madison.

Mary McAvoy is an Assistant Professor of Theatre Education and Theatre for Youth at Arizona State University.

Kristin Hunt is an Assistant Professor of Applied Theatre at Northeastern Illinois University's Department of Communication, Media and Theatre.

Drama and Education
Performance Methodologies for Teaching and Learning

Manon van de Water, Mary McAvoy, Kristin Hunt

Routledge
Taylor & Francis Group

LONDON AND NEW YORK

First published 2015
by Routledge
2 Park Square, Milton Park, Abingdon, Oxon OX14 4RN

and by Routledge
711 Third Avenue, New York, NY 10017

Routledge is an imprint of the Taylor & Francis Group, an informa business

British Library Cataloguing-in-Publication Data
A catalogue record for this book is available from the British Library

Library of Congress Cataloguing-in-Publication Data
Hunt, Kristin.
Drama and education : performance methodologies for teaching and
learning / Kristin Hunt, Mary McAvoy, and Manon van de Water.
pages cm
Includes bibliographical references.
1. Drama and education. I. McAvoy, Mary. II. Water, Manon van
de. III. Title.
PN3171.H66 2015
371.39'9--dc23
2014033802

ISBN: 978-1-138-79950-9 (hbk)
ISBN: 978-1-138-79951-6 (pbk)
ISBN: 978-1-315-75602-8 (ebk)

Typeset in Sabon
by Saxon Graphics Ltd, Derby

Contents

Acknowledgements

This textbook has been in the making for over fifteen years, starting with a draft of the first chapter connecting drama with neuroscientific research based on the data available then. Over the years we have compiled readers drawn from different textbooks and other materials to offer our students a comprehensive course in drama for teaching and learning. Therefore we first and foremost must acknowledge all the drama and performance artists cited in this book, as they have inspired our teaching and research again and again.

We also acknowledge the many teaching assistants for the drama in education course at the University of Wisconsin-Madison, who helped both to shape our understanding of the field and the choice of material that eventually made it in this book: Dixie Beadle, Jessica Berson, Kelly Bremner, Erin Briddick, James Burling, Tracy Burrill, Jennifer Chapman, Heidi Cooper, Steve Feffer, Liz Foster-Shaner, Takeo Fujikura, Jessica Gaspar, Annie Giannini, Katie Gletty-Syoen, Scott Harman, Andrea Harris, Lindsey Hoel-Neds, Erin Hood, Erika Hughes, Lisa Leibering, Megan Marsh-McGlone, Monty Marsh-McGlone, Allison Metz, Joohee Park, Victoria Pettersen-Lanz, Cassandra Proball, Bala Rajasekharuni, Pete Rydberg, Megwyn Sanders-Andrews, Jacqui Scott, Michelle Solberg, Anne Swedberg, Angie Sweigart-Gallagher, Nick Tamarkin, Patrick Tuite, Julie Vogt, Andy Wiginton, and Stepheni Woods.

We thank our students and colleagues at the University of Wisconsin-Madison, Northeastern Illinois University, and Arizona State University for supporting our work.

Lastly we thank Ben Piggott at Routledge for his support and encouragement.

Foreword

Xan Johnson

Drama and Education: Performance methodologies for teaching and learning is an excellent and unrivalled new text packed with twenty-first century *insights* and *incites* that are user friendly. It has been written as a required course text and can be easily adapted as such. The first chapter connects drama with the most up-to-date research on the value of embodied and contextual learning, followed by three practical chapters on linear drama, process-oriented methods, drama for social justice, and performance art methodologies for teaching and learning, and the book ends with two unique chapters on assessment and advocacy. The premise of the book is that to act is to learn and to perform is to teach and that the cultures we live in are innately dramatic.

Those using drama as a tool for teaching and learning bring heightened expertise to the role of teacher. Critically beneficial to drama as a learning medium is the built-in development of metacognitive learning skills. Through drama in educational contexts, both teachers and learners practice, make choices, enact innovative strategies, and imagine new possibilities. Thinking about how one acts and performs to improve one's understanding of human intention and interaction in all its complexity is what actors do and how drama-wise teachers teach.

To this day, many people harbor doubt about the connection between drama and learning. What does this "as if" pretend world of drama really have to do with hardcore cognition? What do acting and performing really have to do with academic achievement? Why study people in a place with a problem to solve as a way to learn? Even more, many educators believe that learners must have isolated focus, silence, and extended concentration time to think and reflect at high cognitive levels. Maybe it is time for some new thinking. Brain researcher Uri Hasson believes that "Cognition materializes in an *interpersonal* space." This quote suggests that many kinds of learning occur in our moments of connection with others. Brains literally attune to each other when students learn through engagement. We are wired to learn and survive by connecting and empathizing with others—we are driven to belong.

As social learners, we learn even more when our bodies and minds work together and with other bodies and minds. This mind-body connection, or *embodied learning*, not only supports empathy, belonging, and collective experience, but it also helps us to understand more fully how drama teaches and why we should value drama-based pedagogy as part of educational praxis in our lives—both in the classroom and beyond.

What Manon, Kristin, and Mary do that is so critically important is "make a case" for drama as an essential tool for teaching and learning by interweaving drama with the emerging research and theory coming out of Social Cognitive Neuroscience. What instantly becomes clear is that education should not be about curriculum border wars over content areas and rigid test initiatives—STEM vs. STEAM, etc. Many brain scientists would suggest curriculum and its combative territorialism has little to do with the purpose of education. Rather, curriculum should be considered a critically rich opportunity for students to explore and experience learning at the intersections of self, community, and culture as a whole—to be free to figure out who they need to become and how to belong.

Brain researchers Antonio Damasio and Mary Helen Immordino-Yang boldly move the paradigm for change in education forward when they state on behalf of Social Cognitive Neuroscience, "the *purpose of education* is to increase children's abilities to recognize the complexities of situations, and to help them develop increasingly nuanced and sophisticated strategies for acting and responding." The new paradigm for drama as a teaching strategy presented in this text fully embraces this neuroscientific point of view. The offerings presented herein are accessible to every teacher, school counselor, parent, applied theatre specialist, theatre education director, recreation professional, Theatre for Young Audiences artist, and pre-K-12 student. How to teach in the New Millennium has arrived, and not a quantum second too soon—it's dramatic and it's fun!

Introduction

Creativity is not an option, it is an absolute necessity.

Sir Ken Robinson (2012)

Creativity is a hot-button issue in contemporary United States (US) education. In the past decade articles, studies, TED talks, and initiatives focused on creativity in the classroom have proliferated (see Pappano 2014; Csikszentmihalyi 1997, 2009; Robinson 2006, 2012). Increasingly, this shifting rhetoric about creative skills occurs alongside discussions of twenty-first century learning, the Common Core standards, innovative thinking, accountability, and other new trends in education. The need for conceiving of new ways to teach and new ways to reach broader populations of students and teachers becomes more salient in light of ever-increasing challenges associated with education funding, particularly in the arts, both in schools and through not-for-profit arts and community institutions. Traditional classroom settings are just one of many possible locations for learning and teaching in the contemporary era. Accordingly, we, as teachers, artists, and scholars interested in drama-based education, created this textbook, a practical guide for integrating drama-based methods into educational settings, in response to ways in which learning and teaching occurs in the twenty-first century.

In this book, we present a diverse sampling of activities that are adaptable for the classroom and beyond. While there are many practical books on drama methods and numerous sources with dramatic exercises available to teachers and teaching artists, we aim to bring these methods into conversation with neurological research, new trends in education, and new paradigms for arts education initiatives. The book is primarily intended for a broad undergraduate population, including students who intend to become professional educators, students who are interested in using drama in recreational settings, students who would like to work with education programs at professional theatres, and students who simply love improvisation, play, young people, and theatre. While we intend for teachers to find relevancy in this book, we also believe that community arts partners, independent teaching artists, theatre companies with education departments, and community groups interested in developing drama-based programs for their specific targeted populations will find it a useful resource as well.

Our text takes into account the aforementioned trends and offers both foundational and innovative approaches for using drama in learning environments. We maintain a focus on practicality while extending and expanding conversations about how, why, and where learning and teaching through performative modes happens. We also include compelling new research about drama's impact on empathic and emotional intelligence and the cognitive dimension of arts-based learning, both of which provide new incentive for examining drama and performance-based learning and teaching in a contemporary context. By discussing both the foundations of the field and the new directions enabled by innovative approaches in the twenty-first century, we provide models for designing drama experiences with diverse populations, subject areas, and drama methodologies. We also connect theories of teaching and learning with practical considerations regarding curriculum, time management, advocacy, and assessment along the way. Given this eye toward practicality, each chapter focuses on resources for teachers, teaching artists, and community organizations, including detailed lesson plans, practical tips, comprehensive descriptions of activities, and planning guides.

Chapters in this book can be used consecutively or in any order, although we designed the sequence deliberately to serve the needs of a variety of facilitators, from artists who hope to teach through drama to teachers who hope to include drama methods in their curricula. Each chapter examines drama methodologies as they relate to education in classrooms and community contexts. Since we firmly believe that research informs practice and vice-versa, we include both hands-on activities and discussion of historical and theoretical works that form the underpinnings of drama, education, and performance as methods for teaching and learning.

Definitions

One important element that sets off drama and informal performance from formal theatre is its vocabulary. Therefore, we encourage you to take note of important distinctions between formal theatre and informal drama. We will use terms associated with drama practice throughout this book.

Another important distinction is that, unlike drama, which is open to all learners, theatre is generally thought of as the prerogative for selected, talented individuals (think of the amount of people who claim "I can't act/draw/write plays"). While we do not necessarily agree with this sentiment as it applies to theatre, we certainly recognize that many people reading this text might believe they do not have the innate ability to take on a drama role or to effectively facilitate the kinds of work described throughout this book. However, we encourage you to think about these methods with a more

Table 0.1

Theatre	Drama
Actors	Participants
Director	Leader/Facilitator
Set	Environment
Rehearse	Practice
Play/Production	Scenes/Scenarios/Situations
Perform	Share
Audience	Observers
Critique	Reflect/Evaluate

open-minded and generous point of view. Drama is for everyone. It relies on universal human skills that we use every day, such as communication, empathy, observation, and improvisation. It is not concerned with creating a polished performance, but with the development of emotional, embodied and cognitive knowledge built on experience. It is also about personal interactions with the environment in specific contexts. We have all used drama methods to learn about and define our specific places in the world. Thus, "talent" is not necessary; you, by virtue of your humanity, are already prepared to do drama. It also bears mentioning that, while drama-based methods as described in this book appeal to many teachers and students, not everyone needs to *like* drama, just as we do not teach math, or any subject for that matter, only to those who like it.

Practicalities

The following chapters will include historical and theoretical information about the field along with lesson plans and specific activities. It is important to note that we, the book's authors, devised these lesson plans for various populations with whom we work. These lessons and activities can be taken as inspiration, just as we devised ours after being inspired by our teachers and mentors, but we encourage readers to adapt them both to personal strengths and to populations with whom you work. We also encourage readers to try out these techniques early and often. Drama is active learning, and it must be practiced alongside reading texts, reviewing lesson plans, or even observing drama sessions. We learn through doing, exploring, and trying out, and by interacting with our peers and our environment. The act of doing is what makes us lifelong learners. Accordingly, we encourage you to take the activities and lessons described within this book and make them your own. Re-imagine them, change them, practice them, and repeat them. Use them to invent new activities or try out twists on existing techniques. Target them to the age group, population, and ability that *you* want to teach. The possibilities are endless if you approach this text as a malleable resource and believe in yourself and the power of your and your students' creativity and imagination.

Lesson planning and practical tips

Throughout this book we include sample lesson plans in different formats from which you may take inspiration. You can also use this format to create your own plans using activities and strategies described in subsequent chapters. Generally, we use written lesson plans not only to prepare our work, but also to keep track of our choices in prior lessons so we can revise and repeat them later. Lesson plans typically include goals (what we hope to accomplish or hope students learn in a lesson), procedures (specific activities), and a reflection or assessment (evaluating what participants learned during the lesson). See Chapter 5 (on assessment) for a more detailed discussion of lesson planning.

We generally work in an open space without much furniture. Chairs are not necessary. Neither are props, costumes, a stage, or scenic elements. Reflections, storytelling, and other down time can take place while sitting, mostly in a circle, on the floor. In part this design is simply practical, but it also allows for creating a safe and equal environment in which all leaders and participants work together.

Doing drama can feel like organized chaos. If you want to free up participants' creativity and encourage embodied learning, you must create room for sound and movement. However, there are moments when you need quiet and attention from participants. We often use an attention-getter that is built into the drama lessons: a sound like a tambourine or a horn, flashing the lights, freezing on the spot, a call-and-response exchange (Teacher: "*One, Two!*" Participants: "*Three, Four, Freeze!*"), or even a gesture (raising hands) or pose (Teacher: "*Freeze like a popsicle!*") are all potential attention-getters. Depending on your comfort level and classroom management style, you may ask students to practice the attention-getter a few times to help ingrain the behavior and support quick transitions.

If your group needs additional support with management issues, you can start each drama with contracting. Contracting, or agreeing on certain principles all participants will abide by while doing drama, is a positive, collaborative management technique that empowers participants to take ownership of how they work together and independently when participating in drama. Respect for others, listening, and working together are often among the guidelines groups agree on. To be effective, and in keeping with the philosophy of this book, the participants must suggest and agree on the rules. Contracting is even more effective if integrated into a ritual (e.g. signing a pledge or pledging aloud to keep the contract). If necessary you can "amend" the contract with further guidelines or behaviors as necessary.

Also, be sensitive to drama's potential to generate strong emotions, especially when dealing with social topics and topics of diversity. Sensitivity to context is key, and this context will differ from group to group. If you deal with a topic that is potentially uncomfortable, talk early on with participants about the need to set personal boundaries and maintain personal safety while sharing and participating. Encourage participants to take safe risks and explore alternative perspectives when taking on roles, but also remind them drama is not therapy and that you are not a trained mental health professional. In fact, if a facilitator plans to address extremely sensitive material, it may benefit them to preemptively seek out support from school counselors or other support personnel. Also, avoid assigning roles that may be potentially difficult for certain students. Instead, if specific roles are necessary, ask for volunteers, have students create their own roles and characters under your guidance, make it a collective role by casting multiple volunteers, or take on the role yourself. In the end, the responsibility to provide a safe, supportive space rests with leaders. Participants may support these efforts, but, as a teacher or facilitator, always feel empowered to take time out or even stop a drama if you sense a need to protect all participants' safety and well-being. Also, always conclude in-role work with an out-of-role reflection period, helping participants to disconnect from characters and process information.

Organization of chapters

We begin this text with a look at "drama then and now:" a survey of cutting-edge neuroscientific, psychological, and sociological research, as well as foundational practices in drama-based education. By putting contemporary science and centuries-old teaching practices into dialogue, we demonstrate the natural relationships between drama-based instruction and human cognitive development.

Chapter 2 discusses the history, theory, and practice of two founding methods in drama-based education: linear drama and process-oriented drama. Through detailed descriptions of techniques and activities common to each method, as well as sample lesson plans, we explore the ways that drama has been practiced in the past, as well as contemporary hybrid methods you can use in your own classrooms, community settings, and workshop spaces.

Chapter 3 discusses the specific application of drama-based learning to issues of social justice, examining the legacy of Augusto Boal's Theatre of the Oppressed methodology as well as contemporary practices in both community groups and standards-based classrooms.

Chapter 4 explores applications for contemporary and historical performance art techniques in drama-based pedagogies. Weaving in methods from path-breaking artists from theatre, British "live art," international "devising" practice, dance, and performance art, we outline strategies for incorporating a broad range of performance methods into educational settings to enable students to explore complex concepts and aesthetic processes. We include lesson plans that involve both performance art as a primary means of learning about a subject, and working through performance exercises in service of other curricular objectives.

Chapter 5 draws on the latest research into effective assessment as a component of arts education to provide you with a variety of practical methods for assessing drama-based learning. We lay out strategies for assessing learning both during and after drama work, as well as provide you with tools to help make the case for drama as a means for valuable and authentic instruction.

Chapter 6 surveys the field of expanding opportunities for practitioners of drama-based pedagogies, from classroom teachers to camp counselors and teaching artists working in schools or community groups. We discuss the ins and outs of advocating for drama-based programs in school and community contexts and provide a practical toolkit for planning, executing, evaluating, and advocating for arts residencies and partnerships.

This text aims to provide you with a foundation in drama as a method for teaching and learning, but the field itself is much larger than we can convey in a concise volume. Therefore, we end the text with an annotated bibliography of further resources. We encourage you to read widely in the field, explore other practitioners' methods and activities, and adapt these strategies to your own purposes.

References

Csikszentmihalyi, Mihaly. 1997. *Finding Flow: The Psychology of Engagement with Everyday Life*. Basic Books.

——2009. *Creativity: Flow and the Psychology of Discovery and Invention*. HarperCollins.

Pappano, Laura. 2014. "Creativity Becomes an Academic Discipline." *The New York Times*, February 5. Accessed 11 August 2014. http://www.nytimes.com/2014/02/09/education/edlife/creativity-becomes-an-academic-discipline.html.

Robinson, Sir Ken. 2006. *How Schools Kill Creativity*. TED talk. Accessed 11 August 2014. http://www.ted.com/talks/ken_robinson_says_schools_kill_creativity.

Robinson, Sir Ken and Adobe Education. 2012. *Why Is Creativity Important in Education? Sir Ken Robinson Video Series*. YouTube video published by Adobe Education. http://www.youtube.com/watch?v=ywIhJ2goiGER.

1 Defining the field

Drama then and now

A mind is so closely shaped by the body and destined to serve it that only one mind could possibly arise in it. No body, never mind.

Antonio Damasio (2000: 143)

In this introductory chapter, we present foundational ideas as well as outline major themes presented in this book. We begin by defining drama as a teaching methodology, discussing its connections to contemporary neurological research. We also provide an overview of contemporary brain-based approaches to learning in order to contextualize the unique role drama plays in learning and provide both a rationale for drama-based learning and teaching and a set of curricular implications and predictions based on the latest research on cognition and emotions. Finally, we introduce you to three pioneering techniques for the use of drama, theatre, and performance in education that will serve as foundations for future chapters: linear drama, in-role and process-oriented drama, and drama for social change.

Drama and performance as educational tools

Drama and performance techniques are well-established tools for teaching and learning. In fact, you may have heard of them during your training as an educator or artist. You may have encountered terms like creative dramatics, drama in education, improvisation with youth, process drama, educational drama, or drama for learning, each of which describes a drama-based method for teaching and learning. Drama-based teaching and learning have a long history. As far back as we can trace, evidence exists to suggest that dramatic activities were used in rituals, ceremonies, classrooms, and daily life to teach and reinforce knowledge, stories, and skills. For centuries, teachers have used drama-based pedagogy to connect with children's inclination toward bodily-kinesthetic imitation as they try on identities and understandings of their world. Over the last 200 years, this process-oriented way of teaching through theatre and performance techniques was defined as *drama*, a word derived from the Greek verb "dran" meaning to do, act, or perform. While we can safely assume that imaginative play as a way to discover, practice, and imitate is as old as humanity itself, drama for teaching appeared as a distinct discipline in the US during the early twentieth century. Early pioneers believed that drama helped learners develop a number of skills in areas like elocution, rhetoric, and presentation, while also supporting development in critical thinking skills, social and emotional well-being, cooperation, and communication.

Drama contrasts with *theatre*, an art form that aims to produce an artistic product for an audience, through its orientation toward process. Unlike theatre, a product is not necessarily the main outcome of drama, even though participants in drama-based learning may share results of their work with co-participants and sometimes with a larger public. Drama-based learning focuses on deepening understanding of self, others, or the subject of the drama; on fostering creativity and critical thinking skills; on exploring modes of expression and communication; and on bringing together the cognitive, emotional, and kinesthetic domains that make us human. Whether drama is used as a teaching strategy in education, in community work, or otherwise, the benefits of drama as a teaching method are multiple. Drama can:

- reach participants who are not served by traditional methods of teaching and learning;
- connect participants to themselves and others;
- transform the learning environment through collaboration and explorations of uncertainty and ambiguity;
- adapt to fit the needs of diverse learners, providing both challenges for those participants who are already considered successful under traditional learning paradigms and support for students who experience difficulties within contemporary classroom settings;
- create space for new modes of creative and critical inquiry and expression;
- enhance understanding of regular curricular subjects, helping learners understand human experiences of heart, body and mind;
- stand as a subject in and of itself;
- advance the goal of metacognition (an awareness or analysis of our own learning and thinking processes).

When we talk about drama methods for teaching and learning, we consider them as a discipline, or a unique field of study. Drama as a discipline is a more recent phenomenon, not fully explored and articulated in the US and English-speaking countries until the twentieth century. Early practitioners in the US, such as Constance D'Arcy Mackay, Winifred Ward, Geraldine Siks, and Nellie McCaslin, as well as practitioners from the United Kingdom (UK), such as Brian Way, Peter Slade, and Dorothy Heathcote, advocated for drama as a means to enhance affective, psychomotor, and cognitive skills. Although the use of drama as a discipline in the English speaking world is often positioned as a US, UK, and later Australian and Canadian movement, the reality is much more international in scope. For instance, in Japan, Shoyo Tsubouchi articulated his Child Drama for Domestic Presentation in the early 1920s. In the Netherlands, Wanda Reumer founded the first teachers' academy in Europe that specifically focused on dramatic education in 1956, attracting and training students from all over Europe. Students of these schools and movements spread their methods internationally, and the use of drama for teaching and learning has thus become a global phenomenon. In response to the increasingly global nature of drama as a discipline, the International Drama/Theatre in Education Association (IDEA) was founded in 1992 and currently has members in over 90 countries worldwide. The members of IDEA are culturally diverse, made up of drama, theatre, and education practitioners as well as artists, pedagogues, and teachers who are united in their commitment to making drama/theatre accessible, significant, and present in the lives of children and young people everywhere.

Despite drama's global proliferation during the twentieth century, this expansion has not occurred without struggle and controversy. As the use of drama as a teaching tool grew in popularity, the assertion that drama enhances learning also generated suspicion. This wariness of drama's value was especially pronounced among educators who maintained behaviorist perspectives (the idea that all human behavior can be explained by examining different stimuli and responses in people, to observe conditioning through pain and reward). Behaviorists were vocally skeptical of drama methods because the benefits of drama were so hard to substantiate, let alone test in a quantifiable fashion. In response to behaviorist critiques, drama researchers set out to prove drama's efficacy for learning. At US colleges and universities, where a number of drama programs were founded, including those at Northwestern University, Emerson College, the University of Minnesota, University of Texas at Austin, Arizona State University, the University of Kansas, and the University of Washington, researchers conducted studies during and after the 1950s to measure the effects of drama instruction on students' learning. Ann Thurman at Northwestern and Geraldine Siks at the University of Washington were particularly influential in providing a rationale for the use of drama as a teaching tool, pointing out its intellectual value and capacity to arouse critical thinking skills. Their ideas, rooted in the Progressive Education theories of John Dewey, William Heard Kilpatrick, and Hughes Mearns, gained traction amongst educational researchers and scholars. Nonetheless, most twentieth-century studies remained inconclusive, primarily describing case studies and offering generalized results (Wagner 1998: 2–3). Consequently, drama remained marginalized in general education despite brief upsurges during the 1960s to 1980s, and its potential advantages were only recognized by a few committed artists and educators.

The cognitive turn in arts education

Despite drama's historically marginalized status in education, in the mid-1990s research from other disciplines (most notably psychology, sociology, and the neurosciences) began to corroborate claims that drama practitioners had been making for decades. However, this field of research is still quite new. In 2014, new studies, research initiatives, and reports are steadily changing our understanding of drama's impact on the brain, and we anticipate more concrete studies to further demonstrate the brain–drama connection in the next ten years. Given the pathbreaking nature of neuroscience and drama-based research, we want to point out a few compelling studies that have direct implications for drama as a method for teaching and learning. Although the scholars we discuss here do not all explicitly address drama or performative practices, their ideas are highly applicable to drama and help underpin a neuroscientific argument for the use of drama as a teaching method. Psychologist Howard Gardner stresses the importance of different ways of teaching and learning in *Intelligence Reframed: Multiple intelligences for the 21st century* (2000), which extends his groundbreaking 1983 study *Frames of Mind*. Similarly, Joseph LeDoux (1998), Antonio Damasio (2000, 2003), Martin Seligman (2002, 2012), and Richard Davidson (Davidson and Begley 2013) have linked emotion and the functioning of the brain in a series of highly successful studies from neurobiological perspectives. Affective neuroscientist and human development psychologist Mary Helen Immordino-Yang is also in the process of publishing new research with compelling implications for embodied learning. Finally, psychologists like Daniel Goleman paved the way for a public understanding of the value of emotional intelligence (or EQ) in learning in addition to IQ (Intelligence Quotient, a number used to express the relative intelligence of a person measured through various standardized tests), in his popular work, *Emotional Intelligence* (2005). Taken together, this research from educational psychology, social sciences, and the neurosciences provides a scientific basis for drama as a valuable teaching strategy. In fact, several of the aforementioned theories closely relate to drama learning outcomes first articulated by drama education pioneer Nellie McCaslin in 1968. McCaslin's goals of drama include:

1   Creative and aesthetic development.
2   The ability to think critically.
3   Social growth and the ability to work cooperatively with others.
4   Improved communication skills.
5   The development of moral and spiritual values.
6   Knowledge of self (added in 2006).
7   Understanding and appreciation of the cultural backgrounds and values of others (added in 2006).

As we will see in the following discussion, multiple intelligences theory, emotional intelligence theory, mindfulness, and brain-based and embodied learning all closely connect with what early theorists and practitioners of drama, like McCaslin, have been advocating for decades. Not only does recent research suggest that McCaslin's seven goals are important for human development, but it also provides evidence of the effectiveness of drama as a tool to reach these goals. The research of Davidson, Goleman, Immordino-Yang, and others suggests that the experience of drama-based instruction can indeed provide learners with opportunities for social growth, emotional development, improved self-knowledge, and a greater ability to empathize with and understand the emotional lives of others. While for the purpose of clarity we discuss the work of these researchers separately, each builds on the others, and new research continues to add to our understanding of the connections between mind, heart, and body. Additionally, remember that these theories are neither universal nor uncontested. As you read on, keep in mind that ideology, cultures, and context also shape these ideas.

Multiple intelligences

Since the early 1980s, eminent psychologist and scholar Howard Gardner has been advocating for the recognition of multiple intelligences. Rather than focusing on the most commonly recognized verbal/linguistic and logical/mathematical aptitudes, Gardner sees multiple intelligences as "potentials [that] will or will not be activated, depending upon the values of a particular culture, the opportunities available in that culture, and the personal decisions made by individuals and/or their families, schoolteachers and others" (2000: 34). While Gardner claims that every human being possesses a basic set of intelligences in a particular blend unique to each person, he also points out that the destructive or constructive use of intelligences does not happen by accident (2000: 44–6). The conception of multiple intelligences is also a matter of cultural circumstance and environment. Intelligences vary from region to region and are dependent on the ideological positions (beliefs, values, norms) and identity locations (social, cultural, racial, economic, ability) of individuals. Thus an awareness and acceptance of a variety of different ideological positions and identity locations is crucial in our multicultural society in order to understand how a learner cultivates various intelligences. By opening space in classrooms and communities for the appreciation of different perspectives and ways of learning and knowing, drama-based instruction helps us cultivate and appreciate the diverse potentialities that Gardner identifies in his work.

While Gardner does not directly refer to drama as a teaching method, in his discussions of multiple intelligences he maintains that "literacies, skills, and disciplines ought to be pursued as tools that allow us to enhance our understandings of important questions, topics, and themes" (2000: 159). Because of drama's performative and interdisciplinary nature, it is a highly adaptable method for approaching complex questions through multiple intelligences, as will be demonstrated in the lesson plans throughout this book. Drama's potential for exploring multiple identities, points of view, and understandings also makes it highly suitable in teaching for inclusion, diversity, and social awareness – all important concerns for twenty-first century education. No matter the specific application, drama techniques directly connect with multiple intelligences.

Verbal/Linguistic	Logical/Mathematical	Visual/Spatial
• Reading • Writing • Speaking	• Sequencing • Analyzing • Generating symbols	• Imagining • Designing • Visualizing • Conceptualizing
Musical/Rhythmic	**Bodily/Kinesthetic**	**Interpersonal**
• Singing • Rhyming • Playing instruments • Understanding musical keys • Demonstrating understanding tempo, pitch, tone, and melody	• Gesturing • Expressing ideas with the body • Moving the body • Building objects	• Cooperating • Empathizing • Effectively communicating with others

Intrapersonal	Naturalistic
• Articulating preferences, values, and morals • Expressing likes and dislikes • Engaging in self-reflection • Evaluating one's own performance	• Classifying and observing natural forms • Feeling most comfortable in nature or outside • Displaying interest in outdoor activities like hiking and gardening

Figure 1.1 Multiple intelligences

Verbal/Linguistic	Logical/Mathematical	Visual/Spatial
• Monologues • Dialogues • Stories • Narratives • Verbal and written critiques • Reflection	• Planning sequential or linear scenes • Analyzing scenes • Building sets or constructing costumes based on patterns • Stage management	• Blocking scenes • Designing set, lighting, costume and props • Directing

Musical/Rhythmic	Bodily/Kinesthetic	Interpersonal
• Singing • Vocalizing • Creating aural environments • Generating a musical score • Sound design	• Tableaux • Pantomime • Finger plays and puppetry • Creating characters through movement • Choreographing	• Planning in a group • Taking on roles • Exploring different perspectives through drama • Making artistic/aesthetic decisions in a group setting

Intrapersonal	Naturalistic
• Expressing ideas about oneself through dramatization • Expressing artistic/aesthetic preferences • Engaging in self-reflection • Evaluating one's own performance	• Relating dramatic process to processes in the natural world • Dramatizing animals, plants, life processes, geological phenomena • Creating outdoor drama and performance

Figure 1.2 Related Drama Techniques

Cognition and emotion

Although the mind–body–heart connection has been a longstanding subject of research and philosophy across the globe, the connection between emotion and reason has been under-researched and relegated to the periphery of contemporary education in the US. Part of this neglect stems from the priorities of the US educational system, which continues to favor objective standardized testing and fairly rigid understandings of knowledge that depend on a limited view of what constitutes learning (see Chapters 5 and 6 for additional discussion). These understandings exert profound influence on what counts as education and how educators measure learning. Thus education has been largely reduced to a very specific, quantifiable skills-acquisition model that evaluates a limited set of abilities while all but eliminating the value differences in backgrounds, cultures, and heritages in the classroom. As Howard Gardner points out, there are three interconnected biases in our society: "westist, bestist, and testist" (2006: 23). These notions of a standardized model of education are not limited to western nations. We see the same phenomenon to varying degrees in many other countries where entrance exams and tests are even more prominent than the US's SAT and ACT college entrance exams. The "testist" paradigm has become an increasingly global feature of formal education. However, these standardized test scores say little about students' quality of life, how they feel and engage with emotions, or how they work with others in their communities. In truth, they offer little data on the many dimensions of life that contribute to a whole and worthwhile existence.

Despite the prevalence of standardized testing models that focus on easily measurable skills, our emotions and the ability to channel these emotions are equally important in learning experiences. The connection between cognition and emotion is especially clear in creative pursuits. Psychologist Mihaly Csikszentmihalyi, one of the leading scholars of happiness and creativity, asserts that the ultimate pursuit and achievement of happiness depends very much on our personal perceptions and goals, with a combination of cognitive and emotional processes happening in tandem with one another. In his influential book, *Finding Flow: The psychology of engagement with everyday life*, Csikszentmihalyi describes the experience of flow, "the sense of effortless action [people] feel in moments that stand out as the best in their lives" (1997: 29). These moments, according to Csikszentmihalyi, occur when we immerse ourselves in tasks requiring a high degree of skill and commitment. In this sense, any task, from skiing to writing a paper to painting or creating a drama, can be both cognitively and/ or physically challenging *and* emotionally rewarding, leading to "flow." Each individual discovers their optimal experiences and where their point of flow lies. Much like Gardner's theory of multiple intelligences, an individual's sense of flow depends on personal, environmental, and cultural factors. However, the experience of flow is directly related to both cognitive and emotional domains.

If we see cognition and emotion as interrelated, then dramatic learning becomes essential: children learn about life through drama by exploring imaginary themes, topics, and issues on both emotional and cognitive levels simultaneously. For example, in drama we create parallel, symbolic worlds and situations. Sometimes they are more literal and sometimes more abstract, but they always involve real thinking and real feeling, embodied to the extent that we are each capable. Drama creates metaphors of our lives, which we lead through both cognitive and emotional domains; the two cannot and should not be separated.

Emotional intelligence

In an extension of our discussion of the importance of learning that connects cognitive and emotional dimensions of the mind, consider the following: "The present generation of children [is] more troubled emotionally than the last; more lonely and depressed, more angry and unruly, more nervous and prone to worry, more impulsive and aggressive" (Goleman 1998: 11). This conclusion by Daniel Goleman, a psychologist who researches social and emotional learning (or SEL), still rings true today. Contemporary news reports and social science research point to a deficiency in regards to SEL (or Emotional Intelligence) in our educational and social systems that cannot be remedied by traditional teaching and learning models. Goleman advocates for curricula grounded in emotional intelligence that support the development of "decent human beings" as "more critical to our future than ever," and articulates five dimensions of emotional literacy: Self-Awareness, Self-Control, Self-Motivation, Empathy, and Relationship Skills (2006: 263). Research suggests that emotional health is fundamental to effective learning (Goleman 2006: 78–95), but our collective emotional health seems to be stagnant, if not in decline. The Centers for Disease Control and Prevention reported (2012) that in the year 2010 suicide was the third-ranking cause of death among persons aged 15–24. A 2011 survey reported that 15.8 percent of youth in grades 9–12 had seriously considered suicide ("Suicide" 2012), and a 2006 study reported that the leading cause of disability in the world today is unipolar depression (Brunette 2006: 36). Furthermore, young people in the US are coming of age with a dire economic picture ahead of them. According to a 2014 *New York Times* editorial report, Millennials (young people born between 1980 and 2000) are

> worse off than Gen Xers (born from the mid-1960s to the late 1970s) were at that age and the baby boomers before them by nearly every economic measure — employment, income, student loan indebtedness, mobility, home ownership and other hallmarks of "household formation," like moving out on their own, getting married and having children.
>
> (The Editorial Board 2014)

Young people are saddled with ballooning student loan debt even as solid, middle-class jobs have evaporated. In many ways, their futures and, by proxy, their emotional lives seem grim.

If we connect these rather sad statistics to Goleman and others' ideas about emotional intelligence, teaching for emotional literacy is a natural and necessary conclusion. Drama techniques such as role-play, image work, spotlighting, hotseating, and parallel play (each of which are discussed later in this book) provide a means to acquire, experience, and enhance the aspects of emotional intelligence that Goleman recognizes as essential to success in today's challenging social and emotional landscape.

Self-Awareness	Self-Control	Self-Motivation
• Cultivating emotional cause & effect • Identifying emotions • Developing emotional vocabulary	• Managing emotions • Choosing appropriate actions • Practicing relaxation	• Setting goals • Monitoring and adjusting behavior • Perseverance • Visualizing

Empathy	Relationship Skills
• Changing perspectives • Demonstrating awareness of others' feelings • Reflecting on the effects of one's actions	• Communicating with the body • Cooperating during activities • Communicating effectively

Figure 1.3 Emotional intelligences

Self-Awareness	Self Control	Self-Motivation
• Analyzing characters • Using the five senses • Reflecting on and enacting emotions • Detecting emotions • Playing roles	• Visualizing real and imagined scenarios • Practicing relaxation and sensory techniques • Reflecting on learning • Taking responsibility in a drama project • Committing and following through to a drama activity	• Selecting, conceiving, and planning a drama project • Discussing, reflecting, and adjusting one's own work • Rebounding after setbacks

Empathy	Relationship Skills
• Exploring multiple perspectives • Trying out roles • Discussing connections between real and imaginary events	• Using face/body to express emotions • Planning and playing characters in relationships • Listening, cooperating, and responding to others • Solving Problems with others

Figure 1.4 Related drama techniques

Mindfulness

In his study of mindfulness, renowned neuropsychologist Richard Davidson has extended work by figures like Goleman and Csikszentmihaly in the facet of emotional intelligence known as mindfulness. In 2013 Davidson, together with Sharon Begley, published *The Emotional Life of Your Brain*, suggesting that different people have different emotional styles and that specific emotional styles can be cultivated by individuals. Moreover, Davidson reveals, with empirical evidence corroborated by fMRI brain imaging, that the brain is a plastic, ever-changing organ whose physiology can be modified through basic practice in mindfulness. Key to Davidson's research are mindfulness exercises which can alter brain patterns that make up a person's emotional style, improving resilience, outlook, social intuition, self-awareness, sensitivity to context, and attention. According to Davidson, all of these emotional dimensions of the mind are founded on habituated patterns of brain activity. Davidson's approach to mindfulness springs from Buddhist meditation practices. Trained by the Dalai Lama himself, Davidson uses exercises in visualization and mental transformation as tools to improve emotional well-being.

Although drama is clearly a collaborative practice rather than an individual, meditative one, drama methods connect to mindfulness in that they not only encourage participants to visualize possibilities in their minds, but also create opportunities for individuals to embody these ideas, try on imagined transformations, and give life to various perspectives and ideas abstractly conceived in the brain. In this connection to mindfulness, drama may help in sustaining general emotional health and even potentially reshaping participants' brains. For example, many drama-based learning activities involve the use of visualization, heightened attentiveness to the senses, exercises in empathy, and awareness of the physical and emotional relationships between self and others. While not itself therapy, drama as a tool for fostering mindfulness can be seen as therapeutic in that it may positively influence the emotional and neurological development of learners.

Brain-based learning

Each of the researchers discussed in this chapter acknowledge the importance of emotional development, and their research can be referenced when making a scientific and/or philosophical case for brain-based learning (see for example Jensen 2008, Weiss 2000, Cercone 2006). According to Eric Jensen, a teacher and leading author on the subject of brain-based learning, brain-based education is a comprehensive approach to instruction using current research from neuroscience (2008: 4). Brain-based learning applies understandings of how our brains work to the design of effective teaching methods. This understanding of learning dictates that physical movement, social development, practicing routines, reducing stress, teaching in small instructional chunks, asking learners to devise new solutions to problems, teaching through and about emotion, and acknowledging differences between learning styles are all essential to effective instruction. Drama-based methods accomplish many of these goals at once, in that they:

- encourage the brain to perform several activities at once.
- engage the whole physiology.
- ask learners to understand and explore knowledge through doing.
- engage the emotions.
- involve learning through both conscious and unconscious processes.
- activate both spatial and rote memory.
- create a learning environment that is non-threatening, yet challenging.
- recognize the unique contributions of each person.
- create a context for active processing of experience.

Drama specialist and professor in theatre at the University of Utah State, Xan Johnson has been researching connections between drama and brain-based learning for decades. He argues that "the brain gives top priority to the most emotionally demanding input at any given moment, [and] this demanding input (emotion) then demands conscious attention, which motivates kinetic and cognitive action leading to new learning and new

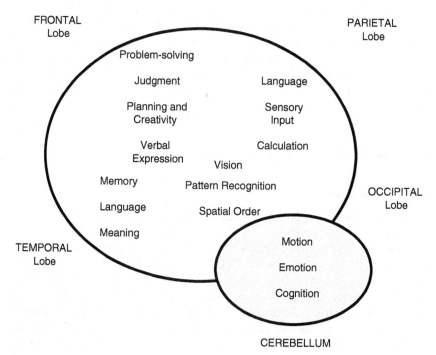

Figure 1.5 The brain

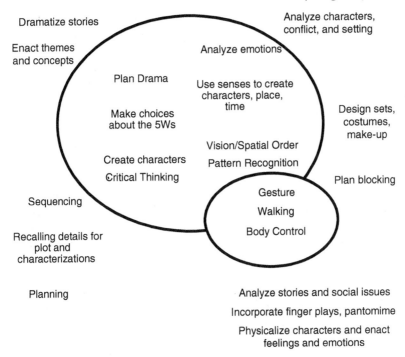

Dramatize stories

Analyze characters, conflict, and setting

Enact themes and concepts

Analyze emotions

Plan Drama

Use senses to create characters, place, time

Make choices about the 5Ws

Design sets, costumes, make-up

Create characters

Vision/Spatial Order

Pattern Recognition

Critical Thinking

Plan blocking

Gesture

Sequencing

Walking

Body Control

Recalling details for plot and characterizations

Planning

Analyze stories and social issues

Incorporate finger plays, pantomime

Physicalize characters and enact feelings and emotions

Figure 1.6 Dramatic techniques

memory formation" (Johnson 2003). Following this reasoning, drama, which is fundamentally tied to human emotions, is not only desirable as a creative medium that connects with brain-based learning, but it might also provide a direct route for engaging learners more deeply by connecting their learning experience to emotional and kinetic experience. Much like Davidson's research on mindfulness, brain-based research makes a compelling argument for conscious integration of drama and performance techniques in education and community work.

Embodied learning

The roles that art and creativity play in connections between the body, emotions, and the mind are perhaps most clearly laid out by scholar Mary Helen Immordino-Yang. As an affective neuroscientist and human development psychologist, Immodino-Yang who studies the neural, psychophysiological, and psychological bases of social emotion, self-awareness, and culture, and considers how these aspects of neuroscience impact education. In her groundbreaking work, Immordino-Yang studied the reaction of young adults to situations that elicit an emotional response, such as admiration, empathy, or sympathy. Through analysis of fMRI data gathered as subjects experienced emotional responses to other people's stories, Immordino-Yang's research reveals that how we experience emotional states is connected directly with culture. In fact, different cultural contexts influence areas of the brain in which we process emotion and thereby influence the ways in which we viscerally experience emotion. Through her research in neuroscience and psychology, Immordino-Yang, much like Gardner and other scholars, suggests that thinking, feeling, and learning do not take place in separate vacuums, but instead within social and cultural contexts: "[a] major part of how people make decisions has to do with their past social experience, reputation and cultural history" (2011: 99).

Indeed, no one learns in a vacuum. We experience and make decisions in context, based on what we believe and how we identify. Furthermore, based on new input from the world around us these values, ideologies, and categories of identity constantly shift. Moreover, learning is an embodied act; our brain, emotions, and physiology constantly connect to one another, interpreting information we receive from stimuli around us. Immordino-Yang's research suggests that our brains simultaneously operate within our bodies, within a culture, and in a world we are trying to understand: "we perceive and understand other people's feelings and actions in relation to our own beliefs and goals and *vicariously* experience these feelings and actions as if they were our own" (2008: 69–70). Ultimately, in presenting research that synthesizes many different threads that relate to education, the arts, and the brain–heart–body connection we have discussed in this chapter, Immordino-Yang's work provides one of the most convincing arguments for the necessity of creativity in education, including drama and performance. Her research suggests that drama, as a creative mode of expression, might be adopted not only as a method for teaching and learning, but also as a way to vicariously experience, practice, explore, and play with real-life situations in a fictional and safe environment. In effect, empathy is essential to learning: "We act on our own accord but interpret and understand our choices by comparing them against the norms of our culture, learned through social, emotional, and cognitive experiences" (Immordino-Yang 2011: 100).

Implications

Why is this research so important for the use of drama methods for teaching and learning? The idea of drama as an effective teaching tool is well-established. However, for the first time emerging research empirically documents the benefits, relevance, and necessity of drama for teaching and learning. Immordino-Yang and Damasio are some of the first to acknowledge that the famous Russian developmental psychologist Lev Vygotsky had a compelling thesis seventy-five years ago when he maintained that the social and cultural dimensions of lived experiences underlie much of our nonsocial brain-based decision-making and reasoning (Immordino-Yang and Damasio 2007: 6). Through their focus on a more complex understanding of the brain, embodied learning, and how the brain acquires knowledge, these scientists, along with many others, also acknowledge and demonstrate the power of broadening the conversation about education, creativity, and the brain across and through increasingly diverse disciplines. This ongoing research needs to be further explored and embraced in conversations by educators, neuropsychologists, and theatre and drama specialists together. As Immordino-Yang points out, we are often so carried away by investigating our own hypotheses that we do exactly what she and Damasio warn against: ignore interdisciplinary ways of thinking that lead to sound and strong theories (2011: 102). We, as educators and artists, might reap great rewards by working together with open minds and a willingness to step out of our comfort zones, particularly for making a case for using theatre and drama methods not simply as a way to make or teach about art, but rather as a way we can improve our lives *through* the arts and education. Above all, we hope you will come to view drama methods as invaluable resources that help us to imagine, create, debate, show, and understand what it means to be human.

Pioneering drama pedagogies

In order to contextualize the different methods included in this book, we turn our attention from neuroscience and cognition toward history, briefly describing four pioneers who influenced how we view drama today. Their theories and practices form the underpinnings of this book, and they all anticipated, to varying degrees, the many connections between drama, emotion, and cognition that are now being validated by neuroscientific research.

John Dewey

To understand drama as a method for teaching and learning, practitioners should look back at the field's history. The decision to integrate drama into education, particularly in K-12 schools, came about in response to several US educational trends at the turn of the twentieth century. Most important for this discussion were developments in Progressive Education pioneered by intellectuals like John Dewey (1859–1952). Education Progressivists generally believe that education should be a tool for societal progress, and pedagogy (the way in which we teach) should be learner-centered in order to help make real-life connections between classrooms and life. Dewey's ideas about education transformed, and continue to exert influence on, the ways in which US teachers and students teach and learn, especially in arts education fields. During the 1920s and 1930s, at the same time that pioneers like Winifred Ward and her contemporaries developed new approaches for drama-based learning, Dewey's ideas circulated throughout education circles. Most importantly, along with similarly minded Progressivists, he advocated for the act of *doing* as opposed to learning abstractly in the processes of both education and art-making. Dewey also believed that learning relied upon specific life relevancy; the mind and body must work together to create relevant experiences for learners. Dewey was profoundly influential for arts learning disciplines since he was among the first US educational philosophers to write explicitly about how the arts connect to education. In his seminal work, *Art as Experience* (1934), Dewey advocated for methods whereby learners practiced skills in understanding and making art, a term Dewey deliberately left open for interpretation, as part of an education in real-life scenarios. These experiences would support learners as they cultivated understandings of life's aesthetic dimensions both in and beyond school. Many drama practitioners embraced Deweyean educational philosophies with fervor and attempted to put his theories into practice in their classrooms.

Winifred Ward

Winifred Ward (1884–1975) is known as the mother of creative drama in the US. Ward joined the faculty of Northwestern University in 1918, and in 1923 she started to experiment with drama at the Evanston Laboratory School. From these experiments she developed her concept of "creative dramatics" (as opposed to production-oriented theatre with, by, and for children) that she described in two widely disseminated publications: *Creative Dramatics* (1930) and *Playmaking with Children* ([1947] 1957). As part of her philosophy, Ward maintained that children should not be in formal productions until they were "ready," basically at high school age, and that creative dramatics helped prepare young people for formal productions later in life. While Ward's creative dramatics approach was process-oriented, her focus on these methods as preparation for formal production also implies that she saw drama primarily as a unique performance discipline and not a teaching tool. Although her theories were not new and often came out of collaborations with colleagues like Rita Christe, who joined Ward on the faculty of Northwestern in 1929, Ward was incredibly influential and tireless in her efforts. She dominated the field of both informal drama and product-oriented theatre for children in the US for the first five decades of the twentieth century.

Despite Ward's pioneering efforts, she did not formulate her theories and practice in a vacuum. Dominant social, ideological, cultural, and economic forces at the end of the nineteenth century created a climate that fostered the development of a unique field focused on drama with children. Specifically, the influx of immigrants, the establishment of settlement houses that helped immigrants adapt to their new environments, the spread of child-centered educational ideologies in Progressive Education, and crusades against the use of children in professional theatre established the necessary social, economic, cultural and ideological circumstances under which a theatre specifically for children could be conceived. With the establishment of Alice

Minnie Herts' Children's Educational Theatre in 1903 and the inception of the Junior League by Mary Harriman in 1901, theatre with and for children was soon associated with educational objectives and established itself as an amateur discipline staffed by volunteers, who were usually women. As figures like Constance D'Arcy Mackay were struggling with this new and uniquely child-centered theatrical genre on a more production-oriented level (see Mackay 1915), other pioneers explored new approaches to theatre for children by introducing creative dramatics activities in schools, community centers, and other social institutions. These initiatives were influenced to a great extent by the Progressive Education movement. Progressive educators like the aforementioned John Dewey, Francis Parker, William Kirkpatrick and William Hughes Mearns emphasized the education of the whole child, which in their theories meant that educating children's emotions was just as important as educating their minds. Thus, from new Progressive perspectives, as soon as drama as a field started to become formalized and defined, it connected to the development of both cognitive and emotional skills.

For Ward, the essence of creative drama was the story. Her approach to lesson planning involved a clear "building block" or linear sequence of activities (see Chapter 2 for examples of this approach). In Ward's linear drama method, the leader is a guide who facilitates the drama from outside, and each drama skill must be mastered before proceeding to the next. Although distinct from formal theatrical production, "story drama," the culminating experience in Ward's method, involves participants enacting stories for themselves or invited guests. In order to attain the skill level necessary for creating story drama, participants take part in four categories of creative drama activities: movement/pantomime, sensitivity exercises, characterization, and dialogue. Work with existing literature, intense focus on characterization, and the use of a culminating performance are all hallmarks of Ward's approach. This approach remained the preferred drama method in the US until the 1990s.

Dorothy Heathcote

Like Winifred Ward, Dorothy Heathcote (1926–2011) is an icon in the field of drama for young people in English-speaking countries. Based in the UK, Heathcote developed an idiosyncratic approach to drama characterized by her taking on a fictional role and facilitating the lesson from within an unfolding dramatic scenario. Through this new method, she positioned participants in roles as "experts" and helped them cultivate knowledge through collaborative improvisation with one another. Her method has been recorded in several works, first by Betty Jane Wagner in *Dorothy Heathcote: Drama as a learning medium* (1976) and later by Gavin Bolton, who corresponded with Heathcote and recorded his correspondence in *Drama for Learning: Dorothy Heathcote's mantle of the expert approach to education* (Heathcote and Bolton 1995).

Heathcote started working as a weaver in a Yorkshire mill when she was fourteen. In 1945 she was accepted at the Northern Theatre School in Bradford when the owner of the mill saw her potential and offered to pay her fees. She initially trained for acting, but her instructors told her she was not the right size and steered her toward teaching. Later she became a senior lecturer in drama and education at Newcastle University, where she remained until she retired in 1986. She continued teaching and lecturing around the world until her death at eighty-five. Like many US practitioners, Heathcote's method was closely connected to her personal style, in this case an improvisational method of working with learners.

From the beginning, Heathcote's approach was considered both controversial and unconventional. A glimpse into her process: she entered a room of participants, and using her actor training, took on a fictional role that steered the development of the day's drama work. While Heathcote fully committed to her in-role work, she did not expect dramatic skills from the participants, nor did she explicitly teach acting techniques. Instead, Heathcote focused on immersion into drama as a method to learn about whatever topic she introduced. Life skills, rather than drama skills, were the desired learning outcome, and the only ability participants needed was firm commitment to the topic. Within this process-oriented work, Heathcote famously maintained that drama was "about a man in a mess." This maxim captured Heathcote's belief that drama helps individuals explore situations of conflict, crisis, and moral complexity. Heathcote believed that drama could connect participants to common human experiences, a concept she referred to as the "brotherhood code." According to Heathcote, participants in drama enter into fellowship with all of humanity when they explore experiences of people who have been in similar situations. By being thrust into a drama, participants must act as individuals in a society that respond to complex situations and problems (see Chapter 2 for examples of this method). During reflective discussion after the improvisational drama ended, Heathcote emphasized the drama's cognitive and emotional elements, asking questions designed to help participants thoroughly reflect on both the drama's events and the emotions and feelings they evoked. Heathcote also included reflection throughout the drama as a distancing technique that emphasizes the significance of what is at stake. For example, Heathcote regularly stopped the drama to ask the participants how they felt in order to encourage the reflection necessary for metacognition.

US practitioners discovered Heathcote's unorthodox methods in the 1970s, and drama programs housed in education departments embraced her work as an important counterpoint to the linear, story-driven approaches that dominated due to Winifred Ward's legacy. In the next chapter we discuss in detail the practices of Heathcote and others who advocate for in-role and process-oriented drama. Even though linear and process-oriented approaches to drama-based learning were distinct approaches that rarely shared much crossover in the US, by the 1990s a more transitional and fluid method that synthesized linear and process-oriented models emerged. This innovation was also influenced by the spread of methods pioneered by Brazilian theorist and practitioner Augusto Boal, another influential pioneer of drama methods in the twentieth century.

Augusto Boal

Augusto Boal (1931–2009) was a visionary, activist, and politician. He was also a theatre director and a dramatist. Although trained as a chemist in his native Brazil, he became attracted to theatre while doing research at Columbia University in New York. After graduate study, he returned to Brazil to work as a director at the Arena Theatre in São Paulo, running workshops for actors and playwrights. A Marxist at heart, Boal took agitprop plays (agitation and propaganda plays with an explicit political message) to the countryside in an effort to politically activate the audience. These experiences led Boal to rethink the purpose and desired effects of agitprop theatre, and, more importantly, inspired him to reconceptualize political theatre into what is now one of his most famous theatrical innovations: Theatre of the Oppressed. Theatre of the Oppressed (TO) consists of socially relevant scenes played out for an audience. These scenes, often referred to as "activating scenes," are designed to engage audiences, exploring different perspectives on the scene, and ultimately to encourage them to take action in response to oppression. Initially, TO consisted of actors taking suggestions from audience members about ways the characters could attempt to address the problems in the scene and playing them out onstage. This format changed when one spectator, frustrated by the actor missing the nuance of her suggested actions, took the stage to show the actors the exact nature of her idea. This performance by a frustrated spectator became one of the hallmark characteristics of TO: an interaction and exploration of relevant themes between the company and the "spect-actors," or spectators who also become actors in the performance. In 1979 Boal published *Theatre of the Oppressed*, a text directly influenced by his friend and mentor Paulo Freire's work in *Pedagogy of the Oppressed* (see Chapter 4 for additional discussion of Freire). Just as Freire wanted to expose the inherent inequalities present in dominant education models and encourage empowered learning, Boal wanted theatre to activate spectators and empower them to find strategies for personal and social change. Over the years Boal wrote several additional books and developed strategies and methods including Image Theatre, Forum Theatre, Invisible Theatre, and Legislative Theatre. No matter the model, his objective was always to empower participants through drama.

Boal's work has been translated in to many languages, and he traveled all over the world giving workshops and lectures. In the late twentieth century he was seen as a leading practitioner in the field, and many followed his theories and practice as a prescriptive approach with a very specific format.

However, Boal saw neither himself nor his drama methods as static, and he continually questioned, adapted, and refined his practice and theories. For example, Sanjoy Ganguly, one of the leaders of the *Jana Sanskriti* Indian TO center and a close friend of Boal, recounts a story of Boal's willingness to adapt his methods. Once, during a workshop, a group of participants asked Boal about a specific detail regarding TO methodology. He responded, "methods are for the people, people are not for the method" (Ganguly 2010: 89). As this anecdote demonstrates, Boal maintained an open mind regarding how his drama methods might be adapted, shifted, and revised to meet the needs of specific communities. Practitioners continue to debate how best to employ these methods for different ends. Boal's methods also directly connect to discussions regarding emotion and cognition as considered earlier in this chapter. His drama methods connect to real life, bring together heart, mind, and body, and focus on both human relationships and the process of social change. In Chapter 4 we expand on Boal's work and discuss his and other drama-based methods for teaching about social justice.

Conclusion

In this chapter we have presented an overview of compelling research in neuroscience and cognition and highlighted foundational figures in the field. In the following chapters, you will learn in greater detail about models that are legacies from each of the pioneers, including linear drama, process-oriented drama, and drama for social justice. You will also have an opportunity to see each of these methods in action.

References

Boal, Augusto. 1985. *Theatre of the Oppressed.* Translated by Charles A. and Maria-Odila Leal McBride. Theatre Communications Group.

Brunette, Lisa. 2006. "New Ways to Explain the Brain." *On Wisconsin* (Summer), 32–7.

Cercone, Kathleen. 2006. "Brain-Based Learning." In Elsebeth Korsgaard Sorenson (ed.), *Enhancing Learning through Technology.* Information Science Publishing, pp. 293–322.

Csikszentmihalyi, Mihaly. 1997. *Finding Flow: The psychology of engagement with everyday life.* Basic Books.

——2009. *Creativity: Flow and the psychology of discovery and invention.* HarperCollins.

Damasio, Antonio. 2000. *The Feeling of What Happens: Body and emotion in the making of consciousness.* Harcourt Incorporated.

——2003. *Looking for Spinoza: Joy, sorrow, and the feeling brain.* Houghton Mifflin Harcourt.

Davidson, Richard J., and Sharon Begley. 2013. *The Emotional Life of Your Brain: How its unique patterns affect the way you think, feel, and live and how you can change them.* Hodder General Publishing Division.

Dewey, John. 1934. *Art as Experience*. Minton, Balch & Company.

Ganguly, Sanjoy. 2010. *Jana Sanskriti: Forum Theatre and democracy in India*. Taylor & Francis.

Gardner, Howard. [1983] 2011. *Frames of Mind: The theory of multiple intelligences*. Basic Books.

——2000. *Intelligence Reframed: Multiple Intelligences*. Perseus Books Group.

——2006. *Multiple Intelligences: New Horizons*. Basic Books.

Goleman, Daniel. [1995] 2005. *Emotional Intelligence: 10th Anniversary Edition*. Bantam Books.

——1998. *Working With Emotional Intelligence*. Random House Publishing Group.

——2006. *Social Intelligence: The new science of human relationships*. Random House Publishing Group.

Heathcote, Dorothy, and Gavin Bolton. 1995. *Drama for Learning: Dorothy Heathcote's mantle of the expert approach to education. Dimensions of Drama Series*. Heinemann.

Immordino-Yang, Mary Helen. 2011. "Implications of Affective and Social Neuroscience for Educational Theory." *Educational Philosophy and Theory* 43 (1): 98–103.

Immordino-Yang, Mary Helen, and Antonio Damasio. 2007. "We Feel, Therefore We Learn: The Relevance of Affective and Social Neuroscience to Education." *Mind, Brain, and Education* 1 (1): 3–10.

Jensen, Eric P. 2008. *Brain-Based Learning: The new paradigm of teaching*. Corwin Press.

Johnson, Xan. 2003. "Violent Prediction." Presentation given at the annual conference of the American Alliance for Theatre and Education, New York. July.

LeDoux, Joseph. 1998. *The Emotional Brain: The mysterious underpinnings of emotional life*. Simon and Schuster.

Mackay, Constance D'arcy. 1915. *How to Produce Children's Plays*. Henry Holt and Company.

McCaslin, Nellie. 1968. *Creative Dramatics in the Classroom*. D. McKay Company.

——2006. *Creative Drama in the Classroom and Beyond*. 8th edn. Pearson.

Seligman, Martin E.P. 2002. *Authentic Happiness: Using the new positive psychology to realize your potential for lasting fulfillment*. Simon and Schuster.

——2012. *Flourish: A visionary new understanding of happiness and well-being*. Simon and Schuster.

"Suicide: Facts at a Glance." 2012. Centers for Disease Control and Prevention Data Sheet. Retrieved at http://www.cdc.gov/violenceprevention/suicide/.

The Editorial Board. 2014. "Recovery for Whom?" *The New York Times*, April 12. http://www.nytimes.com/2014/04/13/opinion/sunday/recovery-for-whom.html.

Wagner, Betty Jane. 1976. "Dorothy Heathcote: Drama as a learning medium." http://eric.ed.gov/?id=ED130362.

——1998. *Educational Drama and Language Arts: What research shows*. Heinemann.

Ward, Winifred. 1930. *Creative Dramatics: For the upper grades and junior high school*. D. Appleton-Century-Crofts.

——[1947] 1957. *Playmaking with Children from Kindergarten to High School*. 2nd edn. D. Appleton-Century-Crofts.

Weiss, Ruth Palombo. 2000. "Brain-Based Learning." *Training & Development* 54 (7): 20–4.

2 Foundational methods
Linear and process-oriented drama

In this chapter we take a closer look at the philosophies, strategies, and objectives of two main drama methodologies practiced in the US: linear and process-oriented drama. Taken together, these two methods form a foundation for drama-based learning and teaching. In order to help teachers and practitioners develop skills in both linear and process-oriented drama, we provide comprehensive discussions of both methods before considering the hybrid approaches which have become most common in contemporary practice. While these methodologies share many similarities, they also differ quite significantly in regard to form, style and content. Accordingly, we discuss elements that distinguish these approaches and explain their value from historical, pedagogical, and practical perspectives. We offer techniques for implementing these methods in a variety of learning environments and provide suggestions and tips regarding how teachers and practitioners might adapt each method for specific populations. Finally, we offer lesson plans that can be easily adapted for various age groups, populations, and learning environments. As you read this chapter, keep in mind these basic definitions:

- Linear drama methods are designed with a clear beginning, middle, and end.
- Process-oriented drama (sometimes also referred to as "holistic drama" or simply "process drama") is open-ended, often with only a skeletal structure of activities designed to evolve based on participants' input throughout the lesson.

Linear drama: history and definitions

Linear drama includes methods organized around specific goals and objectives, with lessons or residencies usually featuring a clear beginning, middle, and end. Also, linear drama methods generally include a sequence of exercises and activities that build in difficulty over the course of a lesson, unit, or residency. These exercises are divided into broader categories related to drama and theatrical skills and may include concentration, sensorial exploration, imagination, character development, and/or guided or independent improvisation. During a lesson, a teacher or facilitator outlines a plan, sets it in motion, and has a clear idea about where she wants to go. She teaches concepts, skills, and terms; introduces and facilitates activities; and provides necessary leadership from *outside* of the drama world. For example, a linear drama facilitator might direct students through a series of exercises related to improvisation with a partner. Unlike many process-oriented drama leaders, a linear drama facilitator will rarely take on a role and interact with participants as a character. Through this facilitation style, participants encounter structured opportunities for input, but these contributions minimally impact the larger structure of the session. Also, since linear drama often includes specific learning goals and/or objectives and a clear beginning–middle–end structure, it more closely aligns with the objective-oriented models of instruction that are most prevalent in contemporary public education. Accordingly, linear drama's complementary qualities make it a natural fit for an integrated approach to drama-based education whereby learners develop skills and knowledge both in drama and in other curricular areas with natural connections to drama, from English Language Arts to Character Education.

Linear drama was the most common method of drama-based instruction in the US until about the mid-1990s, and it continues to be a vital methodology. The aforementioned complementary nature of linear drama with other modes of instruction directly relates to the historical development of the method. As contextualized in Chapter 1, pioneers like Winifred Ward laid the foundation for later practitioners and scholars to refine techniques and articulate several unique approaches that provided the foundation for this methodology. Other than Winifred Ward, some of the most influential practitioners, both past and present, include Rita Criste, Agnes Haaga, Geraldine Siks, Viola Spolin, Barbara Salisbury-Wills, Ruth Beall Heinig, Nellie McCaslin, Lin Wright, Juliana Saxton, Carole Miller, Jonothan Neelands, and Helane Rosenberg, among others. (While a thorough discussion of each practitioner's work is outside the scope of this chapter, see the annotated bibliography for sample texts.) While many early drama practitioners experimented with new methods, we give special mention to Geraldine Siks and Viola Spolin because of their influence on current linear drama practice. Their contributions to the field helped to lay the practical and theoretical foundations upon which contemporary artists and teachers base linear drama methods and practice.

Geraldine Siks (1912–2005) was a professor at the University of Washington in Seattle's Theatre and Drama department and worked in the field of informal drama (drama that has a strong orientation toward process instead of product), a prototype for linear drama. Specifically, Siks looked at the educational dimension of drama in response to behaviorist education theories in the 1970s and 1980s. Noting the increasingly popular accountability models of learning for which behavioral theorists advocated, Siks realized that drama would never be prioritized in education if it were not presented as central to education. Although her larger mission focused on teaching adult students about theatre at the university level, she believed that informal drama was as much an art form as theatre and could be used with learners of all ages. If students worked within dramatic processes they would simultaneously learn about more formal, product-oriented theatre practice and understand its value to a larger education (see Siks 1958, 1961, 1964, 1981, 1983). This idea is now foundational to linear drama.

Siks also articulated connections between drama and other curricula. Namely, she observed overlaps between drama and language arts in the areas of listening, speaking, reading, and writing. Taking these beliefs as core principles of her research, she developed the "process-concept approach" (Siks 1983; Rosenberg 1987). This approach consists of three phases: Plan, Play, and Evaluate. Siks's process-concept model elevated the importance of drama-based play and helped make clear the value of exploring drama concepts through informal activities organized around a central theme. It also supported learning objectives related to reading and communication, linking drama and educational curricula. Furthermore, Siks integrated systematic observation and theories from theatre, education, and child development into her work, creating the first popular research-based approach to drama education in the US. Siks's work directly influenced practitioner/researchers like Helane Rosenberg, Agnes Haaga, and Nellie McCaslin. Rosenberg's Rutgers Imagination Method (RIM), Haaga and McCaslin's approaches to Creative Dramatics, and countless other practitioner/researcher initiatives in drama methods for learning all take inspiration from Siks's research.

Viola Spolin (1906–1994) further expanded linear drama methods under the premise that diverse populations could learn life skills through theatre methods. Spolin was a theatre educator, director, and actress. In the late 1930s she served as drama supervisor for the Chicago branch of the Work Progress Administration's Recreational Project, a government program designed to bring new forms of recreation (including non-professional theatre) to communities throughout the country. In this role she experimented with a system of theatre training that could cross cultural barriers, helping a broader section of US citizens to participate in these recreational drama programs. In looking for new methods to help make dramatic skills and concepts accessible for learners, Spolin adopted a method that now forms the cornerstone of many linear drama lessons: the game. Spolin's habit of developing games as teaching tools has become a widespread method of lesson-planning for drama-based teaching. As she explains, Spolin used games as tools for developing specific skills in her students. "The games emerged out of necessity," Spolin said. "When I had a problem [directing], I made up a game. When another problem came up, I just made up a new game" (Hyams 1974). Spolin's games were widely adopted and incorporated in drama and performance curricula both in elementary and secondary theatre education. Her publications have been foundational for drama and performance teachers and community leaders, and even today Spolin's texts, *Theater Games for the Classroom: A teacher's handbook* (1986) and *Improvisation for the Theater* (1983) serve as comprehensive resources for improvisational techniques for learning.

In addition to her work on the role of games in drama-based learning, Spolin also introduced and refined facilitation techniques which are now ubiquitous in drama methods. Sidecoaching, or "the calling out of just that word, that phrase, or that sentence that keeps the player on focus" (Spolin 1986: 5), occurs in the moment of a dramatic activity. Neither formal instruction nor direction, sidecoaching is a brief facilitator intervention that players hear and then incorporate into their work as they continue the task at hand. Thanks to Spolin, sidecoaching has become one of the most important techniques in drama and performance work, whether using linear, process-oriented, or hybrid methods. However, it is particularly useful for linear drama. We will discuss sidecoaching techniques later in this chapter.

Implications for linear drama: the seriousness of playing dramatically

Linear drama can also be viewed as a set of teaching tools that focus on play as a means of learning. The commonality of play within human development is well documented in fields like psychology and sociology, with scholars like Vygotsky (1967), Moore (1990), and Frost, Wortham, and Reifel (2008) commenting extensively on the subject. As these scholars have noted, people of all ages learn about the world by trying out new ideas and imitating actions through play, and this imitative behavior forms the basis of social learning. Education theorists and psychologists have also taken note of the role of play in social development and applied it to other skill areas and knowledge groups. Almost all formal education, particularly for younger children, includes an element of play, from playing with beads to develop fine motor skills and practice sequencing, to playing in water and sand to learn basic concepts related to science, to playing a game like hopscotch to learn physical dexterity, steps in a process, and skills for collaboration and competition.

If we acknowledge the fundamental role that play plays in learning (no pun intended), then we can see that Siks, Spolin and other linear drama pioneers were sensitive to a fundamental fact of life when they looked at the educational dimension of dramatic play. However, play in linear drama is distinct from other kinds of non-structured play in which children engage. From a curricular perspective, the difference between pretend play and drama is that drama is *structured* pretend play, or play with a purpose. This purpose becomes even more central when we conduct linear drama lessons with participants, since we often follow a specific lesson plan featuring a goal and related learning objectives. Through this playful pedagogy, participants acquire skills not only in drama, but also in a variety of other knowledge areas, from the cognitive to the socio-emotional (see Chapters 1 and 5). Despite the playful dimension of linear drama, we also stress that this work has real and tangible implications for learning, and we encourage you to take seriously the importance of play in linear drama and other forms of drama-based methods.

Linear drama toolkit: techniques, building block activities, and starters

As previously mentioned, linear drama methods work well with a variety of skills and knowledge groups. Often, units, lessons, or residencies are organized around a topic or theme and include specific drama-based techniques. Given the need for linear drama methods to be flexible, based on the wide variety of subjects into which they might be incorporated, we have included key concepts that we find most useful and, perhaps more importantly, most adaptable for different curricula and populations with whom a teacher/facilitator will work. While we sort these different concepts into specific categories like techniques, games, and starters, most of them overlap in some regard, and practically all can be adapted for different purposes. For instance, we describe the "Machine" activity as a game, but we have also incorporated it into residencies as a core technique. Similarly, we describe improvisation as a distinct technique, but practically all drama-based activities involve improvisation-based skills. However, this list is not exhaustive, and we encourage you to investigate additional resources described at the end of this book, as well as Chapters 3 (drama for social justice) and 4 (performance art), which include additional activities that can be easily adapted for linear drama. We also include sample lessons throughout the chapter that include many of these techniques and starters.

Core techniques for linear drama

The following techniques are used to execute linear drama lesson plans. Rather than discrete activities, these techniques can be employed by teachers and teaching artists in a number of ways to facilitate student learning. We also detail ways in which different kinds of practitioners might use these techniques in service of specific learning objectives.

Sidecoaching

As previously described, sidecoaching is the act of facilitating learning without stopping the action of the lesson. When sidecoaching, the leader calls out phrases or words to help participants focus (*"Keep your eyes on a focal point!" "Move without a purpose. Fill in spaces around you."*), create interaction (*"Look for others who inspire you! Take into account what you see as you move."*), refine and revise movement (*"Be bigger! Be wilder!"*), and engage in transformation (*"Explore the space! Choose levels. Find a new way to move!"*). This technique is useful with all age groups, as long as facilitators are careful to use language that your students can easily process in the moment. When introducing sidecoaching to a new group, be clear about how you want students to respond to your prompts. Let them know you will call out suggestions and reminders that they should respond to in the moment without stopping their participation. Unless the majority of a group appears confused or unproductive, try to keep an activity going even if some participants fail to respond to sidecoaching prompts. Monitor the group, sidecoaching with the same prompt again.

Uses of sidecoaching:

- Keeping students on-task during an activity without breaking the flow of the session (*"Remember, this is a silent activity!"*)
- Adding a new challenge to an activity as participants become more proficient (*"When you and your partner are getting good at mirroring each other, see if you can mirror smaller details. How precise can you be?"*)
- Adding in levels of metacognitive reflection during an activity (*"Notice when you and your partner are mirroring each other perfectly. Observe, silently, what you are doing that is helping you and your partner succeed."*)

Spotlighting

Spotlighting allows participants to informally view other participants' work, take inspiration from other ideas, and safely share moments of work in progress. Spotlighting is particularly suited to improvisational work (discussed in more detail below) and provides a structure for groups with limited performance experience to start sharing material.

Procedure: While students are working on short improvisations or other performance activities, call out *"Freeze"* to stop the action in the room. Explain that you will be placing a "spotlight" on each group, one at a time, by pointing at them and calling *"Action."* Each of the other groups should remain in their places but watch the action of the spotlighted group until you call *"Freeze"* again. Allow the spotlighted group to continue their work for as long as it feels productive: a few seconds up to a minute. Then call *"continue"* as all groups continue their action and repeat the same spotlighting process with another group. After spotlighting is complete, you may ask groups to continue their work or conduct a reflection period to discuss what new ideas people saw in each other's work before continuing.

Variation: You may spotlight several participants at once (for example, all participants on one side of the room).

Sharing

Instead of a formal production or performance, linear drama often incorporates sharings at the conclusion of a drama lesson or process. While spotlighting involves sharing work in progress, sharing is typically done at the conclusion of an activity. In a sharing, the rehearsal time is brief, and there exists little expectation for polish and refinement. Mistakes may happen, the group may need to start and stop, or some participants may need to reset and begin again. Through the process of preparing for and executing sharings of drama work, participants think critically about creative and artistic decisions and make choices about how best to communicate their ideas to peers and invited audiences. The sharing gives participants the opportunity to make decisions about how to organize the space, how to sequence events for the sharing, and how to use brief rehearsal time effectively.

Tips for sharing work:

- Before starting an activity, tell participants if they will be sharing at the end. Whether you are conducting a group improvisation or a solo free-writing activity, participants should be informed in advance so they have agency in deciding what kind of material they are willing to share.
- If learning objectives center on participants paying careful attention to the aesthetics of each participant's work, consider reflective discussion or another assessment strategy after each individual performance.
- If learning objectives relate to shared exploration of concepts or curricular material, you may wish to reserve reflective discussion until all performances have been shared.
- Keep reflective questions open-ended to allow the group to process the material. (*"What did you see here?"* before *"What similarities and differences did you notice?"* or *"What different ideas about freedom did you see in each performance?"*)

Storytelling

Stories are integral to most drama-based learning, but were especially foundational in the development of linear drama. The oral tradition of storytelling helps pass along culture, tradition, and wisdom from one generation to the next. It also provides a means to learn about different cultures. Storytelling is an integral component of our lives and social interactions on a daily basis. If someone comes home and is asked how her day was, she tells a story. If you ask a friend whom you have not seen in a while how he has been, he tells a story. We put our children to bed with stories, and we relate experiences in discussions with others through storytelling. Perhaps because we are not aware of the role of stories in our lives, we forget how compelling and entertaining storytelling can be.

Therefore, when integrating storytelling into drama, we encourage leaders to *tell* stories instead of *reading* them to a group of participants. Telling a story involves knowing the narrative arc and recounting it in your own words with your own flourishes and details. A few pointers for storytelling in drama-based lessons:

- Use enthusiasm. Pick a story you like, get to know it inside out, and then, as Winifred Ward said, "Tell it with zest."
- Read your story a few times to understand the plot. Choose five central moments from the beginning to the end of the story and visualize these moments clearly as images. Make them vivid. Pay attention to aural, visual, and oral sensations that the story might evoke. These moments are the backbone of your storytelling and provide a mental outline; as you tell it you move from moment to moment during the telling.
- Structure your story based on the images created in your mind. Start with a hook, like an engaging first line, a sensory experience, or a series of anticipatory questions to hook listeners. Let your story flow from image to image before ending soon after the final climax. Finally, provide a sense of closure at the end.
- Repetition helps listeners follow the story and is especially useful when telling stories to younger children.
- Pay attention to pitch, rhythm, pace, pause, volume, and intensity in your voice.
- Use gestures and facial expressions.
- Make eye contact and/or design moments of interaction to establish rapport between teller and listeners.
- Set a mood. Dim lights, use a flashlight, play background sounds, share an object, close eyes for a moment and create an image in the listeners' minds.
- If your audience is young they may want to help you by offering spontaneous contributions. Acknowledge this input and continue with the story.

The Annotated Bibliography of this book (Appendix A) lists several storytelling and story drama resources. Carole Miller and Juliana Saxton's *Into the Story: Language in action through drama* (2004) is particularly compelling in its detail and meant for novice teachers to use in their teaching practices. Johnny Saldaña's *Drama of Color: Improvisation with multiethnic folklore* (1995) offers a range of stories and strategies.

Image-based activities

Since linear drama focuses on building skills in progression from simpler to more complex, exercises often begin with images before progressing to spoken or written language. Students who begin in silent image work, either creating still pictures with their bodies or through the use of pantomime, can often communicate ideas more freely and without the pressure of clearly articulating ideas through language. This early focus on images helps alleviate any performance anxiety that may spring from the notion of "acting." Also, image-based drama methods can be freeing, making them a standard component of drama for social change, which is explored in detail in the next chapter. For our discussion of image-based drama methods here, we list two core techniques: tableaux and pantomime.

Tableaux

This term, taken from French, simply means frozen pictures that people create with their bodies. Tableaux have many applications for participants of all ages. They are also simple to execute, making them an ideal starting point for groups new to drama-based learning. Tableaux can be quite simple and literal (for example, with teacher guidance a group of younger children may create a tableau from a favorite illustration in a picture book), or they can be complex and abstract (a group of older students generate a series of tableaux based on personal narratives about being a teenager). Tableaux and related techniques are also foundational to theatre for social change and are discussed in this context in Chapter 3.

Procedure: Divide the class into groups (for beginners, groups of one to three). Give each group a short time (five minutes) to collaborate on a frozen picture with their bodies. Ask groups to make their pictures visually interesting and to work together to clearly communicate the group's idea through this picture alone, without any sound or movement. Encourage groups to work on their feet, practicing the tableau rather than simply discussing and planning what they will do. Once groups have begun honing their images, sidecoach them to refine and clarify ideas. As each group settles on a picture, ask them to give their tableau a title before sharing with the rest of the group using spotlighting or a more formal sharing.

Variation one: Have each group create multiple tableaux and link them together by finding visually interesting ways to move from one image to the next. This technique works well as a way to explore the sequence of events in a literary work or historical event.

Variation two: Have each group create a tableau of an individual moment in a story or historical event, using spotlighting to share each image in sequence. After the spotlighting is complete, ask groups to refine their images in order to clarify their part of the story in relationship to the other images their peers shared.

Variation three: Use tableaux as a transition point into improvisational work or pantomime (see below) by asking participants to bring their tableaux to life either silently through pantomime or with words through improvisation.

Pantomime

In its most basic sense, pantomime is the act of dramatization without using words. It relies on gesture, physical movement, and facial expression to convey ideas. Pantomime generally takes one of two forms when incorporated into drama-based teaching: narrative and non-narrative. While particularly effective with populations who may benefit from opportunities for expression beyond the spoken/written word (pre-K children, English language learners), pantomime can be used with all ages to explore concepts, activate bodily-kinesthetic learning, build observational skills in participants who watch and comment on the action, and enhance emotional intelligence in learners.

Procedure: After reading or discussing a story, explain to participants that you will tell the story while the students act it out without words (narrative pantomime). Each participant should find a space in the room to work and imagine herself as the story's main character. Ask participants to imagine the character in a series of prompts related to the story or event (*"How fast is the character?" "How big is the character?" "How does the character feel?"*). Allow the group a moment to practice before explaining that you will now begin telling the story as they use their bodies to act out the character's actions silently. Each participant should work simultaneously, focusing on his own interpretation of the character's actions as you narrate the story.

Uses of narrative pantomime:

- A group of pre-K students simultaneously pantomime a story as the main character while their teacher reads it aloud.
- A teaching artist engages a group of middle-school students in a narrative pantomime about a day in the life of a historical figure.

Variation one: A facilitator might ask participants to pantomime a moment from the story without the guidance of narration (non-narrative pantomime). In this more advanced activity, learners are challenged to recall the sequence of events in the story and assess the relative importance of specific details as they decide what to do and when to place them in a sequence. Simultaneous non-narrative pantomime also gives participants a chance to compare and contrast their choices with those of their peers.

Variation two: During pantomime, participants may work independently, all playing the same role simultaneously (sometimes referred to as parallel pantomime), or together with each playing a different part in the same story or scenario. In variations involving different characters, you can activate students' knowledge of a story or historical event by brainstorming different characters involved in the story before assigning characters and beginning the pantomime.

Improvisation

Improvisation (or improv) is dramatization in the moment. When doing improv, participants have very little, if any, rehearsal time and generally make up their actions and dialogue in the moment. For example, a teaching artist might ask students to act out a scene from a story in real time. Improvisation helps learners to think on their feet; to develop a sense of narrative, environment, and character using quick judgment and intuition; and to collaborate with others. In this section, we share a selection of improv-based activities and games that are hallmark techniques in linear drama. We also encourage you to refer to the appendix of drama resources at the end of this text for a wealth of additional resources for improv games and activities.

Giving a gift: We use this activity to introduce our basic improv rule: accept, do not block. When participants accept during improv, they receive information from their partners and collaborate to create a coherent fictional world based on their and their partners' contributions. For instance, if learner A says *"The storm outside is really terrible,"* and learner B responds *"Good thing we brought these industrial-strength umbrellas,"* or *"Personally I love the rain,"* they are accepting. Blocking would include responses like *"It isn't raining. It's a beautiful sunny day."* This last response rejects learner A's idea. Each participant should listen carefully to their partner, accepting information they provide for the improv while providing their own ideas to build the fictional world together. We usually demonstrate this activity with a volunteer, showing both "blocking" behavior and "accepting" behavior, before conducting the activity as a group.

Procedure: Divide the group into pairs and ask them to designate themselves as partners A and B. The improv will begin with partner A giving partner B a gift. Partner A can indicate information about this gift with movement and dialogue (for example, the student may indicate with their body that the package is heavy or light, large or small, or may say *"I hope this is your size"* or *"Happy Valentine's Day!"*), but should not tell partner B what the gift is. Instead, the pair should collaborate through dialogue to discover together what the gift is, accepting each other's informational cues and building them into the improvisation together. After allowing the groups to work together for a little while, spotlight the pairs to see what they have discovered together.

Environment: Skills developed in this improv game include non-verbal communication, contextualization, description, and observation. We often start with this game as an introduction to improv since it easily adapts to specific curricular areas with the use of appropriate prompts, like *"Pick an environment from our story,"* or *"Show us a geographical location we learned about this week."*

Procedure: Solicit one volunteer and ask them to select an environment without telling anyone else. For example, a student might pick a kitchen. The volunteer begins an activity that he would do in that environment (making a cake or washing dishes). As the other participants figure out the environment, they should join the first volunteer, improvising another activity that fits the original environment (sweeping the floor, kneading dough). After several participants join in, ask the remaining observers to identify the environment. If any member comes up with different environments (for example, someone might think a kitchen is a restaurant), discuss additional activities that would help clarify the environment for people watching.

Sidecoaching prompts:

- *"Make your movements clear and distinct so we can figure out exactly what you're doing."*
- *"What different activities could be happening in this environment? How can you add more detail without copying what you see?"*

The chair: This activity connects with communication, emotional intelligence, and observational skills. It also works well with older populations to break self-consciousness before moving on to free-form improv.

Procedure: Ask participants to form pairs. Each pair will work with a single chair. Ask one participant in the set of pairs to sit in the chair and think of a reason why they need to stay seated in the chair. Ask the other participant in the pair to think of a reason to try to get the seated person out of the chair. Once each participant has a clear idea (allow a few seconds to think), the partners should begin improvising, with each pursuing her chosen goal using only movement and gesture, no language. After the first round, ask pairs to switch roles. Give them time to think of a new reason for staying in the chair or asking their partner to get up, then repeat the exercise, but explain to the groups that they can now use sounds (not words) as well as gestures. Finally, switch roles again but add in language. Spotlight several pairs at each phase. At the end of the activity, reflect together on how each partner used gesture, sound, and language to accomplish the task.

What are you doing?: This is a simple but fun starter for a linear and/or pantomime-based lesson. It is also useful for introducing concentration, movement, and thinking quickly.

Procedure: Solicit a volunteer from the group (A), and ask them to start improvising an activity without making sound. Once the volunteer establishes their activity, ask another volunteer (B) to approach A, and ask, *"What are you doing?"* A should say they are doing any activity *besides* the one they are currently acting out. B should immediately begin to act out the activity A described. For example:

- A – (Pantomimes riding a bicycle).
- B – *"What are you doing?"*
- A – *"I'm planting flowers in a garden."*
- B – (Pantomimes planting flowers in a garden).

This game can be played between two people with others watching, or it can be played with the whole group, passing the activity from one person to the next.

Starters and building block activities

Most linear drama sessions begin with a low-stakes, interactive, and fun game or activity called a starter. These starters serve several purposes. First, they help participants get to know one another and practice necessary skills for a session, from collaboration and ensemble to focus and concentration. Second, they help introduce skills that will be further developed in the session. Finally, they can help link prior learning to a current lesson. Generally, starters contain some element that directly connects with the linear drama session. For example, in a lesson where middle-school English Language Arts students are integrating playwriting techniques, improvisation, and English, students might play an improvisation-based game like "The Chair" (described in the prior section) to help activate knowledge about improvisation and dramatic tension. Most of these starters can also be used later in lessons as ways to build skills and knowledge.

The following are select starter activities we find useful in our own lesson plans. There are many more activities than you will find here, and you may have come across variations of these activities or even created your own. For additional starters we recommend in particular Augusto Boal's *Games for Actors and Non-Actors* and Viola Spolin's books (1983, 1986).

Walking with a purpose: This activity engages the group in collective, movement-oriented dramatization. Similar to parallel pantomime, the activity activates bodily-kinesthetic learning processes and allows a group to collectively explore a concept through movement.

Procedure: Start by asking the group to walk around/through the space, filling the room. Encourage participants to fill the space (*"Go where others are not"*) and to maintain neutrality as much as possible, looking beyond fellow participants even as they sense them while passing. After students are moving about the space, introduce a purpose that should infuse their movement with meaning. For instance, you might ask participants to move as if they were the main character at the start of the story. As the activity proceeds, change prompts from time to time to explore new ideas or perspectives on the topic for the day.

   Tips:

- When first working with walking with a purpose techniques, you may simply want to establish neutral walking without giggling, people walking together, people deliberately running into one another, and so on. This goal is perfectly acceptable and can take time, depending on the group's age and comfort level with one another and with drama.
- After the group develops competency in moving through space, add in different prompts. For example, the group may move like a character (*"Walk as if you're the Weasel, sneaky and suspicious"*), an emotion (*"Walk as if you are completely exasperated"*), a set of circumstances (*"Walk as if you are lost in a cold, dark city"*), abstract ideas (*"Walk purple"*) or even as figures of speech (*"Walk like the moon setting over a fun-filled day"*).
- Consider using music during this activity, either to support thematic elements or to give the participants a sense of time and place.

Cover the space: This activity can be used as a starter for ensemble, body/physicality, and spatial awareness.

Procedure: Designate a playing space. For example, an open classroom, a section of a multipurpose room, or even an area outside will work. If the space is too large, mark off an area with chairs. Ask participants to walk in and through the space with no particular goal in mind. Participants continue to move without talking or touching one another. After the group has started to move freely and quietly and with focus, shout *"Freeze!"* At this moment, everyone should stop and look (*"Look!"*) around to see that everyone has spread out, evenly covering the floor. At your cue (*"Cover!"*), the group moves one leg to cover more of the space. After the group has covered more of the space with a leg, say *"Go!"* The group begins to move freely again. Repeat this sequence (Freeze–Look–Cover–Go) several more times. As participants become more proficient, the leader can simply say, *"Freeze," "Look," "Cover,"* and *"Go"* and accelerate transitions between each action or ask participants to *"Cover"* more than once, extending their reach with each prompt. Once participants have mastered Freeze–Look–Cover–Go, add *"Link!"* When the group hears *"Link!"* they find a way to link with someone near them (you can designate linking as only hand-to-hand or hand-to-body depending on your population's comfort level with physical touch). After the group links, the leader says, *"Go!"* once again. Repeat Freeze–Look–Cover–Go–Link several times, then add *"Move!,"* where linked participants move to cover the entire space.

Sidecoaching prompts:

- *"Pay attention to your body in relation to other bodies in the space."*
- *"Cover the space, fill the room. Go where others are not."*
- *"Avoid a movement pattern. Change the direction you walk. Move away from familiar faces."*
- *"How can you link with more than one person? Can you find new ways to link your body? How can you cover the space while linked?"*
- *"How can you move through the space as a linked group? Is anyone in an uncomfortable position? How can you help them?"*

Groupings: This is a good starter for lessons on non-verbal communication as well as an icebreaker for new classes and groups.

Procedure: Ask participants to form groups without talking, according to qualities you call out. Prompts might include visible attributes of participants (*"Get into a group with someone who is wearing the same color on the top half of their body"* or *"Get into a group with people who have the same eye color"*) or attributes that are not immediately observable (*"Get into a group with someone who had the same breakfast today as you"* or *"Get into a group with someone who likes the same genre of movie that you like the best"*). Remind the groups to be completely silent throughout the game. After the participants sort themselves, have the group call out the common attribute at the same time. They might get it right (everyone yells *"Blue eyes!"*) or they might miss the mark (a group says both *"Bagels!"* and *"Cereal!"* at the same time). There is no penalty for a mixed group, but take the opportunity to reflect on why they may have been confused.

Sidecoaching prompts:

- *"Work silently. Show instead of tell. Communicate through body movements and expression."*
- *"How can you confirm that you all have the same idea? Can you do any double-checking?"*
- *"What are different ways to communicate what we can't see?"*

Map placement: This starter has natural connections to Social Studies/History/Geography or any lesson or drama that deals with diversity issues (identity, immigration).

Procedure: Explain to participants that you will work together to create a map on the floor, using your bodies to determine locations on the map. Start with a small area, such as a classroom, school, neighborhood, or town. Decide as a group where different landmarks are located, then ask the group to place themselves on the map based on different prompts (*"On this school map, show me where you eat lunch/act the silliest/learn the most/feel comfortable"* or *"On this city map, place yourself where you live/go to school/like to visit"*). Ask a few volunteers to share details about their location and/or adjust their position as they learn more about the map from others. You can also move up the map's size (e.g. national map, world map), and ask participants to place themselves in different areas based on prompts (*"Stand where you/your parents/your grandparents/great-grandparents were born"* or *"Stand where you would most like to visit"*). You can also make abstract and/or fictional maps based on narratives or imaginary places (for example, a fictional world in a short story), asking participants to fill in the blanks through prompts (*"Stand where you think the Rabbit made his decision to run away"*) and justify their decisions. Focus on the discussion produced in the activity.

Color touch: This starter is a high-energy, movement-oriented activity that requires quick thinking. It can be used at any point in a unit when you need to shake up participants or generate group energy.

Procedure: Have participants gather in the center of the space and explain that when you call out a color, they should immediately find something in the space that they can touch. When you call out *"Touch Yellow!"*, participants run to touch something yellow in the room. Anything counts, and more than one person can touch the same thing. After everyone is touching something yellow, the leader continues the game with additional rounds, calling out a variety of colors (*"Touch Red!"* or *"Touch Blue!"*) and then adding the element of speed by calling out the colors more quickly. The leader then adds in other qualities (*"Touch Red somewhere over your head!"* or *"Touch Orange with your feet!"*).

Variation one: As the group becomes even more proficient with the game, broaden the categories even further (*"Touch someone on the shoulder who you just met today,"* *"Touch someone as lightly as you possibly can"* or *"Touch your toes to someone's knee"*).

Variation two: After a few rounds, the leader may ask the first, or last, person to "touch" a color to call out the next color or item to touch.

Startle: This starter is an icebreaking activity and a way to license and encourage participants to be silly and loud. It also works within a lesson where you encourage students to take risks responsibly.

Procedure: Ask everyone to stand in a circle, looking down at their feet. The leader counts to three, and on the count of three, everyone looks up at someone else in the circle. If they are making eye contact with someone who is looking at them, they scream (or make some other sound you determine) and then fall to the floor, melt or even die a dramatic death (the more melodramatic the better). The activity continues until there are only two people still standing. Play it multiple times. At first, this game will go very quickly, with participants looking at their friends or in a similar pattern. The more you play, the better the group will be at avoiding the "startle." Reflect on why the group gets better at playing the game despite the fact that it seems random.

People to people: This is an excellent icebreaker for any age level that encourages movement/ physicality, group cohesion, and risk-taking.

Procedure: Ask participants to walk silently through the space with no particular goal in mind. Once the group is silently moving through the space with focus, call out two body parts (*"Elbow to shoulder!"*). Each participant should find a partner, connect these two body parts in some way, and freeze. After they connect, ask participants to unfreeze and walk around the space again. Call out other body parts (*"Hand to head!"* or *"Knee to foot!"*). Increase difficulty by increasing the game's speed, changing group size (*"Knee to foot in groups of three!"*) or add in multiple body part connections (*"Knee to foot and head to hand!"*).
   Sidecoaching prompts:

- *"Spread out! Avoid running into others, but move freely!"*
- *"Connect with the person closest to you!"*
- *"Faster! Find a way to connect!"*

Truth about me: This is a good activity for the beginning of a longer residency or unit, as it helps participants get to know one another beyond superficial observation. It also works well at the end of a unit as informal assessment to evaluate how well participants know each other.

Procedure: All participants except one take a chair and sit in a circle. The one person without a chair stands in the middle of a large circle, surrounded by the rest of the group. The person in the middle states a fact or important quality about themselves (*"I have blue eyes,"* *"I like to sing"* or *"I love eating chocolate"*). Everyone who also shares the same quality (for example, everyone with blue eyes, everyone who likes to sing, or everyone who loves eating chocolate) stands up and moves to a newly vacant chair in the circle. The only restriction is that they cannot move to the chair immediately to their right or left (that would be just a bit too easy, since participants could simply shift to the seat next to them without standing). While other participants are switching chairs, the person in the center also tries to find a vacant seat. Whoever does not find a seat stands in the middle and the activity continues with more "truths" about that individual, repeating the cycle. As the group becomes more proficient at the game, encourage them to include non-visible truths or values/beliefs. The leader should take part in this activity.

Who started the motion?: This starter focuses on concentration and observation skills as well as collaboration and ensemble.

Procedure: Everyone sits or stands in a circle. One participant volunteers to be the Guesser, and that person leaves the room. While the Guesser is out of the room, ask the group to choose a leader. The leader will start a repetitive movement or motion (repeatedly clapping hands, snapping fingers, rolling shoulders or the like). Once the leader establishes the movement, everyone in the circle copies the motion as precisely as possible. After the group starts moving in unison, call the Guesser back into the room. The Guesser stands in the middle of the circle, observing the group to try to determine who is controlling the action. The leader should randomly change the motion as they please, while still trying to keep the Guesser from identifying them. Everyone in the group must work to copy the leader exactly at all times. The Guesser has three guesses to figure out the leader. Select a new Guesser and leader for each round. Encourage participants to reflect on strategies for fooling the Guesser (avoiding direct eye contact with the leader, making sure the leader changes the movement when the Guesser looks in another direction).

Machine: This classic activity is highly adaptable and promotes creative movement, observation, improvisation and cooperation skills. It also connects to concepts like sequencing, mechanization, steps in a process, and analyzing systems.

Procedure: Begin by asking one participant to volunteer and start a repetitive movement and a sound to a steady rhythm (for example, repeatedly chopping with one arm while making the sound, *"Thwack!"*). The volunteer repeats the movement and sound for some length of time as if in a loop. Once the volunteer establishes the movement and sound other participants join in, adding to the "machine" by creating a new repetitive movement and sound in relationship to the first (for example, another volunteer twists at the waist and says *"Boom!"*). You can limit the number of participants, perhaps starting with only five people, then work up to the entire class.

Variation one: Connect to the lesson for the day with specific directions about the machine's quality (for example, *"Let's make an ice cream sundae machine"* or *"Let's make a machine that conveys loss"*).

Variation two: Challenge participants to go faster, slower, louder, softer, and even move as the machine around and through the space.

Friend and foe: This is another good activity that engages with power dynamics. It also helps develop non-verbal communication, patience, and self-control.

Procedure: Begin by asking participants to walk silently throughout the space without a goal in mind. Ask everyone to secretly choose a friend. They should not let their "friend" know they have been selected in any way. After selecting a friend, participants continue walking. Next, instruct participants to secretly choose a foe. As with their "friend," participants should not give hints to their foes. After establishing individual and secret "friends" and "foes," participants move through the space, always trying to keep their friend between themselves and their foe without letting either know their roles. Afterwards, reflect on the activity, asking if participants realized they had been selected as someone's friend or foe and how one might determine their relationship to other participants.

    Sidecoaching prompts:

- *"Keep your friends and foes guessing. Don't let on who you are staying away from and who is helping you."*
- *"Think about eye contact. Notice where you and others look."*
- *"Keep moving. Fill the space."*

Lesson planning for linear drama

While you may use any of the activities discussed above on their own as part of traditional lesson plans involving direct instruction or group discussion, you can also combine activities into drama-based lesson plans. As you decide on a sequence of activities, consider which techniques connect most clearly to your learning goals for the day. Also consider what skills learners will need to successfully accomplish each activity. Linear drama usually involves a progressive accumulation of skills and knowledge, so you may wish to begin the lesson with a starter that develops students' skills in advance of a more challenging activity. Below we provide a sample linear drama lesson plan to help illustrate the process of sequencing drama activities for learning. Later in this chapter you will find additional lesson plans using many of the techniques described above in traditional linear and hybrid linear/process-oriented formats.

A beginner linear drama: feelings

The following drama lesson moves from simple to more complex and exemplifies the lesson-planning mechanics laid out at the end of Chapter 1.

This lesson can be adapted as a first session with any group of participants from third grade to college.

Age group: 4th and 5th grade.

Goal: Getting acquainted, exploration of the expression of feelings and emotions through dramatic activities.

Objectives:

- Participants will develop their skills in imagination, movement, concentration, and simple characterization to explore the expression of feelings and emotions during group improvisational and creative movement activities.
- Participants will create a pantomimed scene based on feelings and emotions with a beginning, a middle, and an end.

Materials: Nametags, paper, markers, masking tape, live or recorded music.

Procedure

Starter—Groupings: Ask participants to form groups around simple prompts related to favorite things (examples: favorite activity, books, television program/games).

Reflection: *"How did you feel when you were able to form a group?"*

Reflection: Follow Groupings with a brief conversation about emotions and feelings, supporting participants as they articulate their own feelings and distinguish them from states of being.
Sample questions:

- *"How are you feeling now?"*
- *"How do you know when you're having a feeling?"*
- *"What is the difference between feeling mad and feeling hot?"*

Walk with a purpose: Ask participants to move through the space. As the group moves through the space, add prompts, including forwards, backwards, toes, heels, round, low, high, and square. Then add feelings/emotions, including happy, sad, angry, distracted, ecstatic, shy, furious, lonely, silly, worried.
Sidecoaching prompts:

- *"Use your senses. Interpret these ideas any way that works for you."*
- *"Create space for yourself. Let yourself work independently. Try different ideas, and find one that works for you."*

- *"Concentrate."*
- *"Show instead of tell."*
- *"Let your whole body get involved."*

Emotion improvisation: Ask groups to form two lines facing each other and assign a side A and side B. Each participant is partnered with the person directly across from them. On your signal, partners should walk to the middle and greet one another using numbers instead of words:

A says "1, 2, 3, 4" ("Hi, how are you?").
B replies "5, 6, 7, 8." ("Fine, thank you").

Ask the groups to switch, completing the same exchange with B greeting and A replying. Next, ask them to repeat the exchange in ways appropriate to different relationships (enemies, best friends, spies, job applicants interviewing for the same position, friends who need to discuss an important secret). Switch between A and B throughout the lesson.

After a few rounds, ask each pair to select their favorite exchange and share through spotlighting.

Reflection: *"How could you tell what emotion your partner was embodying?"*

Drawing emotions: Ask participants to create a literal or abstract sketch of "emotions" as they understand the concept/idea. Hang the pictures on the walls of the room, ask the group to view the pictures and see what they discover (*"See if feelings, colors, ideas, or words pop out to you when you look at these images"*).

Emotion pantomime: After participants have viewed the images, ask them to find a partner. Ask the partners to introduce themselves and engage in a brief discussion about their responses to the images. Next, ask the partners to brainstorm as many different emotions as possible. After their brainstorm, solicit an emotion from the group (*"Did anyone discover an emotion that really stuck out to them as they were talking to their partner?"*). Ask participants to agree on an activity that corresponds to the emotion from the group (for example, if a participant volunteers "fear" as their emotion, the leader would say, *"Decide on something that both of you fear"*). Next, ask the groups to practice pantomiming their activity. After a few minutes, share through spotlighting, asking the group to guess the activity.

Reflection:

"How did you express your emotions/feelings in the activities? What did you use/see? Did everyone look the same or different? How?"

"Was it difficult showing emotions with your body? Why or why not?"

"What happened to your body when you could use language? Did it help? Distract?"

"Would your body have been as expressive if you had used language right away?"

"Why is the expression of feelings and emotions important?"

"Can we always know what other people feel?"

"How do we react when we meet someone who seems sad/angry/ happy?"

Extensions for extra time

Emotion tableaux: Ask participants to form groups of four. Each group chooses an emotion and creates a tableau (literal or abstract) based on the emotion. Tableaux can be scenes (*"Create a family photo from a vacation that shows your emotion"*) or simply the emotions themselves (*"Create a tableaux that shows four different ways your emotion might work in real life"*). Ask the groups to practice and share them through spotlighting or a sharing. Afterwards, ask small groups to make a second tableau using a contrasting emotion with the same characters/situation. Share both tableaux.

Reflection: Ask participants not in the group to reflect on the tableaux: *"What do you see? What sort of emotions? How is this expressed?"*

Group emotion pantomime: Ask participants to forms groups of four then ask each group to develop a scene using the following criteria:

- Create one tableau of a negative emotion.
- Create a second tableau of a positive emotion.
- Generate pantomimed movements that link the first tableau (negative) to the second tableau (positive).

Encourage participants to create a narrative that shows what happened to transform the negative to positive and to include a clear moment of transition. Ask them to practice and then share through spotlighting or a sharing. If time permits, further extend the activity by asking participants to add dialogue, music, or costumes to the pantomimed scene. Conclude by asking participants not in the group to share their interpretations and responses to the pantomimed scene.

Process-oriented drama and in-role learning

Unlike linear drama, which focuses on learning specific skills related to drama and complementary curricular areas, process-oriented drama sets out a main goal of learning about life through dramatic methods. Process-oriented drama is also participant-oriented, with the group being co-collaborators with the facilitator to help shape the drama. Within this model, leaders work from *inside* the drama, functioning as in-role facilitators. Also, process-oriented drama typically avoids a performance or production component; the process is the purpose. For example, process-oriented drama frequently incorporates participants taking on roles within a story or dramatic scenario, determining content and steering the drama based on their input. Building skills in drama or theatre is not generally an explicit goal of process-oriented drama since the method operates under the assumption that drama skills like imitation and imagination are innate within persons and practiced through processes of human development. Given the open-ended and flexible nature of process-oriented drama, these methods work in a variety of educational contexts, from summer camps to classrooms.

In a typical process-oriented drama, participants often find themselves immediately immersed into a story or dramatic scenario (based on real or imagined events) in which they, as players in the drama, directly contribute to the development of events and outcome of the story or scenario. An example: after reading a story about gardening, a group of kindergarteners enter a classroom transformed to look like a garden. Their teacher, wearing overalls, a plaid shirt, and a straw hat, invites them into her garden, saying, "*Oh, hello fellow gardeners! I'm so glad you are here! I'm really having some trouble getting my vegetables to grow! I could really use your help.*" The drama proceeds from the premise that the kindergarten students are now fellow gardeners with the teacher. As this example demonstrates, process-oriented dramas may not have a clear beginning, middle, or end, and may instead focus on a problem or conflict for which there is no clear and immediate solution. Through the process of playing roles, the leader and participants explore a topic together and learn more about the subject and themselves within a specific context.

While linear drama methods dominated the landscape of US-based drama-based methods for teaching and learning, process drama also became a key methodology, particularly after Dorothy Heathcote's methods, pioneered during the 1950s and 1960s, began to circulate internationally (see Chapter 1). Her work also inspired a number of practitioners, including Gavin Bolton, Cecily O'Neill, and Jonothan Neelands. Many of them refined and reinterpreted Heathcote's approach and attempted to provide structure around these initially unorthodox methods. Their revisions not only helped make these methods easier for educators to adapt, but also made clear the connections between process-oriented drama and traditional curricular areas. In the US, Cecily O'Neill has been instrumental in disseminating process-oriented drama.

Cecily O'Neill was particularly influential in the US. She taught at the Ohio State University after receiving her PhD in Exeter, UK. A student of Heathcote's, in 1982 she published *Drama Structures: A Practical Handbook for Teachers* (1982) with Alan Lambert. The book, an attempt to make Heathcote's methods accessible to others, includes fifteen detailed process dramas, from the movement of the settlers going west in the middle of the nineteenth century, to the suffragettes, to an advertising campaign, and is still an excellent resource for in-role drama lessons. Her later work, *Drama Worlds: A Framework for Process Drama* (1995), helped further clarify process-oriented methods for a variety of teachers and drama practitioners. Where Heathcote's original methodology is highly individualized and can be daunting for novice practitioners, O'Neill's work made in-role and process-oriented teaching techniques accessible for a wider audience of teachers and teaching artists by describing the process in detail, with lesson plans that can be replicated by practitioners without years of apprenticeship and study.

Process-oriented drama techniques

Unlike linear drama, in-role and process-oriented drama often treats the learning session holistically, without clear divisions between activities or even between activities and reflection. Learners tend to experience these kinds of lessons as one large session, with the in-role experience evolving from beginning to end, creating an overall learning experience rather than discrete moments of action followed up with specific reflection questions. Thus the techniques of process-oriented drama are the mainstays of the method, rather than individual games or activities. In this section, we describe several key methods used by Heathcote, O'Neill and others, before providing a sample lesson plan that demonstrates the technique in practice.

Mantle of the Expert

Dorothy Heathcote's Mantle of the Expert (MoE) approach formed the foundation of her method. True MoE technique as defined by Heathcote is complex. It involves a lengthy collaborative process between participants and facilitators whereby the group collectively articulates areas of interest, then develops a group-designed fictional world that allows them to explore this interest together. Within this world, participants generate and take ownership of expert roles. Heathcote describes the MoE role as "functional," meaning their foundations are grounded in participants' lived experiences and personal investment in the topic (Heathcote and Bolton 1995: 23–5). MoE techniques do not impose a subject on participants, but instead allow them to decide together what they will explore in the session. The dramas typically take place over numerous sessions and can lead to tangible materials like printed leaflets, letters, artwork, or petitions. However, Heathcote's MoE can be difficult to implement given its need for multiple sessions and for participants and facilitators to collaborate to choose a subject. Many theatre and drama practitioners, particularly those without acting or improvisation background, may not feel comfortable with this free-flowing structure until later in their careers. Contrastingly, teachers or facilitators with long-standing partnerships with participants (for example, a classroom teacher) might adapt MoE methods in their classroom over the course of many weeks. See Heathcote and Bolton's book (1995) as well as Heathcote's collected writings (1991) for additional discussion of her unique and specific approach. While Heathcote's MoE methods may be challenging to implement in pure form, adaptations of MoE techniques have formed the basis of process-oriented drama methods. We will discuss several of them below.

Facilitation

One of the hallmarks of process-oriented drama is the leader as facilitator. Unlike linear drama, in which the leader may steer all activities, provide information, and supervise the lesson's structure from beginning to end, the leader's role as a facilitator in process-oriented drama ensures a more democratic experience. Typically, the leader/facilitator focuses on guiding the drama and offering encouragement and motivation to participants without directly steering their contribution. Through facilitation, the leader supports participants' learning and discovery, leaving room for the drama to change based on student input. While facilitating, the leader might step in and out of role as necessary to question, check on how participants are feeling, provide information to push forward the drama, pause to provide opportunities for additional dramatic exploration, or present research tasks to deepen understanding of the topic. However, their input is rarely prescriptive; instead, participants have choices and independently engage with the drama on their own terms. Facilitators also maintain control and safety in the room, but adjust their leadership and in-role work based on contributions from participants. Quick thinking, listening, and flexibility skills are critical requirements of the process-oriented drama leader. Depending on the leader's role, participants have more or less say in the development of the drama. For example, if the leader takes on the role of a ship's captain she may steer the drama more easily from a power position, while taking on the role of an outsider or disempowered person in need of help allows the participants to take charge.

Role-play

While participants often take on roles in many forms of drama, role-play is a central component of process-oriented drama. Role-play in process-oriented drama is typically grounded in a set of given circumstances (conditions of a real or imaginary world in which participants must operate) with a goal of creating believable and realistic characters with a vested interest in the topic at hand. Role-play involves two components: role-making and role-taking. In order to prepare roles (role-making), participants (particularly older or advanced students) may generate their own roles, completing additional research to help justify decisions about characters and context. They may also engage in extensive character work through facilitated imagery exercises or other improvisation or playwriting-based activities. In other instances, a teacher or facilitator may provide participants with a role. When assigning a role for a process-oriented drama, facilitators may provide important contextualizing information or ask participants to generate this information prior to starting the in-role work. Typically, archetypes and caricatures are discouraged in process-oriented drama role-play.

When embodying a role (role-taking or working in-role) within a process-oriented drama, participants take their extensive character preparation and apply it to a problem or set of circumstances in a believable and realistic fashion (even if in an imaginary world). Embodying a role requires empathy, inferencing, problem solving, and predicting as participants adapt their roles for new information presented within a drama. Embodying a role can be a challenge, and first in-role sessions can be rife with giggles, silly responses, or a general lack of seriousness. Part of this response rests with participants' discomfort; it can be quite challenging to fully commit to an alternative point of view. However, encourage students to commit to their roles even as you acknowledge the challenges they may experience. Also, as the facilitator models commitment, and if necessary, redirects participant behavior from within their role, these issues tend to resolve themselves quickly.

Facilitator-in-role

Facilitators often participate in role-play as well. They may be a supposedly neutral facilitator who steers the drama without offering much in the way of input, a participant with a strong point of view with whom other participants must engage, or any role that best suits the drama. When working in-role, facilitators will likely need to discuss the transition from in-role to out-of-role with students (especially younger children who are still developing the ability to distinguish fantasy from reality). Typically, leaders wear a costume piece like a hat, scarf, jacket, or glasses to distinguish our in-role and out-of-role work. For younger children a facilitator might even model the transition several times to make clear the act of taking on a role, helping them distinguish between the facilitator as a fictional character and the facilitator as herself.

Expert roles

An extension of role-play, expert roles are a foundational technique deriving from MoE techniques. Using MoE techniques, the leader might designate or discuss a topic of exploration. Students agree to take on the role of knowledgeable and skillful experts and work within a dramatic context, integrating their expert knowledge into the larger dramatic context. Examples of expert roles might include students as a team of archeologists exploring an excavation site for a museum, or as city council members offering advice on improving playground spaces. Through the use of expert roles, facilitators empower participants to independently seek out or generate knowledge germane to a topic, while also encouraging an increased level of engagement and confidence within the drama. Expert roles also provide participants with authentic learning experiences with real and tangible purposes for learning and discovering. Finally, through expert roles, participants acquire knowledge and skills that they can apply in everyday life because these roles are grounded in real-world information.

Simulation

Simulation provides a context for participants to work in-role. Simulation, in its basic sense, is an imitation of a real-world experience. In process-oriented drama, facilitators often design simulations based on both real and imaginary events. For example, they might create a simulation from a piece of literature (like the aforementioned example simulation of the kindergarten teacher's garden), a historical occasion, or a scenario based on other real or imagined events. For example, during a residency with undergraduate education students, we developed a simulation of a school board meeting about school choice and race-based pupil assignment. Often, as Heathcote noted, the simulation sets out to inspire action from participants as they work in-role. Typically, this move toward action centers on a decision, and the drama often concludes with a vote, survey, or arrival at consensus.

An example of a simulation that we find very successful is a town meeting. In a large group, the participants either generate roles or the facilitator provides roles based on important representative groups necessary for capturing the nuance of a particular issue. The group comes together, and the facilitator acts as a neutral in-role figure (representative from the mayor's office, school board representative, council secretary), announcing that they have been sent to observe and facilitate the discussion. The facilitator then introduces a specific issue (school assignment, funding of the arts), and the group discusses the issue in-role. At the end of the town meeting, the group takes a vote on the issues, and the facilitator ends the drama.

Interviewing

Interviewing is a simpler version of simulation. A facilitator or participant takes on a role related to a particular topic being presented in a process-oriented drama lesson and other participants interview the person, generating questions either in real time or in advance of the interview. The interviewee responds as best they can in-role, making inferences or filling in blanks to help make sense of the character. For example, during a town meeting about race-based pupil assignment, a facilitator may ask a particularly outspoken in-role participant playing a teacher to be hot-seated. During the interview, other participants (who have stepped out-of-role) ask the participant questions like, *"You seem very passionate about this topic. Why do you care so much?"* or *"How do you see these potential decisions affecting your classroom?"* Interviewing provides an opportunity for participants to explore different perspectives with additional specificity and nuance.

Sound tunnels

Sound tunnels are auditory-oriented in-role activities that help with brainstorming perspectives, synthesizing ideas, or concluding a residency. Ask participants to form two lines facing one another, forming a tunnel. The participants then improvise verbal responses to a prompt (for example, *"What are the inner thoughts of this character at the moment of decision?"*). The group speak their ideas all at once and repeats them until the activity is complete. As participants in line offer their responses, participants take turns walking individually through the tunnel from one end to the other, listening to the various responses, then returning to the line and continuing to share their ideas aloud. Each participant takes a turn in the tunnel.

Writing-in-role

Another method for exploring character outside of spoken language and movement, writing-in-role allows participants to reflect privately on their character's relationship to other individuals and events. You can use writing-in-role to give participants time to further develop their characters prior to improvisational in-role work, to provide reflective closure for a unit or activity, or to develop new ideas to move a lesson forward. Examples of writing-in-role prompts include:

- *"Write a letter in-role to someone who matters to you, expressing your feelings about the situation that is unfolding in the lesson."*
- *"It is the end of the day and you are alone in your room. Write a diary entry recording what you experienced today and how you feel about it."*

- *"Write a note to the main character giving them advice on what to do next."*
- *"You've been asked to write a guest column about this event for the opinion section of the local paper. What do you want to say to the people of the town?"*

A process-oriented drama for older teens and young adults: compassion and agency in crisis

Below is an outline of a process drama aimed at high school students. This lesson plan uses in-role work, a town meeting, and MoE techniques to explore the perspectives of different community members responding to a crisis. This lesson plan also demonstrates the basic character development technique we use in creating roles for process-oriented drama. You will notice that, as opposed to the earlier linear drama lesson plan, this plan does not use starters or many distinct building blocks, instead quickly getting started with the development of a shared fictional world which students inhabit together in-role to explore the central topic of the lesson. However, unlike Heathcote's original lessons, this plan does include the use of tableaux as a way of brainstorming given circumstances early in the lesson.

Goal: Exploring feelings of agency and compassion while being involved in a crisis situation.

Objectives: The participants will take on roles of local and foreign experts, making impromptu decisions in-role, reacting and reflecting on their own and other people's attitudes and actions in the situation as it unfolds in the drama.

Materials: Clipboard, cap, sunglasses, suitable music (classical music, choral music, or hymns works well).

Procedure

Starter discussion:

> *"What is compassion?"*

> *"What do we feel compassionate about?"*

> *"What are some specific instances where compassion might be challenging, but necessary?"*

Defining given circumstances: Building on the prior discussion, select one situation and define a set of given circumstances related to a crisis. Steer participants toward *creating* an original situation and given circumstances, instead of *enacting* a situation from current events. At the same time, encourage participants to take inspiration from current events or lived experience. As a group, decide on and record your given circumstances in a central space in the room (board or chart paper):

- Environment (season, location, region, country).
- Nature of the crisis (What has happened? What has been done so far?).
- Characters/general population (Who are the major players in this crisis? Whose voices are silenced? Who must be present to weigh in?).

Explain in-role and out-of-role work: Distinguish the notions of in-role and out-of-role for yourself and for the group. For example, you may explain that when you, as the leader, put on a scarf and cap and carry a clipboard, you are in-role. Similarly, you will ask students to go into role, embodying someone with very different life experiences. Explain that in-role work requires commitment to making choices that fit your character's given circumstances.

News tableaux: Divide participants into two groups. Ask them to brainstorm headlines from a fictional newspaper published in the location where the crisis takes place. Collect ideas on the board and ask each group to select one. After they choose a headline, ask participants to form a tableau in their small groups based on their fictional newspaper headline. Practice, then share through spotlighting. Discuss if the tableaux added any new details that they would like to add to their given circumstances for the drama.

Contextualizing the crisis: The leader asks for three volunteers to model in-role work and help provide contextualizing information for the scenario. Organize the volunteers in a fishbowl orientation, with the rest of participants in a circle around them. As the leader and the three volunteers develop contextualizing information for the drama, the group listens, observes, and offers input where possible.

Going into role: The leader goes into role as the leader of an emergency operation by putting on the scarf, cap, and clipboard, and gathers volunteers together in a circle. Tell the volunteer group:

> *"We are all called together here as experts in crisis management to leave the next morning to help with the [crisis as defined by the group]. In preparation, we should get to know each other, why we are here, and what we know about the situation, what we need to do to prepare for departure."*

The volunteers quickly decide and improvise their roles, providing an introduction to the group. Accept any role the volunteers offer. Examples may include, but are not limited to, international aid staff members, doctors/medical staff, religious leaders, or politicians. If a volunteer is stuck, quickly step out-of-role and ask observers for ideas, using the brainstormed list of given circumstances to help. (If adapting this lesson for a younger group, consider brainstorming roles ahead of time or having participants conduct research on crisis management professions.)

After participants have introduced themselves, ask a series of questions to help contextualize their experience in relationship to the crisis. Questions might include:

> *"What is your previous experience?"*

> *"Can you brief us on what you know about the situation from your perspective?"*

> *"What are your top priorities upon arrival?"*

> *"What are your biggest concerns upon arrival?"*

> *"Can you articulate what help or support you will need?"*

After the small group contextualizes the crisis, the leader reviews major information, then steps out-of-role and adds details to the given circumstances.

Creating characters: After recording contextualizing information, ask participants to relax and close their eyes. Explain that you will be leading them through a series of questions to help them create a fictional character involved in this crisis. Ask earlier expert volunteers to stay in their original roles, but add detail through this exercise. Remind students to think critically and realistically about the role, encouraging them to create a character with nuance that is deeply invested in this crisis. Discourage caricatures. Questions might include:

> *"What is your name?"*

> *"How old are you?"*

> *"Have you lived here all your life?"*

> *"Who makes up your family?"*

> *"What have you lost in this crisis?"*

"What have you gained in this crisis?"

"How has your day-to-day life changed?"

"How do you view people from the outside entering into this crisis?"

"What do you want the world to know about this crisis?"

Add any questions based on the unique crisis developed by your group. Afterwards, ask participants to open their eyes and walk to a personal space. Ask them to once again close their eyes, and embody the character. Then ask them to open their eyes when fully in-role. Using spotlighting, tap participants on the shoulder, asking them to tell their story. Other participants listen and process. If time is an issue, people when tapped may say one phrase or word that tells how they are feeling.

Volunteer information: After the group shares, the leader solicits a volunteer to give a report from the site of the crisis. The leader facilitates this conversation, asking:

"What did you see?"

"What is the situation?"

"Concretely, how can we help out?"

"What would be the consequences of our efforts?"

"What choices must be made?"

The meeting (Mantle of the Expert): After the volunteer report, ask everyone to remain in-role and silently create a circle, sitting in a spot where they were not previously sitting (selecting a new seat helps everyone disconnect the "real" person from the role they play). Announce that you are here to facilitate a meeting between the crisis management volunteers and the inhabitants of the crisis location. Ask participants to introduce themselves by name and role in the situation. State that you hope the discussion will conclude with a decision about important next steps. Points of discussion might include:

"What does everyone want?"

"What do you personally think will solve the crisis? Is that feasible?"

"Which choices must we make?"

"What is the obvious solution?"

"What resources do we need to solve this crisis?"

At this point the lesson is entirely improvisational, and the leader should monitor the discussion closely but leave room for a variety of perspectives and ideas to circulate amongst participants. Facilitators should use knowledge of the group to support engaged conversation. At the end, ask the group to come to consensus or take a vote on the next major action. After the vote, ask everyone to close their eyes, release the character from their bodies, and open their eyes when they are completely out-of-role.

Note: In practice, we have found that outcomes of this drama run the gamut, from recommendations to shoot the authority, to leaving until circumstances calm down, to forming a private militia. As the neutral facilitator, allow space for all these ideas, using them as points of conversation during reflection of the drama.

Variation: Depending on what unfolds during the in-role conversation, the leader can generate another role based on participants' contributions, thus changing the situation and encouraging different aspects of the conversation. For example, the leader can transform into passport control and arrest one of the volunteers.

Reflection: Process-oriented drama of this nature requires a substantial amount of time for out-of-role discussion. Some guiding questions:

"What were some of the feelings or emotions you experienced during the work?"

"What is the relationship between agency and compassion between volunteers/inhabitants?"

"Did you develop any personal insights about crisis and compassion?"

"Did you learn anything new/different about crisis and compassion?"

"Where were the spaces of ambiguity in this drama?"

"How does the drama relate to real life?"

"Was our solution reasonable and fair? Why/why not? What are other possible solutions?"

Unification: Because the scenario played out above often gets tense, a final group- and community-building activity is advisable. We like Squeeze Pass: The group stands in a circle holding hands. One person starts the process by lightly squeezing a neighbor's hand. The squeeze is then passed hand-to-hand around the circle.

Extension activities: You can break this lesson into two parts, building characters in one session and conducting the town meeting in the next, to allow time for reflection and metacognition between the two lessons.

Linear and process-oriented drama side-by-side: one story, two methods

Our discussion thus far has deliberately attempted to distinguish between linear and process-oriented drama methods to give readers a sense of different techniques and provide some background regarding why they might choose a particular approach for a given topic. However, the two methods are often combined, depending on the make-up of participating groups and according to the leader's comfort level, expertise, goals, and personal preference. This hybrid approach (also called transitional or mixed) allows leaders to mix and match process-oriented and linear methods (in fact, the use of tableaux in the "Crisis" lesson plan above makes even this relatively open-ended plan a hybrid of linear and process-oriented approaches). In practice, you can approach the same topic through many different combinations of linear, in-role, and process-oriented methodologies.

Below we share two contrasting approaches to the same basic material, the famous Japanese folktale, *Urashima Taro* (see Ozaki 1908 for the full story, which is summarized below). In the first lesson plan, we use a linear approach to explore this folktale as a piece of literature, with learning objectives focused on understanding the structure of the original story through embodied learning. In the second, we use a hybrid of linear and process-oriented approaches, combining discrete activities and in-role work to explore moral issues in the story.

The story of Urashima Taro

Note: This is a summary. You should make the story your own and fill it in with imagery and use the storytelling techniques discussed in this chapter.

In a country far away there lives a man named Urashima Taro. He catches fish for a living which his mother sells on the market. One day Urashima Taro comes home and has caught nothing. When he walks over the beach he sees a few children playing with a small turtle. Urashima Taro saves the turtle and puts it back in the sea.

The next morning he goes out fishing extra early. He has just cast his nets when a giant turtle comes up next to the boat and tells him to sit on his back because he is taking him to the palace of the Sea King. After a wonderful underwater journey they reach the palace. The little turtle Taro rescued turns out to be the daughter of the Sea King. She shows him the wonders of the palace. Among other things, Urashima Taro notices that the farmers sow plants, water them, and are almost immediately able to harvest.

Urashima Taro stays a while in the palace. Suddenly he gets homesick and wants to see his mother and his village. He pleads with the King to let him go for one day. The princess gives him a lacquer box that he promises never to open.

The turtle brings Urashima Taro back and he walks to his village but doesn't recognize anything or anyone. Finally he comes to where he thinks his house had been, but he only sees an old man sitting against a tree. He asks the old man "Isn't this the spot where Urashima Taro's house used to be?" The man tells him that he heard a story from his great-great-great grandfather about a man called Urashima Taro who lived in the village and went to the sea to fish one morning and never came back. Urashima Taro looks at the lacquer box, opens it, and out comes a puff of smoke. As his back starts curving and his skin wrinkles and his hair becomes grey, he hears the voice of the princess: "Urashima Taro, it was your life that was in that box. Now we shall never see each other again!"

A linear story drama for elementary students: Urashima Taro

Goal: Exploring the structure of Taro's story and understanding the character's experiences through dramatic play.

Objectives:

- The participants will use imagination and concentration in the dramatization of the story.
- The participants will tell the story through images, in pantomime, and with the use of language.
- The participants will use metacognitive skills to understand the structure of the story.

Materials: Taro's story, note cards labeled with scenes, ocean sounds, and a playback device.

Procedure

Starter—Association circle: Participants lie in a circle on the floor, heads toward the middle, shoulders touching. The leader taps a participant on the foot, saying a word from the list below.

The tapped participant immediately says the first word that comes to mind, creating a word association. The word association should then move around the circle clockwise, with every person saying the first word they think of when they hear the person before them speak. When the association has gone around the entire circle, or when the free association has gotten off-track, stop the group and begin again by tapping a new participant on the foot and starting the free association with another word.

List of words: Sea, Fish, Magic, Secret.

Storytelling: Tell the story of Taro, using recorded ocean sounds to enhance mood.

Reflection:

> *"What images do you remember from the story?"*

> *"Why do you think things happened the way they did?"*

> *"What are the most important moments in the story?"*

Creating tableaux: Divide the class into six groups and assign each group one of the following scenes, either by giving them a notecard with a description on it or by verbal description:

1 Taro returns from fishing and sees the turtle
2 Taro is taken to the palace
3 Taro meets the king and princess
4 Taro is shown around the palace
5 Taro asks to return home for a day
6 Taro is back at his village.

Give each group five minutes to make a tableau of the most important image in their scene. Remind them that they should use their whole bodies and that people can represent objects as well as characters. Remind groups to practice their tableaux.

Spotlighting: When time is up, instruct groups that you will count backwards from five to zero. When you reach "zero," all groups should be frozen in their tableaux images. With minimal "unfreezing," direct learners to look first at group one, then two, and so on.

Reflection:

> *"What did you see in each picture?"*

> *"How could you tell what each picture was showing us?"*

Connecting tableaux: Ask groups to think about what happened just before and just after the images they showed in their tableaux. Each group should create a sequence of three images that demonstrate this before–during–after set of events.

Sharing: Ask each group to share their sequence of images one at a time on your countdown, holding each image for three seconds.

Pantomime scenes: Ask each group to think about how they would bring their sequence of images to life with pantomime. Prompt groups to think about how each character and object in this scene might move. Provide time to practice.

Sharing: Play the ocean sounds as each group in order shares their pantomimed scene.

Adding language: Return to small groups and ask participants to think about ways to add language to their scenes. What would each character say in this moment? What are the sounds happening in this world?

Sharing of scenes: Share each of the scenes with the added language.

Reflection:

> *"What skills did you need to use to tell the story?"*

> *"What did other students do that helped you understand what was happening in their scenes?"*

> *"Why do you think this story happened in the way it did?"*

> *"What do you think would happen if the parts of this story were rearranged?"*

A process drama for elementary students (K-5): Urashima Taro

Taking the story of Urashima Taro as a starting point, the following lesson explores not the structure of the story as above, but instead the emotional and moral experiences of the central character.

Goal: Exploration of anger, loss, and decision-making in the story of Urashima Taro.

Objectives:

- Students will reflect on animal cruelty by exploring Taro's story.
- Students will think of strategies to find a missing person.
- Students will explore the consequences of decision-making through in-role experiences.

Materials: Ocean sounds and playback device, story notecards, big scarf or cape or piece of fabric, staff or cane, soft small foam ball.

Procedure

Starter—Association circle: (see previous lesson)

Tell the story, stopping after the scene in which Taro sees the children tormenting the turtle.

Improvising the story: Ask for three volunteers to be the children tormenting the turtle. Either the leader or a student volunteer will be Taro. Sidecoach the children to think about what it would be like to interact with the turtle and show observers with their actions. At the signal of the leader, Taro enters and begins discussing the sea turtle with the children. Allow for the improvisation to unfold.

Reflection: (out-of-role)

> *"How does this scene make you feel?"*
>
> *"What happened to the turtle?"*
>
> *"What did Taro do?"*
>
> *"Have you ever seen someone bother an animal?"*
>
> *"What did you think about that?"*
>
> *"Can/should you do something about it?"*

Storytelling: Continue the story, starting from Taro saving the turtle. End with the next morning as Taro is casting his net, with your last line being "and suddenly..."

Town hall meeting: Immediately upon completing this section of the story, grab your staff to enter into role as the Village Counselor, addressing the group in-role:

> *"Dear villagers, I am glad you all could come here to this very important meeting. As your Village Counselor, I have the duty to tell you that one of us is missing. Urashima Taro went to sea this morning and has not returned. Now I know some of you have more information than others so we should share what we know and see what we can do to find him."*

The participants are now "in-role" as villagers. Facilitate an initial in-role discussion of what each villager knows about the situation before directing participants toward questions about what needs to be done. Split the villagers into teams, assign them tasks and set the groups to work. Set a time to report back.

This in-role work can go on for the time the leader allows and may even be extended over multiple lessons. Keep in mind that real-life skills are involved but that the world created remains fictional. As long as participants are working with conviction, allow them to proceed together to try to find Taro. Depending on time constraints (in this case a single session), stop where convenient and continue the story.

Storytelling: Tell the rest of the story up to the point of Taro landing back on the beach.

Parallel narrative pantomime: Ask for a volunteer to take on the role of Taro, or allow all participants to play Taro simultaneously. Narrate the story of Taro coming back to the village up to meeting the old man, as the participant(s) pantomime the action. At this point, the leader assumes the role of the old man and begins an in-role interaction with Taro.

Group meeting: In-role as the old man, the leader asks Taro what the box is and calls on all the villagers (participants in-role) to help decide if he should, or should not, open the box. Encourage the group to consider the consequences of different choices and make a decision.

Storytelling: Tell the conclusion of the story.

Reflection:

> *"What were some of the decisions Taro made that led to his adventure?"*
>
> *"When Taro was gone, how did that make you feel?"*
>
> *"Do you think we came up with the right strategies to help him?"*

"What could we have done differently?"

"Would you have opened the box? Why? Why not?"

"What may have happened if Taro did not open the box?"

"Did you learn anything new from this story and the activities that you did not know before? What? How does that make you feel?"

Drama for inclusion and diversity: a hybrid workshop plan

In the previous section we explored two approaches to the same content: a linear drama, and a hybrid drama. As you can see, hybrid approaches are particularly useful for exploring social and ethical issues due to their combination of reflective activities and active, in-role exploration of multiple perspectives. The following longer workshop plan is intended for teens and would be appropriate for either a classroom or a community organization. By immersing themselves in the drama activities the participants will find space to explore their own and others' unconscious biases and presumptions. The lesson includes linear and process-oriented activities, and introduces the field of drama for social justice, which is explored in detail in the following chapter.

A hybrid in-role workshop for teens: bullying and homophobia

Goal: Participants will explore biases and presumptions about themselves and others around homophobia and sexual orientation.

Objectives:

- The participants will take on the perspectives of those involved in Tom's life (use a different name if there is a Tom among the participants).
- The participants will explore homophobia as a social phenomenon.
- The participants will become aware of the impact of ideologies on our actions.

Materials: Markers, chart paper, a life-size outline of a person, an image of Tom's school locker with a homophobic slur written on it, pencils, note cards.

Note: Before beginning this kind of workshop, it is important to point out that participants should focus on exploring characters and actions in-role, independent of our "selves," in part to explore other perspectives. Making a clear distinction between our "selves" and our drama roles helps create a safe atmosphere for drama exploration.

Procedure

Starter—Brainstorm:

Divide participants into three groups. Hand each group a piece of chart paper labeled with the words:

> Homophobia
> Homophobic language
> Turning a Blind Eye

Ask each group to write down thoughts and images based on these words in a free association, building on one another's ideas. After a few minutes, rotate the chart paper clockwise so that each group has another group's work in front of them. Continue the free association. Allow two minutes and then rotate papers a final time for another association period. Finally, rotate the papers back to their original groups and allow groups to discuss what material was added to their ideas.

Tableaux: Ask each group to distill the material on their chart paper into one essential image and create a tableau of that image with their bodies. Encourage participants to work freely; either literal or figurative tableaux are acceptable. Each group should give their tableau a title.

Sharing tableaux: Group by group, share each tableau. As each group presents their image, reflect together on the following prompts:

> *"What do we see?"*

> *"Where do we see that?"* (discuss body positions, expressions etc)

Reflection: After each group has shared, conduct a group discussion about where we see these ideas reflected in real life.

First role-play: Lead participants out of the room. Explain that they will now take on the role of high school students waiting for the bell. Encourage them to pick a role that does not necessarily reflect themselves or their experiences and beliefs, making specific decisions about gender, political beliefs and personal philosophy, favorite activities, and the like.

While participants are outside constructing their roles, enter the classroom and post on the way an image of Tom's locker with the slur plastered over it.

Open the door to the workspace and announce that the bell has rung and it is time for the school day to begin. As students enter the workspace, they should interact with each other and the environment as their characters.

Sidecoach in-role as another student:

"What is that?"

"What does it mean?"

"How do you feel?"

"What do you think is going on?"

"Why would someone do this?"

Reflection: Once the in-role interaction seems complete, go out-of-role and ask participants to exit their roles and form a circle to discuss what happened.

"Is this realistic?"

"Can this happen?"

"Were the students' reactions realistic?"

Visualization: Ask participants to close their eyes for a minute and visualize their characters.

Prompts:

"Think about your character and his/her relationship to Tom."

"How does your character feel about what happened?"

"What would your character say about this incident?"

"What would your character do about it?"

Interviewing: Ask for two or three volunteers to take on the roles of friends of Tom. They sit on chairs facing the rest of the group, who are out-of-role. Introduce these three students as a collective "Friend" and facilitate the interview using questions from the observers.

Sample questions:

"Who are you?"

"How do you know Tom?"

"Do you know what happened?"

"Who did it?"

"How did you react?" "What should happen now?"

Role on the wall: Tape a cut-out labeled "Tom" on the wall and ask participants to write words on the cutout to describe Tom, based on their understanding of him thus far from the Interview exercise and other activities.

Guided visualization: Ask participants to grab a pencil and paper and return to their roles as students. Begin guiding them through the following visualization:

"Look at the locker again. Look at your classmates. Keeping the situation in mind, close your eyes. You're lying in bed at night. Think of what happened. How do you feel about it now, alone in your bed? For some of you it may be confusing, for some crystal clear. You feel you have to write to someone about it though. Ask yourself, to whom must you write? What do you have to say? You turn on your light and pick up pen and paper. Open your eyes and begin your letter. "

Allow enough time to write, monitoring to see when the majority of participants have completed the task before asking the group to finish up their final sentence.

In-role, each participant should read what they have written and find the one sentence or phrase that best expresses their thoughts and feelings about this situation. Ask participants to underline and memorize that phrase.

Voice collage: In-role, ask students:

"Imagine you are back in your bedroom. When I touch your shoulder, say your word or phrase."

Create the voice collage by touching students on the shoulder one at a time. After the collage is complete, ask participants to come out-of-role and speak in pairs with someone near them about what they heard.

Tableaux: Divide the participants into two groups. Each group designates a "Tom" (let someone volunteer for this role; never assign it). "Tom" should take up a neutral stance (no need to be in-role). One at a time, each participant should position themselves in a tableau around "Tom" the first time they see him again after the locker incident. Discuss each tableau.

Collective improvisation: As a group, select one of the two tableaux to use to explore conversations that may have taken place between Tom and classmates just after the locker incident. Take three volunteers to go into the tableau as "Toms." Just as the earlier exercise built one collective "Friend," this exercise will build a collaborative "Tom" (instruct volunteers to accept the other "Tom's" answers and build on them.) Place the three "Toms" in the middle of the tableau, back to back in a triangle, and have all participants place themselves in the tableau in-role. At your signal, bring the tableau to life and allow the group to explore the conversations that Tom and his classmates would have in this scene.

Note: The "Toms" are designed as a collective to diffuse any personal associations between participants and this role. Nonetheless there are ethical issues involved in impersonating people other than ourselves, especially in sensitive and vulnerable situations. Always make sure you have volunteers and never require the "Toms" to react fully in-role but encourage them to stay neutral and think about what Tom might say. Depending on group make-up, talk about risk-taking, safety, and personal boundaries.

Conscience alley: Divide the group into two lines, facing one another. Instruct them to think of some thoughts/questions/feelings Tom may have. Each participant should pass as "Tom" through the alley while the rest of the participants utter these thoughts. One by one participants move through the alley as "Tom," listening before returning to the line.

Role on the wall: Return to the cut-out of Tom on the wall, and ask participants to silently fill in what we didn't know before but know now. When the activity is complete, allow time for everyone to read the new material.

Visualization: Ask participants to close their eyes for a visualization:

> *"It has been over fifteen years since this incident happened at your high school. You are now adults, teachers or administrators at schools, school board members, social workers, or members of the community. Some of you are married or live with a partner. Some of you have children who are freshmen in high school. Your viewpoints may have totally altered or not. Create your adult character."*

Give participants some time to think, sidecoaching toward questions about character traits.

> *"When you open your eyes, you are at an open high school board meeting. Think about why you are at that meeting and what your role is here. Although you can build off your student character, your*

characters do not know each other, nor will you bring up the incident of fifteen years ago in the meeting."

Board meeting: Leader-in-role as the Board President makes the following announcement:

"An incident has happened at North High School. There has never been an act of violence quite like this, and the board is very concerned. We would therefore like input from the community on how we could respond."

Allow for discussion and points of view to be voiced. Use your role to encourage everyone to get involved in the discussion and build the scenario together.

After the board meeting has reached a conclusion or the in-role work feels complete, ask the participants to close their eyes and reflect silently. After a moment of silent reflection, read the following aloud:

"Bullying is the ongoing physical or emotional victimization of a person by another person or group of people. Cyberbullying is an emerging problem in which people use new communication technologies, such as social media and texting, to harass and cause emotional harm to their victims.

Thirty-two percent of the nation's students (ages 12–18) reported being bullied during the 2007–2008 school year. Lesbian, gay, bisexual, and transgender (LGBT) youth experience more bullying (including physical violence and injury) at school than their heterosexual peers.

Both victims and perpetrators of bullying are at higher risk of suicide than their peers. Children who are both victims and perpetrators of bullying are at highest risk.

Young people who are the victims of bullying are at increased risk for suicide as well as increased risk for depression and other problems associated with suicide."

(Substance Abuse and Mental Health Services Administration 2012)

Reflection in-role: Ask each participant to choose a character who has somehow been involved in the locker incident. After a moment to think, each participant should take a note card to write a message to Tom. Take the cut-out and tape it in front of Tom's locker. One by one, allow each participant to read their message and tape it to Tom's cut-out.

Take a moment of silence. Take participants out-of-role and ask them to reflect together with someone next to them.

Reflection out-of-role:

"How did this drama relate to our lives and experiences?"

"Is it realistic? Why? Why not?"

"In creating and hearing the different characters, what insights did you gain on the role of bias, privilege, and power?"

"What was the impact of ideological positions and identity locations in this drama?"

"What stereotyping did you see in the drama? Is it possible that Tom was a completely different character? Could he have/gain power?"

Linear and process-oriented drama with different age groups

While all of the activities and lesson plans in this chapter can be used with diverse age groups, here we discuss a few considerations for drama with specific populations. Keep in mind that most activities can be modified not only for different content areas, but for different age groups and skill levels.

Early childhood

Linear drama with early childhood populations typically involves creative movement, simple stories, and activities that provide opportunities for multimodal engagements with a topic (visual, aural, verbal, tactile). Imitation and repetition are also important components of early childhood linear drama. For example, tell a story, sing a song about the story's main character, dramatize the story through narrative pantomime, then repeat the cycle. Pre-K and kindergarten participants are also in the phase of emergent literacy (developing early literacy skills including pre-reading, phonemic awareness, independent expression, basic comprehension, and retelling), so look for opportunities to communicate information through multiple strategies (for example, reading aloud and showing pictures, then asking learners to share what they saw and heard). Also, very young participants have smaller worlds than other age groups. Highlight narratives that relate to their life experiences (self, school, family, play). Lessons should typically be shorter for young learners.

Key techniques:

- Narrative pantomime
- Songs and poems
- Teacher-in-role
- Parallel play
- Creative movement.

Early elementary

Children between first and third grades have developed increasing competencies in literacy. Many are beginning to read with greater fluency, and they are beginning to work with higher-order cognitive processes like making inferences and predicting outcomes. They are also more adept at navigating multi-step processes. This age group has also developed more sophisticated interpersonal skills. Thus this age group often enjoys work in improvisation and more sophisticated story drama in which they develop characters and reinterpret stories. They will also likely enjoy multi-step drama games. This age group still learns a great deal through embodied learning and repetition, so prioritize linear drama activities that provide opportunity for movement and do not worry about boring a group by repeating an activity several times.

Key techniques:

- Improvisation
- Story drama
- Games
- Teacher-in-role/student-in-role
- Town meeting
- Non-narrative pantomime.

Upper elementary

Upper elementary students are in the process of developing skills in abstract (as opposed to concrete) thinking. They are becoming more skilled at making connections between academic subjects (for instance, the connection between music and math), and they are often more interested in issues beyond their immediate worlds (the environment, political issues) than younger learners. They are also increasingly social and are beginning to develop personal values and morals. For linear drama with this age group, try small group work and activities that support project design (for example, planning, rehearsing, and sharing a story dramatization with peers). They will also enjoy games that allow them to create in the moment (like What Are You Doing?). Also, this age group will likely respond well to drama that deals with social issues.

Key techniques:

- Improvisation
- In-role work
- Multi-step image work
- Games.

Middle school

Middle schoolers often display an increasing level of independence and likely will attempt to define themselves in relation to others (including peers, parents and teachers). Sometimes, middle school participants may be outspoken or even argumentative as they develop critical, independent thought. In linear drama, they will likely respond to opportunities to reinvent stories/narratives, add complexity to topics, and/or articulate aesthetic values. They are intensely social and may appreciate opportunities to explore relationships (familial, authoritative, and romantic) and work alongside peers. Above all, they will respond most positively to being taken seriously, being given opportunities to apply their knowledge to real-world situations, and to having their opinions heard and respected.

Key techniques:

- Improvisation
- Formal sharing
- Social drama
- Town meetings.

High school

High school participants are swiftly approaching the autonomy of young adulthood. Accordingly, they appreciate opportunities to take leadership roles, with adult facilitators acting as mentors and supporters instead of supervisors. They will often have complex and nuanced ideas about the world and their place within it. They are also social, but may have more complex relationships with peers and family than middle school students. High school students often have a strong sense of self, and self-determined ideas about their competencies. For example, a student may say, *"I'm not creative at all."* However, highly motivated high school students will be deeply invested in drama programs. Many high school students are also beginning to think beyond their school as they prepare for life after high school. In drama, they will respond to opportunities to devise new work based on abstract ideas (hopes, fears, dreams, aspirations). They will also look for opportunities to show their life as they experience it (as opposed to how media and adults conceive of high school experiences).

Key techniques:

- In-role work
- Mantle of the Expert
- Town meetings
- Advanced character development activities

- Devising/production processes (see Chapter 4)
- Advanced social issues through drama (see Chapter 3).

References

Frost, Joe L., Sue Clark Wortham, and Robert Stuart Reifel. 2008. *Play and Child Development*. Pearson/Merrill Prentice Hall.

Heathcote, Dorothy. 1991. *Collected Writings on Education and Drama*. Northwestern University Press.

Heathcote, Dorothy, and Gavin Bolton. 1995. *Drama for Learning: Dorothy Heathcote's Mantle of the Expert approach to education. Dimensions of Drama Series*. ERIC. http://eric.ed.gov/?id=ED378628.

Hyams, Barry. 1974. Stage. *Los Angeles Times (1923-Current File)*, May 26, 1974. http://login.ezproxy1.lib.asu.edu/login?url=http://search.proquest.com/docview/157486036?accountid=4485. Accessed August 12, 2014.

Moore, Robin C. 1990. *Childhood's Domain: Play and place in child development*. MIG Communications.

O'Neill, Cecily. 1995. *Drama Worlds: A framework for process drama*. Heinemann.

O'Neill, Cecily, and Alan Lambert. 1982. *Drama Structures: A practical handbook for teachers*. Nelson Thornes.

Ozaki, Yei Theodora. 1908. "The Story of Urashima Taro, the Fisher Lad," *Japanese Fairy Tales*. Lit2Go Edition. Accessed August 10, 2014. http://etc.usf.edu/lit2go/72/japanese-fairy-tales/4881/the-story-of-urashima-taro-the-fisher-lad/.

Rosenberg, Helane S. 1987. *Creative Drama and Imagination: Transforming ideas into action*. Holt, Rinehart, and Winston.

Siks, Geraldine B. 1958. *Creative Dramatics: An art for children*. Harper.

——1961. *Creative Dramatics for Children*. 26. Ginn.

——1964. *Children's Literature for Dramatization: An Anthology*. Harper & Row.

——1981. "Drama in Education – A Changing Scene." *Children and Drama*, 15–28.

——1983. *Drama with Children*. Harper & Row.

Spolin, Viola. 1983. *Improvisation for the Theater*. Northwestern University Press.

——1986. *Theater Games for the Classroom*. Northwestern University Press.

Substance Abuse and Mental Health Services Administration. 2012. *Preventing Suicide: A Toolkit for High Schools*. HHS Publication No. SMA-12-4669. Center for Mental Health Services, Substance Abuse and Mental Health Services Administration. Accessed August 12, 2014. http://store.samhsa.gov/shin/content/SMA12-4669/SMA12-4669.pdf

Vygotsky, Lev Semenovich. 1967. "Play and Its Role in the Mental Development of the Child." *Journal of Russian and East European Psychology* 5 (3): 6–18.

3 Drama for social justice

This chapter discusses tactics for incorporating drama methods into curricula devoted to social justice issues. We start with a discussion of Augusto Boal's Theatre of the Oppressed methodology, with a nod to contemporary practitioners like Michael Rohd and Chen Alon, who have adapted Theatre of the Oppressed techniques for new work on social issues specific to young people (see Alon and Kuftinec 2007; Rohd 1998). We also approach this chapter inspired by the work of scholar-educators like Alison Dover and Elinor Vettraino, who explore ways that teachers have responded to the need to integrate issues of social justice into their lesson plans while also keeping in mind the dictates of state and nationwide standards (see Duffy and Vettraino 2010; Dover 2013). We include tactics for designing workshops and lesson plans that engage with specific social issues for a variety of age groups. We conclude with a discussion of teaching for social justice within standards-based education models for different grade levels.

Drama for social justice: Is it necessary?

One of the first questions teachers and artists interested in drama for social justice education must ask is: Is social justice education necessary? We believe so; however, we also recognize that social justice education for young people is an especially contentious issue (see for instance Manzo 2008). Some parents may be concerned about children being indoctrinated into value systems they may not share. Others may fear that social justice education takes valuable time from the core curriculum at a time when testing-based accountability measures increasingly drive instruction. Still others may be concerned that teachers who engage with social justice pedagogy are critiquing traditional values or even undermining students' patriotism by discussing negative aspects of local or national histories. While manipulating or indoctrinating students should not be the goal of teaching for social justice (and runs counter to most social justice education values and goals), interactive drama can help teachers and facilitators to directly engage with issues of equality, diversity, and justice while creating necessary space for dialogue.

It may seem like common sense that young children are innocent and should not be spoiled by discussion of issues related to class, race, or gender. Likewise, we may wish to believe that by being color-blind in the classroom we can teach all children to treat all people equally. However, research appears to show just the opposite. For example, studies indicate that ignoring social issues leaves young children particularly vulnerable to stereotyped beliefs and behaviors (see Winkler 2009; Patterson and Bigler 2006). Children also see the impact of systematic oppression on people's lives and, in the absence of open discussion, make sense of it as best they can, often by deciding that unjust treatment of a specific individual or group of people is somehow warranted. Furthermore, research consistently shows that children recognize oppression. For instance, children recognize racial oppression and begin developing racial biases as early as age three (Van Ausdale 2001). These facts make social justice education essential for young people.

Historical and theoretical foundations

What does it mean to teach for social justice? While definitions vary, notions of social justice depend on the idea that all individuals in society should be treated fairly and have mutual interest in, and responsibility to, one another. Dr Martin Luther King, Jr. described the impulse toward social justice education when he declared, in his Letter from Birmingham Jail, "I am cognizant of the interrelatedness of all communities and states. ... Injustice anywhere is a threat to justice everywhere. We are caught in an inescapable network of mutuality, tied in a single garment of destiny" (King 1963: 80). Teachers or teaching artists concerned with social justice education may build into their curricula examinations and dialogue about social issues. Teachers may also focus on helping their students cultivate skills to become fully engaged citizens with a strong sense of social awareness and responsibility to broader communities. Thus in teaching across units and curricular areas they might use techniques to encourage empathy, listening skills, appreciation of diversity and difference, and awareness of social and political power structures.

Most contemporary practitioners of social justice pedagogy have been influenced by Brazilian educational theorist Paulo Freire (1921–1997), author of *Pedagogy of the Oppressed* ([1970] 2000). A transformative figure in modern education, Freire argued that traditional methods of education rely on students passively absorbing knowledge, a mode he called the "banking method" of education because of the way in which teaching resembled making deposits into students' mental bank accounts. Freire also argued that this banking method reinforces the status quo in societies, teaching students to know their place in a rigid and hierarchical system of power and discouraging them from thinking critically about their world and their place within it. Freire suggested that the banking method instilled in students the idea that society is static and that oppressive structures cannot be changed. As a counterpoint, Freire advocated for an educational system that would help students develop skills to both think for themselves and challenge the status quo, seeing society as constantly growing and changing. He believed in teaching and learning models that encourage dialogue, problem-based learning, and cooperation. Moreover, he set out to change the educational system through a fundamental shift in how students and teachers engaged with knowledge. The result, his "pedagogy of the oppressed," focused on empowering the oppressed (students and beyond) rather than reinforcing the status quo, in which teachers held the power of knowledge and deposited it into the minds of their students. Many social justice educators today draw inspiration from Freire's focus on dialogue, cooperation, and problem-based learning, as well as from his beliefs about the relationships between power and knowledge.

Taking inspiration from Freire's philosophies about education, the use of drama as a method of teaching for and about social justice takes many forms. The most prominent tradition in drama for social justice, Theatre of the Oppressed (TO), involves collaborative exploration of specific issues of oppression and power imbalances. The originator of TO, Augusto Boal (1931–2009), was a Brazilian theatre artist, politician, and writer, and Paulo Freire's student. Boal's interest in drama as a tool for social change sprang from his experience of living under military dictatorships. In 1964, Boal was a young man when Brazil experienced a military coup. The Junta Militar exiled many artists, including Boal, in an attempt to silence any voices of opposition. During this time of exile, Boal wrote *Theatre of the Oppressed* (1985), his first and most influential theoretical work. In addition to writing *Theatre of the Oppressed*, Boal also used his time in exile to develop and refine Theatre of the Oppressed techniques in other South American countries and, later, throughout the world. He used theatre games, activities, and short scenes to create a "forum" for public debate. This technique, now known as Forum Theatre, focused on transforming the idea of theatre from an actor–audience model that encouraged passive reception of dramatic performances to a "spect-actor" model in which audience members were encouraged to debate character choices and take an active part in solving problems posed by scenes presented to them, even taking over the role of the actor by substituting themselves in scenes. Boal was finally allowed to return to Brazil in 1986 after the demise of the military dictatorship, at which point he established a center for the study of Theatre of the Oppressed in Rio de Janeiro. In addition to his internationally recognized work in theatre, he also became a city councilperson in Rio de Janeiro and was nominated for a Nobel Peace Prize in 2008. He was an extremely active practitioner until his death, and his legacy continues in the form of conferences, institutes, actor and practitioner training, performance paradigms, and scholarly interest.

The TO approach takes Augusto Boal's work in books like *Theatre of the Oppressed* (1985), *Games for Actors and Non-Actors* ([1992] 2002), and

The Rainbow of Desire (1995) as its primary inspiration, but it also includes theatre artists and educators who have adapted his techniques into new forms. The TO model often takes the form of workshops with community groups. These workshops usually focus on empowering participants to explore specific problems related to power and oppression in their lives or communities and set out to develop possible solutions, either through image-based work, games, improvisation of scenarios, or a combination of all three. Workshops may last an hour or extend for multiple days or weeks. Usually a highly trained facilitator called a "Joker" oversees Theatre of the Oppressed work. TO techniques can form the basis of short units or a day's lesson plan, but they can also be foundational to a teaching artist or teacher's entire pedagogical philosophy. Many practitioners have adapted Boal's methods to their own purposes, such as Michael Rohd's Hope is Vital ensemble, which applied these techniques and other theatre tactics to create dialogue between and among teens about issues surrounding HIV and sexuality (Rohd 1998). Former Israeli soldier Chen Alon and Palestinian activist Nour Shehadah adapted Boal's method to create Combatants for Peace, a group that uses personal storytelling and TO techniques to explore polarizing conflict (Kuftinec 2009). TO techniques have also deeply influenced Theatre for Development work in developing nations around the world, in which non-government organizations (NGOs) create performance work aimed at educating communities and addressing social issues from domestic violence to gender-based oppression. If teachers or artists are committed to learning environments characterized by open dialogue, student-directed learning, and empowerment of all participants, TO techniques may even become a central feature of their teaching and pedagogical philosophies. Boal continued to revise and refine his methods throughout his life, developing a family of TO approaches that includes:

- Image Theatre, in which participants use activities to create, discuss, and transform images of oppression.
- Forum Theatre, in which participants see and discuss scenes of oppression before using substitution to try out different ways of dealing with the oppression represented, facilitated by a highly trained leader known as a "Joker."
- Invisible Theatre, an activist mode of performance in which actors present realistic scenes of oppression in public places without letting audiences know they are viewing a performance.
- Legislative Theatre, a method that uses performance to discuss and refine proposed laws.

Beyond Boal

Outside the formal tradition of TO, teachers may also use a broader repertoire of drama methods and techniques as tools for exploring issues of social justice. Leaders of drama for social justice neither require the formal training that TO typically expects of "Jokers," nor do they necessarily follow the format for Boal's Forum or Image Theatre techniques when applying drama methods to social justice education. Nevertheless, TO and drama for social justice do substantially overlap, although there are also some significant differences. While TO workshops tend to focus on the participants' personal and specific lived experiences, drama for social justice often frames issues more broadly, using the lesson plan format to explore issues related to a topic. Sometimes these lessons generate personal responses, much like TO. At other times, a social justice lesson will include or even prioritize critical distance from the topic under consideration. Scholars and teachers from Dorothy Heathcote (see Chapter 2) to Sharon Grady have advocated the use of drama-based pedagogy to explore issues like class, privilege, race, gender, and ability in the classroom and have adapted drama methods, from Boal and beyond, to help in these endeavors.

Related methods

Theatre and drama for social justice fall under a larger umbrella known as "applied theatre." Applied theatre refers to theatre and performance techniques used to address specific issues or contexts, from education to therapy. Below we list a few specific types of applied theatre with a social justice orientation:

- Sociodrama, a method of using dramatic play to explore and resolve conflict and build empathy, was a related technique developed in part by Patricia Sternberg, author of *Theatre for Conflict Resolution in the Classroom and Beyond* (1998). This approach helps participants to share information and increase awareness of facts and debates around social problems, in addition to engaging with personal connections to social issues.
- Drama therapy, practiced by licensed therapists, uses methods similar to Boal's, but instead of directing this work outward toward the community or larger groups, the work is focused on generating opportunities for self-knowledge and healing on an individual level. Take care not to dabble in drama therapy without proper training.
- Playback theatre, a form of theatre used to start dialogue and build community, features audience members telling their stories before seeing them immediately reenacted by performers. Active in over fifty countries, Playback theatre has been adapted in educational settings, prisons, community centers, summer camps, and other contexts to create interactive performance events centered on participants' stories. As with drama therapy, Playback theatre practitioners need thorough training to ensure the desired results and safeguard participants' emotional and psychological well-being. See http://www.playbacktheatre.org/ for more information.

- Theatre for Development (TfD), the use of theatre as a tool in educating communities for social justice, is especially popular as an approach used by NGOs in areas of extreme poverty or unrest. While TfD can be either "traditional" or "interactive" performance, Boal's Theatre of the Oppressed has been particularly influential on interactive TfD (see for example Sloman 2011).
- Drama in Healthcare includes the use of improvisation techniques to improve doctor–patient communication as well as Clown Care, an international program that sends specially trained clowns to provide therapeutic entertainment and interactions with patients and families. Many healthcare organizations consider applied drama techniques foundational to positive patient outcomes (see for example Spitzer and Warren 2013).

Lesson planning considerations

Below we list a few suggestions for addressing social issues through drama. Perhaps the most important rule of thumb for this work is to practice, practice, practice. Listening, facilitation, and workshop design are all skills that can be honed through repetition and reflection. As often as possible seek out feedback and ask for observation from peers and experienced mentors as well as from workshop participants. Make a habit of keeping notes about elements of your programs that work and areas for modification to help you keep refining your technique and lesson plans. Also, review the assessment and advocacy chapters (Chapters 5 and 6) for additional information regarding how you can prepare, execute, and reflect on your lessons and residencies.

Knowing your audience

You may be conducting activities focused on drama for social justice with a group you have known for weeks or months, or you may walk into a workshop full of new faces. In either case, try to avoid assumptions about your group, their lived experiences, their abilities, or even their interest in drama and/or social justice education. Getting to know each group and each individual within the group with an open mind helps you adapt and adjust based on participant needs and interests. If you are providing a commissioned workshop for a community organization, this process will likely start well in advance of the workshop as you determine the organization's goals, evaluate the nature of participants' prior experience with this type of drama-based work, and investigate group demographics.

If you are working with students or participants you already know or have collaborated with during previous lessons or residencies, you will have come to know quite a bit about them individually and as a group. Sometimes, prior knowledge of a group can short-circuit the process of shared discovery that is meant to happen during the session, since teachers and facilitators hold unavoidable preconceived notions about their students. While prior knowledge of participants can be handy in lesson planning, especially in terms of choosing activities appropriate to the group's skills and experiences, maintain an open mind and stay attentive to group dynamics as they evolve in the new context of collaborative drama work. For example, a regular classroom of high school English students is not necessarily prepared to engage with social justice issues simply because they have shared a classroom for a semester. Similarly, a group of middle-school summer camp participants (or their parents) might express questions or concerns about exploring tough subjects during their "fun" summer program.

We recommend evaluating all groups with one of the "temperature taking" or "values inventory" activities, like the Continuum activity, listed later in the chapter, to help facilitators understand the range of attitudes in the group as well as help the group begin the process of thinking through social issues together. Building in getting-to-know-you activities and integrating different ensemble-building games not only helps groups develop communication skills and build comfort with one another, but also assists facilitators in reevaluating any preconceived notions about their students.

Demographic concerns

When planning a drama session based on social justice issues, take into consideration the demographics of your group. However, approach these demographic observations with care. Participants' responses to social issues will rarely break down neatly along lines of race, class, ethnicity, gender, sexuality, religious belief, or political affiliation. While you should take care to treat all participants as individuals rather than making assumptions about their points of view, being "color-blind" is not a reasonable or responsible position to take as a session leader. Playwright August Wilson famously explained the problems of the "color-blind" stance:

> When white people say, "I don't see color," what they're saying is "You're affected by this undesirable condition, but I'll pretend I don't see that." And I go, "No, see my color. Look at me. I'm not ashamed of who I am and what I am."
>
> (Wilson 1998)

In espousing a false color-blindness (or any other kind of identity-blindness), you deny individual participants' unique experiences and imply that difference is best ignored. Privilege, bias, and different life experiences are facts of life in a diverse society, and ignoring these issues not only fails to neutralize them, but also prevents you and your group from examining them directly in order to understand and address their effects.

A few recommendations regarding group demographics:

- Avoid making those in the minority in the room (whether or not they are part of a minority group in the local, regional, or national community) spokespersons for an entire group of people. Doing so trivializes their individual experiences, often makes the individual and others uncomfortable, and might even lead other members of the group to reduce the individual's complex identity to a single attribute.
- Acknowledge your own position and privilege where appropriate. While workshops should focus more on participants' experiences and less on your experiences as the leader, disclosing details about your life and background in simple statements helps participants contextualize your perspectives and potentially helps them feel more comfortable with your leadership. Offering participants a glimpse into your life is preferable to donning a mask of false neutrality.
- Think critically about how to engage with issues in homogenous groups. For instance, you might work with a group of mostly middle-class white US citizens engaging in a drama-based lesson that examines race relations during the US Civil Rights Movement. In order to help a group of students develop critical understanding of issues surrounding this complex historical event, you will have to think carefully about how to approach source material, discussions, and dramatic representation. Specifically, be careful with performance-based learning that might lead to stereotyped representations, or what we call "stereotype mining," in which a group with little knowledge of a subject or category of identity draws on limited and at times erroneous understandings to create stereotyped representations of other people's life experiences. Stereotype mining can lead to students simply recreating stereotypes they have heard about with regard to issues or groups, often reinforcing the very assumptions the lesson is designed to allow students to rethink. We have led workshops in which participants improvised scenes without proper preparation and have been shocked to see stereotyped accents, racist assumptions about characters, and incorrect information about events or people creeping into the material. These experiences provided a rude awakening regarding the complex nature of drama-based social justice education and the importance of rigorous preparation and reflection to a successful residency. To avoid stereotype mining, think about how and when to use performance activities as you plan lessons in order to maximize learning and keep the group on track to interrogate rather than rely on or reinforce stereotypes and biases. While taking on roles outside our own experience can be a pathway to new insights, avoid asking students to "play the part" of a person without giving them appropriate time to prepare and develop a deep understanding of the complexity of a human identity (see also Chapters 1 and 2).

- Do your research before, during, and after a lesson. Especially in lesson plans involving specific historical or contemporary events, use the wealth of information accessible to you to invest your workshop with voices and details connected to the reality of those events. We love using historical newspaper articles, first-hand accounts, period-specific advertisements, and news broadcasts to give participants a taste of the real events to be explored in the lesson. This strategy can help immensely with avoiding stereotype mining.

Defining a workshop topic

You will often enter your classroom or workshop space with a topic already established. Perhaps you have been hired as a teaching artist to work with a community group on issues surrounding women's health. Or you're a middle school teacher planning to use drama as a tool for exploring social justice issues during a unit on the US Civil Rights Movement. At other times, however, you may want to offer participants a chance to tackle an issue of their own choosing, giving them space to develop the topic for the day in collaboration with you and with each other. Below we offer some tips for getting started, either with an established topic or a topic decided upon in collaboration with participants.

Starting with participant concerns

Tackling issues that interest participants is one of the biggest rewards of planning a social justice drama residency around participants' actual lived experiences. Many practitioners begin drama workshops or lesson plans by collaborating with the group to decide on a topic. Augusto Boal used this format in many of his workshop models, ensuring he was working with participants on issues that truly concerned them. However, drawing from participants' experience presents some challenges, including less time for advance research, the need to do a bit of lesson planning on the fly, and the added time needed to adjust plans each day based on group contributions. For some, it can be unsettling to say, *"We'll need to leave open that section of the plan until we know what the group wants to do."* However, these challenges can also be viewed as opportunities for a more democratic process. If you decide to let participants dictate the topic for the day, remember to slow down and consider the process of choosing a topic to be part of the workshop.

Be sure to consider power dynamics in communication during the process of deciding on a topic. The phenomenon of groupthink can be very powerful in large-group discussions, leading participants to refrain from offering alternative ideas if they perceive the group to be moving in a different direction. If you begin with large-group discussion, be aware that one of the first few ideas is likely to "stick" for the day unless a very strong-willed group member decides to go against the flow. In order to gather a diverse set of ideas from the beginning, we recommend starting with a brainstorming activity that helps the group generate an abundance of different ideas. We like using a pair/share procedure in which participants partner up to think of an issue they would like to explore before offering it for group consideration. Alternatively, the popcorn activity also allows participants to share initial ideas anonymously (see Chapter 4 for a description). No matter the activity you choose, brainstorming encourages a wider array of suggestions and potentially helps generate a richer workshop topic.

Consider creating a shorter lesson to decide on a topic, breaking the process into steps like these:

- Ten minutes: Sculpture Garden (see description of the activity later in this chapter): In pairs, have Partner A sculpt Partner B into an image that evokes the word "oppression." After a walk through the "garden," during which sculptors discuss together what images of oppression they see, allow partners to switch roles and repeat the activity.
- Five minutes: Brainstorm some meanings of the word "oppression" on the board.
- Five minutes: Return to pairs to discuss a specific issue of oppression they would like to focus on for the remainder of the workshop. Have pairs share their ideas with the group.
- Five minutes: Decide as a large group what issue is of most interest, and proceed.

Starting with a preexisting issue

We often begin social justice-oriented drama lessons with an issue in mind. In some cases, your workshops will be commissioned by a specific constituency, such as a community group or elementary school, who will choose an issue in consultation with you (see Chapter 6 for more on this process). At other times, classroom dynamics, current events, or curriculum may dictate an issue for exploration. Starting with an issue in mind, such as bullying or gender-based discrimination in schools, allows for greater specificity in lesson planning and is essential for Forum Theatre work in particular, since this process requires a well-rehearsed set of activating scenes to work properly. Work based on a pre-set idea or issue also allows participants to include a shorter workshop within a longer process, which might accompany prepared packets of information, websites, or discussion forums for participants to use in their ongoing thinking about the issue after your work together is finished.

Even if a workshop or residency topic is commissioned or predetermined, leaders should still be mindful about building in plenty of room for participants to make choices, ask questions, and take control of their own learning during the workshop. A rule of thumb we like to use: avoid beginning your workshop with a short set of bullet points in mind that you want all participants to agree with by the end of the day (for example, "*I want all participants to agree with me that recycling is important, that they should be actively engaged in advocating for green energy sources, and that we should set home air conditioners to seventy-five degrees in summer*"). Doing this orients your lesson toward indoctrinating participants into a specific value system. While these may seem like positive outcomes to you, they are prescriptive rather than open-ended (think back to Freire's banking system of education) and will be unlikely to provide participants with the room to explore a diversity of perspectives on the issue. While these prescriptive learning outcomes may sometimes be mandated, we encourage you to seek out topics with greater nuance and room for debate or discussion. We like to take inspiration from Dorothy Heathcote's maxim about drama as "a man in a mess" and look for issues that are, indeed, messy. Messy topics for drama lessons usually involve conflict and complexity, allowing participants to grapple with several perspectives and issues simultaneously. Focus your lesson-planning process on providing a space for shared exploration of gray areas in complicated social issues. After all, Freire set out to stop educational indoctrination with *Pedagogy of the Oppressed*. Instead of indoctrinating students, drama for social justice works to open dialogue and allow participants to think critically about issues by collaborating, listening, creating, and reflecting together.

Questions to guide your planning

With the goal of collaboration and creation in mind, consider starting with questions rather than with answers as you design your lessons and workshops. A few questions to ask yourself as you begin your work:

- What power imbalances occur in this scene (or event, interaction, story or novel)?
- What systems of oppression are involved in this power imbalance?
- What choices did individuals make to address these power imbalances?
- What other options did they have?
- What relevance does this situation/issue have to my students' lives today?
- What contemporary or real-life parallels can we draw?
- What skills does this group already have?
- How might I challenge them further?

If you'd like to give your participants freedom to choose a topic, but do not have time to undertake a full collaborative decision-making process, consider a hybrid approach. Prepare two or more basic plans centered on issues that you think will resonate with your group and allow the group to choose one, gaining the benefits of preplanning while still allowing space for group decision-making.

Drama for social justice toolkit

This collection of activities will help you plan a drama lesson or residency focused on social justice, but these suggestions represent only the tip of the iceberg. We recommend reading widely in the field, starting with the sources mentioned here and in the book's annotated bibliography (Appendix A), to access hundreds of exercises, games, and activities designed by leading practitioners in the field. Most of these exercises, like many theatre games, exist in nearly countless variations. They are highly adaptable, and you should be open to adjusting them as you learn your own strengths and needs. You can tailor these activities to your lessons by changing names, procedures, or reflection strategies. You can also borrow or modify many of the activities in the other chapters of this book for a social justice lesson. We list activities here that will make good building blocks for linear and process-oriented lesson plans, but you can also use these activities individually as games or as short experiences that can generate reflection that feeds into class discussion.

Starters

Starters work not only to engage participants, but also to spark ideas and questions that can grow into longer conversations during the reflection period. We use at least one starter in each of our full-length lessons, and vary activities according to lesson goals. You will find that two starters often work well; one starter primes students to think about the issue of the day, and one starter helps students get in touch with their bodies as creative tools. Boal emphasized the importance of using the body and voice creatively as a way to help participants cast off the restrictions and self-consciousness of everyday life; do not underestimate how freeing these simple acts can be!

One Up: This game does triple duty as an exploration of power, a tool for increasing observational skills, and a fun way to generate group cohesion. Adapted from Anne Bogart's "3 Up, 2 Down" exercise for actors.

Procedure: Ask all the students to move around the space, attempting to cover any empty areas of the room. Have students begin to notice the idea of levels, stretching their bodies tall and then crouching low. Call out percentages, with zero being the absolute lowest level achievable (lying or sitting down for most participants), 100 percent being as tall and high as possible, and everywhere in between interpreted by the participants. Explore the space in this way for a while until the group develops proficiency with the exercise, then introduce the "one up" concept. At any given moment, only one participant may be at 100 percent. All others must stay below 60 percent. The group must work together to follow this rule. Insist on silence during the activity. The goal is for the group to pay attention to one another and keep the one-up rule working organically. If a participant is dominating the one-up position, remind the group that they should all collaborate to vary who is in the "one up" role.

Variations: Greater complexity can be achieved through the use of bigger numbers, like "seven up" in a group of twenty.

Continuum: A discussion made physical, the continuum activity works in some cases as a standalone lesson plan in itself. Expand or contract the opportunities for verbal reflection as needed to fit your goals and available time.

Procedure: Line up students in the space from one end of the room to the other. In cramped classrooms, use a diagonal from corner to corner to achieve the greatest amount of space. Explain that one end of the line will represent "strongly agree," the other end "strongly disagree." The midpoint of the line is "neutral" or "not sure." Every position in between these two points represents differing levels of agreement or disagreement according to how close or far one is from strong agreement or disagreement. As you call out declarative statements, students should position themselves along the continuum according to their agreement or disagreement. We recommend at least ten statements to start. The group will work more efficiently as the activity progresses, so you may find you can use more than twenty different prompts for a longer discussion.

Sample statements for a lesson relating to issues of gender:

"Women are nicer than men."

"When I meet a new baby, I care whether it's a boy or a girl."

"If a man and woman go on a date, the man should pick up the check."

"There are natural differences between men and women."

"I fit perfectly with society's expectations for my gender."

"I am comfortable calling myself a feminist."

Tips:

- You might want to avoid singling out individuals for responses, but when large divergences in position occur, take a moment to ask if anyone would like to explain their reason for choosing a particular spot on the continuum. After hearing from a few participants, ask if anyone in a very different position is willing to share as well.

- After hearing someone's reasoning, a student may decide to change position. Allow this to occur naturally; adjusting placement on the continuum is not cheating, but rather a sign of a dynamic conversation.
- This activity works well with a great deal of reflection. If your group is trying Continuum for the first time, let participants know that all positions on the line are to be accepted and heard without judgment or critical comment. The activity's goal is not to encourage participants to change one another's position on the line, but to allow the group to explore their different positions.
- Participants may engage in critical interrogation of the key terms in your statements as the activity evolves. You may wish to clarify for the students, but if your statements are clear, you may instead ask students how they interpret the statement and allow discussion to evolve accordingly. Often, as the group interrogates the meaning of words or phrases, a deeper discussion will naturally emerge.

Movement in space (basic viewpoints): One of the most common starter methodologies encourages participants to move in the workspace, often with musical accompaniment to help inspire tempo and rhythm. Adding in Anne Bogart's Viewpoints of repetition, tempo, duration, and kinesthetic response (Bogart and Landau 2005, see also Chapter 4) can help open the group to a heightened awareness of the body as a creative entity, which comes in handy in later activities that depend on participants making strong, confident choices in creating images, sounds, movement, or characters.

Materials: Music and a sound delivery device.

Procedure: Ask the group to spread out in the room, attempting to cover the entire space as much as possible. When you start the music, participants should begin moving about the space, both exploring the area and also trying to cover the entire space. At first let participants move naturally, then sidecoach them to explore Viewpoints such as tempo (the pace at which participants move), duration (the amount of time between changes of tempo or other choices), direction (forward, backward, diagonal), shape (the shape of the participant's body in space or the shape she makes with her path through the space), and kinesthetic response (the way the participant lets other stimuli, like noise or interaction with another participant, influence her movement choices). Coach participants to try to see how many ways of moving about the space they can find. We like to use the sidecoaching cue: *"See if you can surprise yourself! Break out of established patterns!"*

Cocktail party: Another discussion tool for breaking out of "sitting in a circle and talking" or "pair/share" procedures, this technique relies on movement as a way to get participants thinking actively. Adjust the name as needed for populations ("Dinner party" or just "Party" works well too). Cocktail party works especially well with untrained groups who are meeting one another for the first time.

Age group: Elementary and up.

Materials: Music and a sound delivery device.

Procedure: Give participants a question related to your lesson to think about or even free-write about for a minute or two. For example, in a lesson about gender and power, you might ask participants to write about a time they experienced or witnessed someone being corrected for "inappropriate" gender expression. After the group has had a moment to think, explain that you're hosting a cocktail party for the next ten minutes. Students should circulate in the space as the music plays, acknowledging one another's presence. When the music stops, ask participants to find a partner and discuss the question together for a short time. When the music starts again, participants should break away from their partners and circulate to find a new discussion partner. Start and stop the music several times, allowing groups a minute or two to talk with their partners each time.

Variations: This activity works as a get-to-know-you game when participants are asked to think about a prompt relating to their lives, such as *"Think about the story behind your name or nickname."* You may want to give participants two different prompts, allowing the pairs to choose one as a focus each time the music stops. You can also adjust the group numbers, encouraging members to discuss the prompts in groups of three, four, or five.

Games for social issues

Each of the following games can be used as a starter, a building-block activity in a linear or hybrid lesson plan, or as a standalone activity to explore power dynamics.

Power play: As one version of a great many games that explore space as a mode of understanding power dynamics, Power play uses materials readily available in your classroom or workspace. You can play for five minutes or conduct multiple rounds, either on the same day or as a warm-up/starter that you repeat several times throughout a unit or semester.

Materials: Whatever is already in your workspace. Chairs, tables, and rehearsal blocks all work well. Be creative.

Procedure: Set up a group of chairs or other materials in an open space in your room. You can either arrange the space to mimic a known location, like a classroom or boardroom, or simply create a visually interesting arrangement. Allow the group some time to look at the space before asking for a volunteer to enter the arrangement and take up the position that she thinks gives her the greatest possible power. Allow time for the rest of the group to discuss the choice made by the volunteer, and then ask for another volunteer. This participant should enter the space and take up a position that gives her greater power than the first volunteer. Once a participant has entered the space, she should hold her position throughout the game. Allow as many volunteers as wish to play; the game gets most interesting when a large number of people have taken up positions, as the options participants will exercise to seize power become more nuanced and inventive.

Reflection: After each new volunteer, ask, *"What do you see?"* and *"Who has the power here?"*

    At the close of the activity, have the group reflect on the changing power relationships.

    "Who has the most power?"

    "Who has the least?"

Ask the volunteers to share how it felt to seize power. *"How did you decide what to do?"*

Variation one: Once you've exhausted the first set of volunteers, allow the first volunteer to change position to reclaim power. Rotate through each volunteer in order, allowing them to change position.

Variation two: Once all participants have taken a position, give them a moment to think about their relationship relative to other players. Ask each participant to think of a single word or phrase that sums up his or her relationship to the others. As you walk through the space, tap each participant on the shoulder and ask them to state their word or phrase.

Eye contact tag: We adapted this game from British devising group Frantic Assembly, who use it as a warm-up (see Chapter 4 for more on devising techniques as teaching tools). You can use any variation on a game of tag to explore power relationships, especially with appropriate reflection time. This version of tag works especially well if personal space is a concern, as it is played without physical contact among players. This activity requires an odd-numbered group. If you have even numbers, play along with the group yourself or break the group up and have a section observe while others play.

If you have a single group member who is much shorter than the rest of the group, this game may not work well.

Procedure: Create an open space in the center of the room. Start with the group moving about in the space, trying to cover any open areas. At your signal, ask participants to look up. The first person with whom a participant makes eye contact becomes her partner for the activity. One player will be left without a partner. This player is "it." The objective for those in pairs is to maintain eye contact with their partner at all times while exploring the space together, while the player who is "it" attempts to steal eye contact from one member of a pair. The rule: if you make eye contact with the "it" player, he is your new partner and your old partner is now "it." Players must be honest about acknowledging making eye contact with the active player; it is impossible to deny. Allow the game to go on as long as you like.

Reflection: Ask participants: *"What strategies did you try to maintain or steal eye contact?"*

If there are observers, ask them: *"What social dynamics did you see as the game progressed?" "How did groups manage to stay together?" "How did 'it' players interrupt partners?"*

Pushing hands: A partner exercise to generate focus and group cohesion, this activity also develops bodily awareness, trust, and observational skills. Similar activities include Boal's Colombian Hypnosis (a favorite starter, see *Games for Actors and Non-Actors* for a description) and the Mirror Exercise (a common theatre game, see variations by Boal and Viola Spolin for ideas).

Age group: 5th grade and up.

Procedure: Organize the group into pairs. One participant will be the leader and one will be the follower. The follower should place his hand palm up, and the leader should lay the palm of her hand on top of it. The follower should press upwards with steady, even pressure. The leader will return this pressure to create equilibrium. The leader is now "in charge," and can move the follower about the space, starting slowly. The follower must maintain the same equilibrium of even pressure between his palm and the leader's throughout the activity. Remind participants that the purpose of this activity is not to "trick" or "catch" one's partner by doing things he cannot handle, moving too quickly, or otherwise making the activity harder. The goal is for pairs to get better at doing the activity together. As the group develops proficiency, introduce new challenges. Remind the group to explore all levels, directions, and tempos that their bodies and the space allow, while maintaining eye contact.

Variations—Obstacle course: Do the procedure above, but place obstacles throughout the space so that pairs must be more careful and conscious of the space around them as they work. Encourage the pairs to find interesting ways to use the obstacles as they explore the space.

Trust push: Do the procedure above, but have followers close their eyes.

Image work

One of the foundations of Boal's theatre practice, image work is more than just a set of activities. By starting with images rather than improvisation of scenarios, character, or traditional discussion, leaders can open space for participants to share ideas in a way that highlights group interpretation, creating an atmosphere of collaborative exchange. Because most of these activities involve participants silently creating images for other participants to interpret, image exercises provide many opportunities for groups to collaborate while they make meaning together.

Image work is especially useful in situations in which opinions are sharply divided, since interpreting images can help draw out nuances of issues and thus get groups past black-and-white thinking. Image work also helps younger learners express ideas without struggling with language, letting the group interpret together by looking and exploring what they see. While these activities are great as starters for almost any lesson, do not sell image-based techniques short; some of our most successful work with students has involved hour-long lesson plans using only two to three image activities in multiple steps with lots of reflection along the way.

Tableaux evolutions: Creating tableaux is a foundational skill for image work that we incorporate throughout this book. See Chapter 2 for detailed discussion of the basics. This activity uses tableaux to quickly generate a variety of images and interpretations of an issue before thinking critically about those issues through image transformations.

Procedure: Either work with a predetermined topic or ask the group to identify an issue for exploration. If working with a piece of literature or a historical event, start by asking students to identify an issue of power or oppression that occurs in the material. Split into groups of three or four, and ask the groups to quickly create a tableau that captures an important aspect of the day's issue or topic. Share tableaux one at a time, allowing observers to discuss what they see in each tableau. Be sure to ask those in the tableau to remain frozen and silent during the discussion, even if they feel their work is being misinterpreted. It's about what the group sees, not necessarily the image creator's original intention. Questions to guide this discussion include:

"What do you see here?"

"Who has the power?"

"Who is disempowered in this image? How do you know?"

At the end of the sharing period, ask each group to think of a way to change their original image in order to begin to resolve the issue. Make clear that changes should be realistic and not shortcuts in which all problems are easily and quickly solved. Give students extended time for this activity. When each group has developed a new tableau, ask the groups to come up with a way to move from the first tableau to the transformed tableau. Present the tableaux transformations one at a time, discussing the choices made in each.

Reflection: As with all TO practices, reflection should focus on issues of believability and power while leaving room for interpretation from observers. A few examples:

"Does this situation seem believable to you? If not, what can we change?"

"Is this the best solution to this problem?"

"Are there other approaches to this issue?"

"Is this solution realistic?"

"How have the power dynamics shifted in these images?"

Tableaux variations—Worst to best: Ask small groups to stage the worst possible version of a common event, like a family vacation, a meeting with a teacher, or a first date. Then ask the group to transform the tableaux to the best possible version of the same event. Tune your choice of event to the topic for your lesson.

Essence of the issue: Ask groups to create a tableau that represents the core of a social issue or kind of oppression. As each image is shared, ask participants if the image is realistic. Allow discussion of each image in detail, then give groups time to revise their images in response to the discussion. Share and discuss a second time, reflecting changes.

Thought bubbles: Once participants present a tableau, ask the group to ponder what each character in the scene is thinking. As you place a hand above each character's head, ask participants to call out possible phrases that could fill in a cartoon thought bubble for that character. Allow several responses for each character as a means of active reflection on the scene.

Hotseating: Hotseating, a form of Interviewing, is a technique developed by Russian actor and director Konstantin Stanislavski and later adapted as a core technique for TO practice by Augusto Boal. This activity allows participants to probe a character's inner motivations and works especially well with material inspired by works of literature, in which participants have a strong depth of knowledge about characters. Let the group choose a character from a tableau that they would like to hotseat. Ask that character to unfreeze and take questions from the group. The participant on the hotseat should answer truthfully according to their understanding of the character. Hotseating can also help students work on making inferences, as the interviewee improvises to fill in gaps of knowledge and the interviewers delve into other issues with their inquiries during the question-and-answer session.

Conscience talk: Focus on a character in the tableau who is facing a difficult moral decision. Ask two volunteers to become the conscience of the participant, with one volunteer giving voice to the positive impulses the character feels and the other voicing negative impulses (depending on your group you may refer to "good or bad" impulses or refer to cartoon representations of the "angel and devil" on the character's shoulders). Have the two volunteers take positions on either side of the central character and talk to the character as the character's conscience. At any given point you may bring the scene to life and have the participants begin acting out the scenario while the character hears his conscience and obeys one or the other, or neither, set of impulses.

Substitution: A cornerstone of TO and Forum Theatre, substitution is a key technique for transforming "spectators" into "spect-actors." This method can be used either in performed scene studies or in image work. After participants present a tableau or scene, begin reflection. As the group discusses the issues being represented, sidecoach them to think of what characters might do differently or how the scene might work differently. When a participant has an idea, ask her to tap one of the original performers on the shoulder, signaling that participant to give up his spot and allow the new volunteer to replace him, demonstrating her idea for a new interpretation by substituting herself into the tableau. In scene work, you can intensify the process by instructing audience members to call out "stop" at any time they like, at which point they can replace an actor in the scene and try a different strategy for dealing with the issue unfolding onstage. This technique can work well in combination with Hotseating, Thought bubbles, and the others described above.

Statues and sculpting variations: A variation of tableaux, statues are frozen images made using our bodies. We often use statue and sculpting variations as starters in image-based lesson plans. They also work well as a brainstorming tool in discussions of literary characters, historical figures, or abstract ideas. A quick round of statues can help students to collectively toss out a range of ideas and interpretations of a concept or question, a few of which can spark longer-form discussion.

Statue garden: A solo activity that can be used as a prelude to the partnered sculpting variations below.

Procedure: Divide the class into two groups. The first group will be active participants, while the second will be audience members (conduct the activity twice to allow everyone a chance to take on both roles). Explain to participants that they will be creating a "sculpture garden" for their peers. The theme of this garden will be determined by the lesson plan for the day. Themes can include a concept (like freedom, tyranny, power, or injustice), an exploration of a literary character (perhaps "the character's deepest desire" or "the character's greatest fear"), or anything else that works for your lesson. Instruct participants to think about levels, size, shape, the arrangement of their bodies in space, and smaller details like facial expression. Give them a moment to think (not too long—thirty seconds works well), and then instruct the group: "*I will now count down from five to one. When I get to one, you should be frozen in place as part of the sculpture garden.*" Count down, then ask participants to hold their positions while the audience walks through the garden. Discuss what you see (remind the "statues" not to speak). Repeat the activity so that each group can experience the exercise from the other point of view.

Variations—Group photo: Ask a volunteer to enter the workspace and create a frozen image of a single person or character from the material being studied. This image should communicate something essential about the individual being represented. Ask another volunteer to choose a new character or person with a relationship to this first character and add himself to the "group photo." Continue until a "group photo" is assembled. Ask the audience to share observations about power relationships in the image. Incorporate the Thought bubble exercise to add language to the activity. After the group photo is complete, incorporate Substitution by asking a new volunteer to tag out any one person in the photo, taking a new pose that reveals something else about that character. Continue with the transformation of the photo until something particularly striking occurs, then do further reflection.

Group sculpture: Do the procedure described in Group photo, but this time ask participants to create a large scale sculpture in response to a theme, using their bodies as the material. The first volunteer should enter the space and take up a position he or she can hold. The group should observe the choice made, and then a second volunteer can enter the space and take up a position relative to the first volunteer, adding to the sculpture. Continue the process until the group is satisfied with the piece. The leader should ask appropriate questions to spur volunteers to action, like *"Does this piece represent the issue completely? Is anything missing?"*

Partner sculpting: In this method, the group divides into pairs, agreeing on Partner A and Partner B. Partner A must become "clay," allowing Partner B to "sculpt" his body into any form he chooses through the use of touch. You can use sculpting prompts exactly the same way you used them for the statue activity. Since successful sculpting requires a bit more comfort and familiarity between group members, consider starting with statues and working toward sculpting as a new challenge.

Group sculpting: As the group becomes proficient with paired sculpting, move on to collaborative group sculpting exercises. In these activities, pair participants as sculptors and clay, but ask sculptors to work collaboratively to make their human clay creations relate to one another. Group sculpting exercises work well with larger groups if you divide the group, asking one half of participants to watch while the other half completes the exercise. Afterwards, switch to allow audience members a chance to try as well.

Forum theatre tactics: Scenarios

The most famous of Boal's TO techniques, Forum Theatre, involves the presentation of scenes or improvised scenarios to highlight social issues. Participants then examine these scenes through a range of techniques like substitution and hotseating, collaboratively trying out ideas and strategies for dealing with oppression. Boal's Forum Theatre method is quite complex. Practitioners spend years honing their skills in the design and execution of Forum Theatre workshops; achieving mastery in this practice is thus beyond the scope of this book. However, you can borrow Forum Theatre scenarios and techniques and adapt them in your own teaching and workshop design, keeping in mind that facilitation of TO work requires continued learning, practice, and reflection.

Designing effective scenarios for Forum work

You can design Forum Theatre scenarios on your own and then rehearse them with a group of actors, or you can collaborate with students or participants to create new scenarios for Forum Theatre. If you are working with a group to create new Forum Theatre scenes, be prepared to spend several sessions developing and refining them. Improvisation often makes a better starting point than writing a script, as individual performers can find the truth of a character through trial and error, as well as constructive feedback from peers. The work of developing a scene is in itself a helpful exploration of issues of oppression, and should not be rushed.

Beginning with character

After you've determined a topic of interest, consider starting with character exploration. Incorporate free-writing exercises into drama sessions to encourage participants to flesh out a character, then use techniques like hotseating to further develop ideas. A sequence for the first session might follow a format similar to the one outlined below:

- Warm-up: complete the image
- Free-writing on topics of interest
- Paired discussion of possible topics
- Group discussion to choose a topic
- Board-facilitated discussion of people who might have experience with this issue
- Participants select a character to develop
- Participants complete a character bio for their characters listing age, occupation, and other basic information
- Free-writing to explore character attitudes about the issue
- Hotseating session
- Discussion of possible scenarios that could emerge from the work.

Developing a scenario

After a character development session, participants can think independently about scenario development before the next session. Having participants return with the outline of a scenario helps give the group creative control and opens space for multiple ideas at this critical development stage. The next session should be devoted to sharing and beginning to develop scenarios together through performance. Ask participants to write scenarios on the group's chosen topic inspired by the ideas and characters explored in the previous session. We like to use the following simple scenario format, developed by Professor Emeritus Lin Wright from Arizona State University. Students should list the following components in detail on a sheet of paper to create the outline of a scenario for improvisation:

- Characters (specific individuals with names, ages, personality traits, and a clear relationship with one another)
- Preceding action (what happened prior to the start of the scene)
- Central problem or conflict (a problem to be solved, featuring high stakes for the characters involved)

- Setting (the location where the scenario takes place)
- Initiating action or opening line (A character enters the space and delivers a line or does an action. The line or action must demand a reaction from another character. For example, a character might enter and ask another character, "*Where have you been?*")

Scenarios are not complete scenes or scripts. Rather, they are the seeds of an improvised scene with a central conflict that the entire group can explore together through TO tools like Substitution, Hotseating, Thought bubbles, and Conscience talk. Therefore participants should only provide the material required in the checklist, rather than write a complete script. Characters need to be believable and playable (for instance, characters should not be young children). We find the best scenarios start with three characters. All characters need to be in the same setting to allow them to fully interact (for example, scenes with characters on the phone together are too limiting for improvisation). Scenarios should also be realistic and the dramatic situation and characters should have meaning for the participants. Also, point out the danger of stereotype mining here. For example, rather than creating a character of a specific race and ethnicity as the "oppressed" character, ask participants to write a scenario with characters (of any race and ethnicity) who have to face an incident of racism.

After participants develop initial scenarios, ask for volunteers to improvise the scenarios. Encourage participants to act in a scene they have not created, allowing the creators some critical distance to observe their ideas in performance. Once scenarios have been performed for the group, use reflection to decide if the central conflicts are clear and believable enough to inspire participants to care about what happens. We ask questions like "*Is this scenario realistic and believable?*" If participants do not agree that the scene is realistic, ask the group to give feedback and adjust the scene until it is satisfied that the scene is realistic before proceeding to activities like Substitution, Thought bubbles, and other techniques.

A sample scenario developed through this process

We developed this scenario for a workshop on homophobia. We provided it to actors playing roles well in advance of the workshop, and we prepared and rehearsed the scene prior to staging it for a Forum Theatre session.

Characters

Sarah: You are a sophomore college student. You're majoring in English, and you have an internship planned for the summer. You and your boyfriend, Mike, have been dating since high school. You're pretty happy together, but things have been a little tense lately.

You've been spending a lot of time with Melissa, a self-identified lesbian. You two have a lot in common since you're both English majors, you both played soccer in high school, and you both like to work out at the gym, and run. Mike doesn't seem to like Melissa much and he's sent a few texts joking about Melissa, reminding you not to "go gay" or if you do, asking if he can watch. You've laughed them off, but his behavior is starting to bother you.

Mike: You are a junior in college. You're majoring in Communication Arts and hoping to get into the highly competitive business school next year. You've been dating your girlfriend, Sarah, for four years. Recently, she started spending more time with Melissa, a lesbian. While you don't consider yourself homophobic, you're concerned about the amount of time they spend together, and have made some casual jokes about Sarah not going gay.

Joe: Joe is Mike's best friend at college. They play intramural flag football together and are in the same Communication Arts program. You know Sarah and Mike have been a little tense lately, and Sarah can get on your nerves because she is always worried about studying and working out. You don't want Sarah to ruin the day with relationship drama.

Elizabeth: Sarah's roommate, a Sophomore biology major. You and Sarah have been roommates since freshman year, and although you aren't best friends, you really enjoy hanging out with one another. Sarah's told you that Mike's been weird and possessive lately.

Preceding action: Sarah, Mike, and Mike's friends are hanging out at Elizabeth and Sarah's apartment before a football game. The group has made plans to go to the game together.

Inciting incident: Sarah receives a text from Melissa asking if she can join everyone to go to the game. When the group seems uncomfortable, Sarah asks what the big deal is. Mike says it's either Melissa or him.

The improvisation starts from this outline. The scene begins with small talk to establish character, and then the inciting incident occurs. As the improvisation plays out, the character playing Sarah must try to deal with the conflict as best she can. For instance, Sarah might try to convince everyone that Melissa should come along. The other actors should play the scene as true to their understanding of their characters as possible. For instance, Mike should not have a "magical" change of heart and accept Melissa right away. In the end, Sarah should make a choice the character is clearly uncomfortable with, for instance deciding to lie to Melissa to keep her from coming over. This unsatisfying end is essential to inspire the participants to propose alternative strategies for the main character, leading to discussion and fueling activities like Substitution and Hotseating.

Other sources for material

Literature and life are great sources for scenarios. Consider pulling a scenario from a story or event that students are already studying, allowing a working session to develop character and rehearse scenes before using those scenes as the basis for forum work. For instance, we developed improvised modern-language versions of scenes from Sophocles's *Antigone* for a workshop with high school students, using Hotseating and Substitution to work through issues of oppression in the play.

Strategies for facilitation in Forum Theatre

Once a scene has been presented, the real work begins. You can either present your scenario in full, asking follow-up questions afterward, or inform the group that they may call out "stop" whenever they'd like to discuss an issue in the scene. Once the action has stopped, lead the group through a few questions to draw out their ideas before continuing with activities like Substitution, Hotseating, or Thought bubbles.

Facilitation is a delicate process. You should remain in control throughout the process, but focus on finding and drawing out the group's ideas. Your own opinion on the scene should be considered irrelevant. Be wary of asking leading questions; they often work to influence the group to your point of view. Instead, use open-ended questions like *"What do you see here?"* or *"What's happening in this scene?"*

Suggested facilitation prompts to use after the presentation of a scenario:

"Was this realistic?"

"What was happening in this scene?"

"Who was the main character?"

"What did the main character want?"

"How did she try to get what she wanted?"

"What prevented her from getting what she wanted?"

"What else could she have done to get what she wanted?"

Using scenarios in lesson plans

Rather than writing out a script, consider integrating scenario and improvisation work into lesson plans in order to create realistic dialogue and action that will engage the group of participants watching the scene.

You can either work through the scenario with the facilitation prompts above, using activities like Hotseating, Thought bubbles, and Substitution to facilitate discussion, or you can build a lesson plan around the scenario, beginning with image work or games that prime the group to think critically about the chosen issue before moving on to the presentation of the scenario and subsequent discussion and activities.

For more resources on Forum Theatre, we recommend Augusto Boal's *Theatre of the Oppressed* (1985) and *Games for Actors and Non-Actors* (1992) and Michael Rohd's short and accessible *Theatre for Community, Conflict and Dialogue: The Hope is Vital training manual* (1998). For those interested in expanding their skills, we recommend attending several Forum Theatre workshops and seeking out training in Theatre of the Oppressed via the many organizations that continue Boal's work, including Theatre of the Oppressed Laboratory (TOPLAB), Theatre of the Oppressed NYC, Jana Sanskriti, and CTO-Rio.

Drama for social justice: three lesson plans

After you have completed your research and have a topic or approach in mind, you will need to make a general plan for your work. For a more detailed discussion of lesson planning, see Chapter 2 as well as the discussion of assessment in Chapter 5. In this section, we offer three sample lesson plans to give you the sense of a few applications of drama for social change in classroom and workshop environments. The first plan incorporates drama techniques into a content-centered lesson plan for a middle school history class. The second uses Image Theatre techniques to help a kindergarten class explore their understanding of gender roles in fairy tales. Finally, the third plan outlines an extracurricular Forum Theatre-inspired workshop to help high school students work with issues in a shared work of literature. Though we designed each of these lessons to work within a single class session, you could also expand any of these lessons into longer workshops.

Building social justice into lesson planning: exploring historical events

Techniques described in this chapter can form the basis of dedicated workshops on social issues, but in the standards-based traditional classroom, teachers can also carve out space to focus on issues of oppression and injustice in core content. Far from a distraction, these techniques can encourage critical thinking, create space for students to connect more deeply with material, and provide inspiration and engagement for projects and papers. The following lesson plan is designed for a history or civics class in which students have already studied the events surrounding a major legal change or Supreme Court ruling. We have based the lesson on the historic 1954 Brown vs. Board of Education ruling that declared segregated schools unconstitutional. This plan uses the process drama-oriented model described in the previous chapters.

Age group: Middle school.

Goal: To explore the experience of citizens, government officials, and aid workers in a moment of legal and cultural transition related to school segregation and integration.

Objectives:

- Students will explore multiple perspectives on a historical legal ruling and subsequent events through reading and discussion.
- Students will take on roles of characters involved in a segregated school district, exploring a plan for integrating schools.
- Students will reflect on their own and other people's attitudes, needs, and experiences during a major cultural shift like the end of segregated schooling.

Materials: Relevant news clippings and interviews, whiteboard or chalkboard, index cards.

Procedure

Engagement activity: Provide each student with a packet of news clippings and interviews to read and explore for 5–10 minutes.

Discussion: On the whiteboard, record students' brainstorming ideas about people involved in a school district that will make plans to integrate schools (sidecoach toward parents, school officials, community leaders, religious figures, teachers, and administrators).

Discussion: After identifying characters, brainstorm issues and concerns that come up for each character during the transition to integrated schools.

Character creation: Ask each student to select a character from the board that interests him or her. Use process of elimination to make sure most characters are represented. Give each student several minutes to do free-writing that develops further ideas about his or her character. Use the following prompts, giving students two minutes or more for each prompt:

"Describe a typical day in your life."

"Write about what matters most to you in life."

"Describe your experiences on the day of the decision."

"Write about how you feel now. What are your biggest concerns right now?"

Character visualization: Ask students to close their eyes and visualize their characters' home or current residence. Where do they sleep? Is it comfortable? How much sleep do they get? What is the immediate environment like? How does it feel, sound, and smell? What do they eat for breakfast? Where do they go first in their day? What do they plan to do today? Who do they see along the way? How are they dressed? How do they feel?

When the visualization is finished, ask students to open their eyes in character. Explain that you will also be taking on a role as the town mayor, and that today we will hold a special town hall meeting to discuss next steps for integrating schools in your small school district.

Town meeting (teacher-in-role): Introduce the given circumstances, such as the amount of time that has passed and what steps have already been taken to integrate schools (you can develop this with the group or provide it to participants as part of contextualizing information). Introduce an appropriate central issue that relates to school integration before opening the floor for comments and questions from the group (for example, access to busing, re-evaluating district lines, or notifying parents of students affected by the redrawn district line). Moderate discussion as needed, including giving a student the floor and allowing the others to question her in-role if the situation seems appropriate. Steer the group toward a central conflict and allow as many students as possible to weigh in on the situation before closing the meeting.

Small group meetings: Divide students into four small groups to work on proposed next steps in the integration process. Give students 5–10 minutes to work in-role to come up with a plan of action and a rationale.

Town meeting: Return to the large group and ask a representative from each smaller group to present their plans of action. Moderate large-group discussion to decide on a next step.

Reflection (out of role):

> *"How did our next steps differ from those that were taken in this situation?"*

> *"How do you think our solution might have worked?"*

> *"What feelings do you think your character would have had about this solution?"*

> *"What feelings did you experience during the drama?"*

> *"What personal insights did you gain?"*

"Did you learn anything new/different?"

"What possible alternative solutions can you think of to problems you encountered in this drama?"

Extension: After this session, have students do independent research into the approaches that specific communities (perhaps your own community) took in response to this decision. Discuss the differences between the decision the group came to in the drama and the historical decision made.

Image-based lesson plans for young learners: fairy tales

This lesson plan uses Image Theatre techniques to open up dialogue about traditional gender roles roles in fairy tales. Image work often comes naturally to very young children, who are developmentally predisposed to showing rather than, or in addition to, telling when communicating ideas and stories. The use of images helps younger learners communicate the nuances of their ideas and also gives participants valuable experience interpreting one another's ideas collaboratively during the reflection period. Be careful not to short-circuit this process during each reflection phase; allow the entire group of participants to share their interpretations of others' images freely so that multiple ideas and interpretations emerge. This lesson plan may be spread out over several sessions depending on the group.

Goal: Through Image Theatre techniques, participants will examine and engage with fairy tales' complex roles in our society.

Objectives:

- Participants will analyze fairy tale attributes.
- Participants will recall and synthesize their knowledge of fairy tales to generate embodied images of oppression.
- Participants will evaluate and analyze images generated by themselves and their peers and articulate meanings conveyed by the images to audiences.
- Students will generate and dramatize new images that respond to images of oppression and power present in fairy tales.
- Students will assess how Image Theatre techniques modify their understandings of fairy tales during reflection.

Materials: Paper/whiteboard, markers.

Procedure

Starter—Prime the pump: Use large sheets of paper or a chalkboard to collect ideas about fairy tales. Have students call out words they associate with the concept—traits, emotions, desires, actions—there are no wrong answers. Sidecoach students toward a large volume of responses.

Reflection:

> *"What are some kinds of characters we find in fairy tales?"*

> *"What kinds of things happen to each character?"*

> *"What do girls do in fairy tales?"*

> *"What do boys do in fairy tales?"*

Starter—Movement in space: Ask participants to move around the space, taking up all available room. Once the group is moving freely, ask them to add on attributes from the list generated during Prime the pump.
Sidecoaching prompts:

> *"See if you can move equally far from and close to everyone else."*

> *"Move like a rescued princess."*

> *"Move as though you are on a quest."*

> *"Move as if you are a mouse who has become a king!"*

Fairy tale character sculptures: Model guidelines for sculpting with a student volunteer.
Sidecoaching prompts:

> *"Sculptor: Sculpt your partner with hands, or use mirror language, through showing, instead of telling."*

> *"Clay: Allow yourself to be sculpted."*

> *"Respect the clay: Help your clay keep its pose with thoughtful uses of balance and shape that respects your image and your partner's body."*

> *"Sculpt the entire body, head to toe."*

Phase one—Partner images: Split the group into teams of two, assigning an A and a B. Have A be clay. B sculpts A into a fairy tale character at a moment of conflict, crisis or tension.
Sidecoaching:

> *"Think about both the most important thing about this character and what happens to her."*

"Create strong poses that tell us as much as possible about the character."

"Give your sculpture a title."

Share the sculptures in a sculpture garden, allowing each sculptor to introduce the sculpture.

Switch roles and repeat the activity.

At this point, each pair should have two sculptures. Ask pairs to combine their sculptures into an interesting composition, and give their two-person sculpture a title.

Sidecoaching:

"You may have to change your fairy tale a bit or imagine a new scenario to make it work. That's ok!"

"Think about how these two characters would come to be in this situation!"

Ask teams to share their titles and sculptures with the larger group.

Reflection on the images:

"What images are the most powerful to you?"

"What similarities and differences do you note between the images?"

Phase two—Group images: Work with participants to decide on two categories of characters related to the initial brainstorm (e.g. Evil Witch and Kind Princess). Ask a volunteer who had a strong image related to one of these characters to start the activity, recreating their statue. Facilitate four to five additional participants joining in to help create a tableau that completes this image.

Use the Thought bubble technique to explore the inner thoughts of each character and discuss what emerges.

If time allows, have those who have not yet had a turn create a new tableau, showing us a different perspective on these characters. Share and repeat the Thought bubble activity.

Reflection:

"What is happening here?"

"Who has the power?"

"What does each character want?"

"How can we tell?"

Phase three—Transforming images: Participants divide into groups of three, then spend one to two minutes generating a story in response to the prompt *"How would you write a fairy tale in which things turn out differently for the main character?"* The groups generate a new tableau based on this story.

Have each group share their new images one at a time. After all groups have shared, discuss the differences participants may have seen from the first set of images.

Conclusion and reflection:

"What changes did you see?"

"Did you discover any new ideas you have about fairy tales?"

"If you could change one major aspect of fairy tales, what would it be?"

TO techniques for literature: The God of Small Things

We developed this lesson plan as part of a one-day symposium for the University of Wisconsin Center for the Humanities' Great World Texts program, which brings high school students from across the state together to explore a common text they have studied for an entire school year. We enacted this one-hour Forum Theatre workshop with several hundred students and teachers, with the help of a group of ten high school students who volunteered for a one-hour morning training session. Because of the large group size and short lead-time, we focused on image-based techniques, which are great discussion starters, while using the Forum technique of Substitution to encourage group involvement. Witnessing hundreds of teens clamoring to express their ideas about images of oppression in a work of literature both inspired us and demonstrated the utility of this method for exploring subject matter that may feel somewhat unfamiliar to participants.

Goal: Exploration of power and oppression in *The God of Small Things* by Arundhati Roy.

Objectives:

- Participants will connect with their bodies and their peers through "knowing the body" exercises.
- Participants will make connections between the book and their lives through discussion.

- Participants will reflect on the themes of the book through image work.
- Participants will use substitution work to explore alternative options for characters.

Procedure

Starter—Push not to win: A favorite short starter developed by Augusto Boal, this game is played in pairs. Partners should face one another and place the palms of their hands together. Each partner must push against the other, but the objective for the pair is to keep their hands in exactly the same place (i.e. not to "win" by pushing either partner backwards). Ask participants to try to explore what happens as they engage with pushing while also trying "not to win."

Reflection:

> *"What does this exercise tell us about power?"*

Brainstorming on large chart paper:

> *"What issues of power did you notice in the book?"*

> *"Who had power?"*

> *"Who did not?"*

Statues and sculpting: Whole group—partner sculpting into characters from the brainstorm.

Reflection:

> *"What do we see in the sculpture garden of characters we created?"*

Tableaux: Note: We worked with our student volunteers to develop four tableaux with the volunteer actors featuring a major image that related to a moment of oppression from the book.

The volunteers present an image of oppression, then the leader facilitates a group discussion, asking the audience to discuss what they see while sidecoaching to help identify issues of oppression within the image.

Facilitation prompts:

> *"Is this realistic?"*

> *"What is happening in this scene?"*

"Who is the main character?"

"What does the main character want?"

"How did she try to get what she wanted?"

"What prevented her from getting what she wanted?"

"What else could she have done to get what she wanted?"

The leader further facilitates the discussion using the following techniques:

Thought bubbles: As the leader places her hand over a character's head, audience members shout out possible thoughts. After each engagement, stop and discuss what thoughts we heard and which we think might be most realistic.

Conscience talk: The leader asks the group to identify the person facing a decision in the image. Two volunteers are selected, one to express the thoughts of "Angel," urging that character to a good decision, and one to express the thoughts of the "Devil" thwarting those urges. The leader encourages each volunteer to be bold and speak loudly so the group can hear. Allow more than one round if the group has other ideas about character motivation.

Hotseating: The leader allows characters from the tableau to break out of the frozen image to answer questions from the audience (note: volunteers were trained in this activity in the morning session).

Image transformation through substitution: The leader asks the audience to change the original image to show an ideal image in which the issue is resolved. Volunteers are allowed to substitute for people in the tableau to change the image. After each transformation, the leader facilitates discussion of the proposed change and whether it is realistic. Through Hotseating of the volunteers, the leader allows the audience to ask about each character's motive and ideas, as well as other characters' responses to the new choice. Allow several substitutions before settling on one.

Once the group has decided upon a realistic transformation, the actors move from the first to second tableau in slow motion. The leader facilitates discussion of how this transformation could take place in a realistic way.

Social justice drama with different age groups

How does teaching for social justice fit into an increasingly circumscribed curriculum? Recent work on the intersection of standards-based curriculum and social justice education shed some light not only on the challenges for teachers, but also on the opportunities creative teachers have found to incorporate social justice methods into standards-based classrooms (Dover 2013; Johnson, Oppenheim, and Suh 2009). Drama-based teaching and learning has become one of the primary ways in which teachers are tackling this challenge. Scholars like Dr. Ruchi Agarwal-Rangnath have already highlighted the utility of arts-based education methods for satisfying Common Core standards regarding citizenship, listening, and language skills (Agarwal-Rangnath 2013). Drama-based techniques are especially applicable to problem-solving, communication, interpretation, and language skills. Teaching for social justice has also become an established workshop tactic for after-school programs, community groups, religious organizations, and summer camps, aligning with the embodied learning practices discussed in Chapter 1.

Early childhood: It is never too early

We made the case for social justice education for the very young earlier in this chapter. Remember that research shows that children as young as three demonstrate awareness of and even participate in social power structures that create oppression. For instance, young children use race, class, and gender as ways to negotiate status in shared play. Since children are already learning about and participating in these social structures, dramatic play and dialogue can help them begin to think critically about their experiences and the world around them. Preschoolers' innate interest in improvisation-based play and games makes the activities in this chapter especially useful for this age group.

Key techniques:

- Image work
- Daily or weekly games
- Open-ended reflection
- Leader-in-role techniques.

Lower elementary: Social drama for content knowledge and social skills

If teaching for social justice is a part of your community's general practice, then kindergarteners will already have experience with this mode of learning. However, teaching for social justice is often an individual choice that varies from teacher to teacher, so you may be the first to take up these issues with your students outside of their home environments. As children begin to read, learn about national and world history, and encounter the arts, issues of social justice naturally come to the fore. Much of the content children encounter in literature, history, and the arts centers on human conflict. Mine this content for issues of oppression and injustice to create opportunities for

TO work, or use social drama as a way to cover specific content while addressing and discussing the social issues inherent in the material. TO and social drama also come in handy for addressing local issues, such as power and oppression within the classroom itself. TO games make for a great five-minute break when attention is flagging, and a quick reflection period after each game can help students learn to understand one another's feelings, develop empathy, and improve social skills that can enhance your students' relationships with one another.

Key techniques:

- Image work
- Daily or weekly games
- Social drama for content knowledge.

Upper elementary: Social drama for preteens

Preteen's social structures grow in complexity as they age, making drama for empathy a potentially important element of lesson planning. Social drama also makes an effective technique for exploring the more complex literature students encounter in fifth and sixth grades. Fifth and sixth graders can also process ideas effectively through improvisation-based exercises, giving them access to a skill set while addressing curriculum standards related to speaking and listening. Longer units involving research to create characters and scenarios are appropriate for this age group, and can be combined with holistic in-role techniques to explore historical and contemporary events from multiple angles while engaging social issues.

Key techniques:

- Daily or weekly games
- Character work.

Middle and High school

For Middle and High School students, longer units focusing on development of TO skills can make a great way to provide service-learning options for your students. Developing a workshop for a community organization helps students build social skills, while generating the content required for effective advocacy work can enhance students' research, critical thinking, and communication skills.

Key techniques:

- Character work
- Forum Theatre development.

Adults

While all the techniques in this book can effectively be adapted for adult learners, TO specifically addresses adults in its design. The learner-centered approach common to all TO methods helps take adult expectations of autonomous learning into account. Adult learners have a wealth of life experience to draw upon in the creation of scenarios for improvisation, which makes Forum Theatre a rich area to explore with this population. We recommend starting with activities to build bodily awareness before moving to image work and finally Forum Theatre when working with adults, who benefit most from dedicated work to reduce shame and embarrassment associated with "standing out" or "acting different."

Key techniques:

- Group games
- Image work
- Forum theatre.

References

Agarwal-Rangnath, Ruchi. 2013. *Social Studies, Literacy, and Social Justice in the Common Core Classroom: A guide for teachers.* Teachers College Press.

Alon, Chen and Sonja Kuftinec. 2007. "Prose and cons: theatrical encounters with students and prisoners in Ma'asiyahu, Israel." *Research in Drama Education: The Journal of Applied Theatre and Performance* 12.3 (2007): 275–91.

Boal, Augusto. 1985. *Theatre of the Oppressed.* Theatre Communications Group.

——[1992] 2002. *Games for Actors and Non-Actors.* Routledge.

——1995. *The Rainbow of Desire.* Routledge.

Bogart, Anne, and Tina Landau. 2005. *The Viewpoints Book: A practical guide to viewpoints and composition.* Theatre Communications Group.

Dover, Alison. 2013. "Getting 'Up to Code': preparing for and confronting challenges when teaching for social justice in standards-based classrooms." *Action in Teacher Education* 35(2): 89–102. DOI: 10.1080/01626620.2013.770377.

Duffy, Peter, and Elinor Vettraino. 2010. *Youth and Theatre of the Oppressed.* Palgrave Macmillan.

Freire, Paulo. [1970] 2000. *Pedagogy of the Oppressed.* Translated by Myra Bergman Ramos. Bloomsbury.

Johnson, Elisabeth, Rachel Oppenheim, and Younjung Suh. 2009. "Would that be social justice? A conceptual constellation of social justice curriculum in action." *The New Educator* 5: 293–310.

King, Martin Luther Jr. 1963. "Letter from Birmingham Jail." *The Atlantic Monthly* 212.2 (August): 78–88.

Kuftinec, Sonja. 2009. *Theatre, Facilitation, and Nation Formation in the Balkans and Middle East.* Palgrave Macmillan.

Manzo, Kathleen Kennedy. 2008. "Election renews controversy over social justice teaching." *Education Week* 28.10 (October 29): 1, 12–13.

Patterson, M.M. and R.S. Bigler. 2006. "Preschool children's attention to environmental messages about groups: social categorization and the origins of intergroup bias." *Child Development* 77.4 (Jul–Aug): 847–60.

Rohd, Michael. 1998. *Theatre for Community, Conflict and Dialogue: The Hope is Vital training manual*. Heinemann.

Sloman, Annie. 2011. "Using participatory theatre in international community development." *Community Development Journal* 47(1): 42–57.

Spitzer, Peter and Bernie Warren. 2013. *Smiles Are Everywhere: Integrating clown-play into healthcare practice*. Routledge.

Sternberg, Patricia. 1998. *Theatre for Conflict Resolution in the Classroom and Beyond*. Heinemann.

Van Ausdale, Debra. 2001. *The First R: How children learn race and racism*. Rowman & Littlefield.

Wilson, August. 1997. "The ground on which I stand." *Callaloo* 23.3 (Summer): 493–503.

Winkler, Erin. 2009. "Children are not colorblind: how young children learn race." *Practical Approaches for Continuing Education* 3(3): 1–8.

4 Performance art in the classroom

This chapter provides both rationales and techniques for using performance art to unlock new ideas in the classroom. We build on foundational work by Laura Gardner Salazar and extend her ideas to include the methods of Anne Bogart and other contemporary theatre artists. This chapter also discusses the potential pitfalls, challenges, and, most importantly, rewards associated with approaches to drama-based learning and teaching oriented to performance art. We dispel myths and empower teachers and students to incorporate non-linear, experimental, and abstracted methodologies into their teaching and learning. We explore educational applications for performance art and contemporary techniques for developing performances, including collaborative devising, a process in which groups work together to create new performance. Finally, this chapter prepares readers to integrate performance art immediately into their learning and teaching. We describe specific tools for implementing performance art as a reflective and creative pedagogical tool, drawing on established techniques for working with poetry and performance art with young people and incorporating contemporary activities and techniques used by artists from Goat Island to Siti Company.

What is performance art?

Operating outside the longer tradition of Western theatre, performance artists rethink the so-called rules of performance, often stripping down performance to the simplest terms: a performer, an audience, and an action. The term "performance art" (sometimes also referred to as "live art") is commonly used to describe performance events that occur outside traditional theatrical spaces and traditional playwriting techniques. The form's emphasis on interactivity, interpretive openness, and creativity makes performance art a method that is particularly useful for teachers. Performance art also naturally connects to the methods of embodied and contextual learning explored in earlier chapters, offering students new ways of experiencing and exploring ideas. Many of the tools and procedures pioneered by performance artists are designed for non-artists and novice performers to use, making them readily adaptable to classroom and workshop applications.

You can use performance art techniques to create new performance art with participants, in which case any of the processes discussed below might be employed. However, creating performance artworks is just the tip of the iceberg. You can also use these processes as structuring devices for lesson plans, as alternatives to large- or small-group discussion, or as tools for generating other kinds of performance, such as public service announcements, commercials, speeches, or demonstrations. Performance art also works well as a vehicle for exploring ideas that are hard to articulate in language or that individuals might feel uncomfortable sharing with groups. In total, performance art provides a wealth of path breaking techniques that enliven classrooms and reframe our understanding of drama-based learning and teaching.

A brief history of performance art

Before discussing applications for education, we will outline a history of major performance art movements and practitioners. Since the turn of the twentieth century, performance art has challenged distinctions between the visual arts, dance, and theatre, combining art forms to produce refreshing or confounding juxtapositions and challenge existing definitions of art. F.T. Marinetti and the Italian Futurists created exciting performance art events called "syntesi" in the early twentieth century, combining performed poetry, live painting, music and even food to create live performance events. Through these performance events, the Futurists shunned expected dramatic and theatrical elements like linear narrative in favor of surprising combinations of sounds, shapes, ideas, smells, and tastes that could stimulate new ideas and reactions in their audiences. As this example demonstrates, performance art has been both a prime arena for avant-garde artmaking in the last 100 years and an umbrella term that encompasses all sorts of procedures for creating art events that hinge on interactions between artists and audience members. In the remainder of this section, we will focus on influential performance artists who have explored several key approaches to the form.

Performance art has a long tradition in the US as well. Considered some of the earliest postmodern performance artists, dancers and choreographers associated with the famous Judson Dance Theatre worked in the Judson Memorial Church performance space in Greenwich Village, New York. There, in the 1960s they experimented with techniques for democratizing choreography and dance. For instance, filmmaker, dancer, and choreographer Yvonne Rainer created the dance *Trio A* (1966) in an attempt to distill dance to its essential features (Rainer 2009). The five-minute dance is choreographed using everyday movements like walking, hopping, and standing on one leg. In addition to using everyday movements, Rainer added a unique twist to *Trio A*; dancers are encouraged to teach the piece to others, spreading the choreography from person to person across the globe. Non-dancers have even been taught the choreography, which takes only a short time to learn, and then encouraged to perform the dance onstage themselves. *Trio A* has been performed by thousands of people in thousands of different contexts, thus redefining contemporary dance from an elite artform reserved for very few to an activity in which anyone can participate. This democratic impulse, common to many of the performance art practitioners we discuss here, makes many performance art techniques relatively accessible to non-artists, contradicting the assumption that it is elite or difficult for the average person to grasp. In fact, much performance art challenges the line between "artist" and "non-artist."

Performance art is often also grounded in personal interaction between the artist and her audience. For example, Yoko Ono, best known outside the art world as the wife of John Lennon, is a highly influential performance artist in her own right. Her performance work *Cut Piece* (1964) features the artist seated in a gallery space with a pair of scissors on the floor in front of her (Bryan-Wilson 2003). Audience members are invited to take up the scissors and cut sections from Ono's clothing as the event unfolds. Ono allows audience members to cut as they wish, ceding control of the event to the audience, who become participants in making the event and in determining what it "means." Often referred to as relational art, performance pieces like Ono's depend on the artist initiating social interactions between audience members and performers. Techniques employed by relational artists, like Ono inviting audiences to cut pieces of her clothing, lend themselves easily to learning environments in part because they are already quite similar to pedagogical practices; like relational artists, teachers set up provocations that inspire participants (in this case, learners) to interact, react, and create new ideas.

Performance art may also focus on creating events for audiences to experience. Celebrated twentieth-century choreographer Merce Cunningham and composer John Cage worked together in the 1950s at Black Mountain College in Asheville, North Carolina, to teach and collaborate with students in making new music, dance, and performance art. One of Cage and Cunningham's most innovative approaches to artmaking was the use of "aleatory procedures," techniques for allowing chance to determine artistic choices. Strategies like the use of dice, playing cards, or other chance procedures allowed students to make art through impulse and response to "random" stimuli. For instance, artists might roll a die to determine how long a piece of choreography would be, or draw from a deck of cards to determine what movement came next in a dance. Through the addition of chance, Cunningham and Cage attempted to open their students to the ephemeral excitement of "happy accidents." Their work led to a performance of the first "happening" in August 1952 (Harris 2013). In this live event, students and faculty performed actions determined by chance for an audience surrounded on all sides by activity. The event, the first of its kind, led to multiple genres of path breaking performances, such as flash-mobs, that use surprise and the reversal of audience expectations and expectations about audiences to create new and exciting experiences. The use of aleatory procedures in classrooms can be a helpful tool for teachers committed to collaborative learning; by giving up absolute control of the creative process, teachers allow students to take the reins in class activities.

In other instances, performance art is a conglomeration of different approaches, deliberately designed to avoid strict categorization. Devising artists and directors in theatre, including Anne Bogart, Goat Island, Mabou Mines, and others, have used the concept of collage-style remix to generate art in which multiple reference points exist in contrast, creating "intertextual" pieces. Siti Company, an international performance group founded by Bogart and Tadashi Suzuki in 1992, often works with existing stories from myth, literature, or history as the basic framework for a play, weaving in material from other sources to create a new work that is a collage of old and new, fact and fiction. Intertextual strategies, discussed below in more detail, involve creating new art from existing texts, films, songs, and other work. In our contemporary media landscape, students are often quite familiar with techniques like sampling and remix, making intertextual art tactics accessible ways of critically engaging with literature, history, and media content.

Performance art as a teaching tool: a reflective method

You can use performance art as a tool for exploring concepts, events, social structures and relationships, or artistic processes themselves. One of the most exciting benefits of using performance art techniques in lesson planning is the opportunity these processes create for reflection. Unlike many standards-based learning experiences, when students experience a performance art activity, they reflect in multiple stages. Often this process begins with interpretation of the assignment itself. We advocate the use of performance art assignments that challenge students to interpret instructions and examine their values and boundaries, much as Ono does in *Cut Piece*. In these kinds of experiences, participants are encouraged to reflect on the meaning of their choices during each phase of an activity, rather than saving reflection for the end of the day. Further, the qualities of abstraction and openness found in a great deal of performance art means that students will likely create work in these lessons that requires imaginative interpretation on the part of peers and observers. In the space between creation and interpretation, students have room to spark new ideas in one another as audience members and identify nuances that the performer herself could not fully articulate. These levels of reflection can happen naturally during the flow of the lesson, priming participants to think deeply about the material being explored for the day and often yielding a greater depth of discussion during the closing reflection period.

Performance art techniques can round out a lesson plan, offer learners a shift in routine, or provide a chance for lateral thinking in an otherwise linear lesson plan. We encourage you to try using a short activity inspired by performance art as one element of a lesson plan. The rewards include renewed enthusiasm for a topic, new approaches and ideas, and a chance for students' creativity to shine. Performance art tactics also lead to free and open exchanges of ideas as students realize that there are no right answers in interpreting this kind of work. Often, a quick performance art activity will jumpstart groups that feel stuck or struggle to discuss hard topics. Performance art techniques can also serve as effective starters for lessons that may be mainly structured around linear or in-role techniques, or as an engagement strategy for a lesson that will involve lecture and discussion.

Below we describe several broad categories of performance art, devising, and "live art" procedures that we find most useful in teaching situations, with sample activities for each method.

Iterative processes

Iterative lessons involve participants creating short performances which they then edit and revise multiple times, creating variations on the original performance. Each "iteration," or repetition, of an activity creates a new variation. Groups like Chicago's Goat Island used iterative processes to explore complex concepts over long periods of time, often working with the same ideas for years before moving on. *Trio A*, described in the introduction to this chapter, used the iterative process of teaching choreography based on simple, everyday movements to create an ever-evolving piece of postmodern dance, democratizing the artform in the process.

Iterative procedures might include creating a one-minute performance in small groups, then sharing and commenting on that work in the large group. Afterwards, participants "steal" one thing from another group's work to incorporate into their original piece before re-performing the new work. You could also ask performers to work on a simple performance piece in many variations with multiple different interpretive prompts. These processes are especially useful in lesson plans designed to draw out critical thinking, as they can help learners share ideas in a different format than traditional discussion. By interpreting information through words, body, and mind, performance art techniques encourage students to make connections among multiple interpretations of an idea or set of instructions.

Here are some examples of iterative strategies for lesson plans.

Escalating challenges

The sample lesson on "The Jabberwocky" below uses multiple iterations of a soundscape activity, with each new repetition adding a new element to challenge students' interpretive skills. Between the soundscape iterations, participants reflect on one another's work and receive new instructions to guide their next engagement with the poem. This strategy of "perform–reflect–perform-again" can work well with interpretations of literature for all ages. Young learners often respond especially well to iterative processes, which give them more time to explore the nuances of an activity and "catch on" to the procedure.

Repetition with a difference

Repeating an activity multiple times helps participants delve deeper into a simple idea. Have students generate short performances (one minute works well) based on a prompt or question related to a day's lesson. After an initial round of sharing performances (we often do this simultaneously to decrease nerves and manage time effectively—see also Chapter 2 on sharing), ask learners to revisit their performances, creating a new one-minute piece that highlights their favorite aspect of the original. Share again, then give learners a new prompt to work with, repeating as many times as you or participants like. In the final sharing portion of the lesson, allow students to share the version of their performance they think is most significant or interesting.

Combining performances

Combining solo performances into group performances makes for a fun challenge and can lead to fascinating discoveries. After creating short solo performances using any of the procedures discussed in this chapter, pair students and have them combine their solo performances into a new duet performance (if you have uneven numbers, try also using groups of three). Instruct students that any combination can work (side-by-side performances, interwoven performances, or swapped performances) as long as the resulting piece interests them. We recommend keeping the "run time" of the new performances the same (e.g. if solos were one minute, ask participants to keep their new performances to one minute as well) in order to avoid students simply performing two solo performances back-to-back. If time permits, combine these performances into quartets and so on, with the whole group creating a final performance (see Goat Island's *Schoolbook 2* for a multi-day lesson plan that uses a similar procedure).

Aleatory processes

Aleatory or chance procedures, like those pioneered by Cage and Cunningham, use carefully designed structures to create performance art determined at least partly by chance. Aleatory procedures can often feel and work like games, making them a great option for groups with little performance experience who can benefit from having lowered decision-making pressure. Aleatory procedures also allow the leader to invent overarching structures for a lesson plan but still infuse a sense of play, surprise, and risk in the learning session. Chance can be employed not only to generate short or longer performance art pieces, but it can also be used to structure other lesson plans, such as in-role dramas. Using a roll of a die or a deck of playing cards to determine characters or plot points is an aleatory procedure.

Here are some examples of aleatory strategies for lesson plans.

Found texts

Give students a limited set of parameters in which to search for text for their performance art pieces. The parameters for the assignment can vary as necessary to connect to the lesson plan. In a lesson on gender stereotypes, for example, ask high school students to look through a contemporary magazine and gather the first four sentences they find that convey assumptions about gender performance. These four lines then become starting points for composition work. For a lesson on storytelling structures, send participants on a five-minute search around the room, hall, or other limited geographical area with the instruction *"Find a sentence to use as the start of a story."*

Exquisite corpse variations

This procedure, originally played as a party game by the French Surrealists, involves students collaborating to tell a story or generate other creative work, often with surprising results (see Friswell 2010). Send participants into the hallway, asking them to enter the room one at a time. Upon entrance, the student must contribute one line to a story or poem. As the next student enters, the prior speaker repeats only the last line of the piece, to which the next student responds by contributing a new line. The next student enters, hears the last line, contributes his or her own, and so on until all have participated. This process can be done on the board with the aid of a paper or cloth to cover all but the last line contributed, or you can assign a student to write down the composition as it is developed. Students will make interesting observations about the process if you do this procedure twice, with half the class as audience and half as participants each time. The same procedure may also be used for collaborative drawing, dance, and other creative activities.

Procedures with cards or dice

These processes allow the leader to set parameters while still allowing for improvisation and play in the lesson period. Use cards or dice with student names associated with numbers or cards to decide who will lead each section of an activity, assign cards to determine plot points or characters in in-role dramas exploring literature, or roll a die to determine movement or sound choices in lessons that involve generating new performance.

Intertextual activities

Intertextual lesson plans play on the performance artist's tendency to appropriate and re-combine existing material in new ways. Just as postmodern playwright Charles Mee uses existing texts, from fiction to poetry to horoscopes, to create collage-style dramas (Mee 2002), intertextual activities allow students to create new works out of old material. Composition work (see below), iterative processes, and many other activities in this chapter can use intertextual techniques as a way of exploring curricular content or combining material from more than one learning unit in new ways.

Here are some examples of intertextual strategies for lesson plans.

Materials round-up

Help students connect the material for the day with their own lives by asking them to bring in the words to a favorite song, poem, short story, or other piece of written material. Use this material in developing the performance work for the day. We often use this strategy for composition work, handing out a set of composition instructions (described later in the chapter) and asking students to incorporate at least one element from every member of the group's contributed materials to generate the performance. You can guide students' choices with a prompt. For instance, the day before a lesson on citizenship, ask students to bring in their favorite piece of writing having to do with "responsibility."

Instant experts

Today's media connectivity allows students to become "instant experts" through in-class research using mobile devices. While working with a text or idea, have students use their mobile devices to gather content that connects thematically, geographically, culturally, or temporally to the subject and ask them to plug that material into the day's lesson. For instance, in a lesson on World War II, students might research advertisements, popular music and news stories from the era to find material to create a soundscape using their voices, bodies, and even YouTube resources delivered via mobile phones.

Relational processes

Relational art creates a social relationship between participants or between artist and participant. Yoko Ono's *Cut Piece*, discussed in the introduction, is a classic example of relational work. Most drama-based lessons could be considered relational practices in the sense that they often feature teachers setting up scenarios and structures in which students experiment together to make meaning, but specific strategies borrowed from relational artists like Yoko Ono can be employed to great effect in lesson plans.

We use relational practices in two main ways. First, teachers can take on the mantle of the relational artist, creating provocations to which their students then respond. For example, to begin a unit on food politics, you might rearrange your classroom into a long dinner table configuration, offering each student a chance to sample from a shared bowl of simple food and allowing them to choose how much to take without prescriptions or rules. After students have taken from the bowl as they wish, encourage students to discuss how they chose how much food to take and what their choices mean to them. These types of engagements work well with any age group, though older students will be able to sustain longer discussion after the initial event.

Second, we often use relational practices as a structure with older students (middle school and older), asking students to take on artist roles, then conceive and execute a relational project after modeling one like the dinner party described above. These types of assignments can unlock student creativity, opening spaces for learners to consider their own values and deeply held beliefs. Units with connections to contemporary social issues are particularly well-suited to these methods. In longer units, we like to challenge students to create an experience for their peers that will deepen their learning. For example, instead of a traditional book report, ask students to create a participatory relational experience for peers that will take them inside the world of the story.

Below is a relational strategy for lesson plans.

Instructions exchange

Particularly good for groups with some experience of using composition, this technique allows students to use what they've learned to unlock others' creative impulses. Assign each student a recipient, or have participants draw names from a hat. Ask them to think about the person whose name they've drawn and create a performance assignment that will help that person explore something new, highlight a talent, or have an experience that will be beneficial to them. Give participants some time to think. When they are ready, each participant should write down instructions for their recipient that will allow them to execute a performance act of some kind. Participants should deliver the instructions to their recipient. Give recipients an appropriate amount of time (twenty minutes or overnight both work well) to think about and prepare their performance. Share and discuss the process of making and interpreting the instructions.

Environmental processes

Environmental performance techniques use found spaces to inspire new performances. Often relational in their structure, environmental performance asks questions about the character of spaces around us, allowing aesthetic and practical elements of classrooms, cafeterias, sports facilities, libraries, and other everyday spaces to become the basis for performance. Our high school and college students have enjoyed re-purposing their learning environments, hallways, outdoor courtyards, libraries, and even bathrooms for performance art. Public spaces, when used to create art, have the unique advantage (and challenge) of creating new audiences out of passersby. When challenging students to create "found space" performances, consider other users' needs regarding the spaces in question. We once arranged a very successful collaborative performance art piece that included math performances in celebration of Pi Day (March 14 or 3/14), but found out afterwards that scientists in the building were disturbed by laughter in the hallways while they tried to teach laboratory classes. Make sure you are reasonably certain that the spaces you select can be used without serious disruption. Also, when sending students out of the classroom to work, consider how you will reflect on the activity. Try sending students out in groups so that some can observe while others work, creating greater opportunities for reflective discussion in the post-activity period. In contrast, complete these activities in stages, with a session devoted to planning, one to execution, and one to reflection, with time for writing and thinking in-between sessions.

Here are some examples of environmental strategies for lesson plans.

Invisible theatre

Augusto Boal regularly used this technique to highlight social issues in a unique public space. In invisible theatre, performers prepare a provocative scene to perform in a public space, never letting those around them know that the scene is a performance. The resulting display is designed to provoke passersby into intervening in the scene or discussing its consequences with one another. A famous example involved two actors entering a hotel restaurant, ordering food, and then professing they were unable to pay (see *Theatre of the Oppressed* for a full description). When their server protested that they must pay for their meals, the actors began a dialogue with the server and the patrons of the restaurant about the fairness of the establishment's prices, noting that the dish they ordered was so expensive that even workers at the hotel itself could not afford it. Taking this model as inspiration, have groups of students select a social issue and a nearby space connected to that issue, constructing a short scene designed to attract attention and inspire passersby to react or engage in discussion with the actors and each other.

Incendiary moments

We sometimes use this technique in our own lecture-based classes, assigning students the challenge of interrupting our lectures to present a short, provocative speech or piece of performance that provides a counterpoint to the point of view we are presenting as a way to disrupt classroom power dynamics. Ask students to identify a place in need of an intervention, then plan and execute short performance pieces in that place. Flash-mobs, short speeches, and guerilla performances are all great choices. Ask students to be creative when designing their performance and encourage them to keep in mind their place and purpose. If using incendiary moments as part of a longer unit on public protest, consider having students research techniques for art-based political action and select a style to emulate. Some great starting points include Group Material, Critical Art Ensemble, RepoHistory, and the Situationists.

Dance and physical theatre

Recent scholarship reminds us that movement helps us think in different ways (see for instance Ambady and Slepian 2012, along with further discussion of embodied learning in Chapter 1). Movement can help learners break through mental blocks, unlock creativity, and collaborate with others, in addition to being good for our bodies. While pre-K and early elementary students are usually comfortable exploring what their bodies can do as part of their daily routines, middle school and older learners can be preoccupied with issues of body image, perceived competency or lack of ability in specific movement disciplines, or fear of embarrassment. Techniques from contemporary dance and physical theatre offer us alternative methods for movement that help break some of these expectations and open up possibilities for anxious participants to move without self-consciousness.

The following are examples of dance and physical theatre strategies for lesson plans.

Starting with movement

In lessons that involve creating characters or scenes, consider starting with movement rather than with scenarios. Similar to Augusto Boal's famous "complete the image" exercise, techniques that start with movement help participants explore deeper ideas or impulses that they are not yet able to articulate in words. Movement techniques can also be a helpful tool for collaboration among participants. The following technique, an example of this collaborative movement, is based on Frantic Assembly's devising exercise, Hymn Hands (Graham and Hogget 2009).

Procedure: Divide the group into pairs. Ask each pair to come up with a series of "moves" in which partners make contact with one another. For example:

1   Partner A places a hand on Partner B's shoulder.
2   Partner B reaches up to touch Partner A's hand.
3   Partner A removes her hand.

While "Hymn Hands" involves ten moves of the hands, we find allowing partners to experiment with what constitutes a "move" to be a fine choice for our purposes. Give the pairs a set number of moves to complete, then allow a few minutes for rehearsal so the know their sequences well. Have the groups "loop" the moves so they can be performed continuously. You now have a movement "text" to work with for the rest of your lesson. Some options for exploration include:

- Have a pair volunteer to share their movement sequence. Ask participants to offer their observations about the perceived relationship between the two figures based on the movement. Use this information to help develop characters for a scene.
- Start the sequence of moves with a prompt (use a word connected to the theme of the lesson or choose an emotion). Once groups have developed their sequences, share and reflect on what ideas emerge from the movement pieces.
- Take the initial movement piece through an iterative process by asking partners to use the same movement but add improvised language to the scene. Each time groups share their work, conduct a large-group reflection to discuss new ideas made by observers after watching the scene. Allow partners to work again based on the feedback they receive from peers.

Contact improv: A simple starter for dancers, contact improv is a technique that helps participants develop comfort as a group and explore bodily-kinesthetic collaboration. As Boal pointed out, breaking the constraints of "expected" movement can be especially liberating for participants used to conforming to a narrow set of behaviors every day, so we like this starter for lessons involving critical thinking, creativity, or collaboration, each of which is a skill primed by the focused work of contact improv. Participants also develop spatial skills and listening skills as they work with their partners to succeed in the activity.

Materials: Music and a playback device.

Procedure: Ask participants to work in pairs and collaborate on movement through space in response to music. They must maintain one point of contact at all times. To start, ask participants to place together the palms of their hands. As the participants begin exploring the space together, instruct pairs to begin to transition from palms of hands to other points of contact, without ever disconnecting from one another. At first, participants may just switch hands to other points of contact like shoulders, but encourage partners to experiment with ways to explore the space unconventionally: back to back, toe to toe, forehead to forehead, rearranging themselves as often as they like. As partners develop competency with the exercise, challenge them to continuously move and realign themselves. Keep contact improv a silent activity to encourage collaboration and careful attention to other's actions as cues. After a session, reflect together on discoveries, strategies for cooperation/collaboration, and surprising bodily-kinesthetic collaborations.

Variation—Movement free association: Start a lesson with a brief contact improv session focused on a word or pair of opposites as the inspiration for the students' movement (for instance, round/sharp, free/bound, gargantuan/ tiny). Ask students to explore multiple levels (standing, tiptoe, crouched, lying down), tempos, rhythm of movement, and relationships with their partner. Add related music from a period, composer, tradition, style, or geographical location that relates to the lesson for the day.

Activities for generating new work

In the previous section, we defined several activities for lesson plans inspired by performance art. In this section, we outline methods for creating new short performances with learners. We first describe a collaborative technique for making performances in groups known as devising, and follow with a description of writing or text-based methods for creating individual performances. As with all activities, fine tune details of an exercise to specific learning objectives. For instance, focus on individual work like free-writing as a starting point for creating material for performance if writing and communication skills feature prominently in your goals. On the other hand, techniques like composition highlight collaboration, interpretation, and synthesis of new ideas in groups.

Composition

For a more thorough introduction to this method, see Anne Bogart and Tina Landau's text, *The Viewpoints Book* (2005), especially the chapters on composition (the Viewpoints techniques developed by Bogart, based on her mentor Mary Overlie's work in choreography, can also be adapted to lesson planning). In Bogart's composition technique, participants create short performances that combine multiple elements, much like a collage artist uses multiple images to make a new work of art. The composition format is simply a set of instructions or list of ingredients that varies according to your learning objectives and curricular goals. You may find using the word collage is often better than the term "composition" for younger learners or those who do not identify with the label "artist." One of our favorite aspects of composition is the way that it provides multiple opportunities for reflection. Students inventory their values and ideas in their initial response to the instructions, then do so again in creating and sharing a composition. Then they have another opportunity to reflect and interpret as they watch their peers present performance art pieces based on the same set of instructions. Finally, the entire group has an opportunity to reflect together on the new ideas that emerged from the session. Use compositions to help students let go of concern for narrative or character and focus on ideas and concepts; it is an especially useful tool for exploring critical questions and big issues as a supplement or alternative to discussion.

Materials: Composition instructions (either one set per group or a set for each participant).

Procedure: Divide the class into the desired number of groups for the activity. Explain to the group that they will be creating short performances in groups using a set of instructions you will provide. Emphasize that performances should focus on communicating an idea or feeling and can be abstract. The activity's goal is to create sound and movement collages rather than narrative scenes. Give groups a specific amount of time to work (twenty minutes works well) and pass out instructions. After the work time concludes, ask groups to present their compositions one at a time. Observers discuss their impressions and ideas after each presentation. Consider allowing free commentary from the audience rather than asking groups to "explain" their work, since free association can yield more exciting interpretations.

A simple composition template for use with novices or as a short activity:

Create a one-minute performance art piece using the following ingredients:

- your favorite character in the book;
- your favorite line;
- three abstract movements.

Your piece should answer the question: *"What does this character fear most?"*

A complex template for use with experienced students or as a longer activity:

Create a performance using the following guidelines:

I. The piece should be made of two distinct sections. Each transition from one section to the next should be clearly marked in some way (a pause, a repeated movement, a word, a blackout, etc.).

Section 1. Our World as It Is
Section 2. Our World as We Wish It To Be

II. The following is the only text you can use. Feel free to repeat single phrases, perform them out of order, use only some of these lines, or use no text at all. Anything goes:

[here we would use lines from the text of a current news story we had explored in class].

III. You must incorporate at least ten of the following twelve items at least once. They may be repeated. You may also use them all.

- A moment where everybody is looking down
- One moment of great contrast (dark to light, loud to soft, stillness to great movement)
- Use your body to create music (percussive sounds, singing, whistling)
- Twenty consecutive seconds of laughter
- Repeat a movement six times in a row
- A surprise
- Movement in unison by everyone in the group
- Fifteen consecutive seconds of top-speed talking
- A staring contest
- A moment in slow motion
- Change of light in the room
- Lift one person into the air

Decide where you want the audience to be and how you will begin and end your performance.

Anything is possible; try something new. The composition is completely open to your interpretation. It does not need to make sense or tell a story, though it can. It can be funny, serious, or anything in-between. You cannot be wrong.

Short prompts for written work

From solo artists like Holly Hughes to groups like Forced Entertainment, performers often generate new work through the use of free-writing prompts. Similar to prompts used in creative writing workshops, these prompts can take many forms and function as starters, as writing-in-character engagements, or as jumping-off points for creating and sharing performances relating to class material. After working with free-writing for a few sessions, we recommend also allowing participants to suggest their own prompts, even using the popcorn activity described below as a way to add an aleatory element to the process. Be sure to alert students in advance if work they create in free-writing sessions may be shared with others.

Sample prompts:

For a unit on poetry: *"Write for two minutes, listing all the clichés you can think of."* Have students create a spontaneous poem by cutting their list into pieces and drawing them out of a bag or hat to create a new set of phrases.

For a unit on cause and effect: Pass out photographs, and give students the prompt: *"What happens next?"*

For a unit on a work of literature: Have students select a main character, and give them the prompt *"Write for two minutes in the voice of the character, starting with the question 'What do I most want people to know about me?'"*

Creating performances using free writing

After working through several free-writing prompts, give participants a few minutes to review what they have written. Ask participants to identify anything they find especially interesting or surprising in the writing they generated. After processing time, ask participants to use their free-writing as raw material for a one-minute performance text.

    Variation: Ask participants to pass their new performance text to a classmate for interpretation and performance. After sharing performances, reflect together regarding new ideas emergent from the process of interpreting someone else's work.

Performance art as an alternative to traditional reflection

Lessons based on performance art often produce abstract or impressionistic responses to activities. Creating short pieces of movement, performing original poetry, or group compositions can serve as the basis of an hour-long lesson plan, but performance art could also be adapted as a means of reflecting on work completed in a more traditional lesson. Consider taking ten minutes at the close of the lesson for the creation of thirty-second performances that respond to a reflection question related to lesson content. After a round of presentations, allow students to discuss what they saw in their peers' responses. This reflection technique, like many others using performance art, help teachers empower students who are afraid to voice opinions or hold positions that diverge from the norm. By presenting ideas in an abstract or unusual format, students can feel freed from the constraints of traditional discourse typically integrated into classrooms.

While performance art can be used as a reflection strategy in and of itself, some teachers may feel that this abstraction makes thorough lesson reflection all the more important. We recommend a hybrid model in these instances. Traditional discussion works well to unpack ideas explored in the lesson, and performance techniques help create new reflection strategies, either for performance art-based lessons or for any of the other lesson plans discussed in the book. These performance art reflection strategies provide a change of pace that encourages student thinking after a traditional lesson or are an open-ended method to end a performance art lesson.

Composition for reflection

Give students a short set of composition instructions and ask them to add in three elements from the day's class, their peers' work, or from group discussion. These elements could be words, phrases, small bits of movement, or ideas.

Short performance responses

Many techniques discussed in this chapter can be adapted to reflective purposes, but if you use performance art often in your classes, you may also find that giving students a general prompt like *"Make a one-minute performance"* in response to a reflection question can yield fruitful results. Once students gain proficiency with making performance choices and develop evaluative skills through reflecting on others' work, try giving them free rein to create performance art within a time-limited format. When reflecting on these short performances, ask participants to highlight ideas they saw in others' performances that either surprised them or connected with their own ideas in some way.

Five-word responses

A quick, silent reflection strategy when a group needs to regain composure or when time is short, this tactic creates space for students to experience one another's observations without judgment or cross-talk. This activity is adapted from Goat Island's *Schoolbook 2*, in which it serves as a technique to help reflect on peer artwork and generate a starting point for new work.

Age group: Middle school and up.

Materials: board and writing implements.

Procedure: After presenting performance pieces or any other sharing of work or ideas, ask participants to remain silent and, one at a time, record a five-word response to what they have just seen on the board. Emphasize that these words do not need to form a sentence. They may be associations, images, feelings, or any other reactions participants experienced.

Reflection strategies: Once everyone in the group has written five words, allow time for discussion of ideas. After the activity, ask each student to free-write for two minutes in response to a peer's five-word response.

Allow five-word responses to be the absolute last word of the session by dismissing class immediately after the activity, with no additional commentary from the leader.

Popcorn

A favorite with our college students as a framework for discussion or as an introduction to the topic of a lesson plan, this technique allows a measure of anonymity through a simple aleatory procedure. While the event created through this activity is performative, it need not generate performance. We often use it to reflect on art processes in a way that continues the spirit of energetic exploration learners have experienced during a lesson.

Age group: Second grade and up (reading competency is important, though this activity may be modified through the use of drawings).

Materials: Small scraps of paper, writing instruments.

Procedure: Gather learners in a circle. Give them a few minutes to write comments or questions on small slips of paper. Instruct them to crumple their papers into balls and toss them in the center of the room when they are finished. Once a substantial number of comments are piled in the center of the room, it's time to make popcorn! Simultaneously, each participant should dart to the center of the room, grab a piece of paper, open it, and shout out what is written on it. Once this is done, crumple the paper again, toss it in the center, and grab another to shout out. Everyone works simultaneously. Allow this process to go on until a satisfactory amount of energy has built up and the soundscape has reached the desired level of complexity.

Reflection questions:

"What words or phrases stood out to you?"

"What surprised you?"

Variation: Use this activity to generate further discussion. After the popcorn session ends, ask participants to return to the circle. Have a volunteer grab a paper ball from the center and use it to start discussion. Instruct participants that once they feel the prompt has "run out of gas," someone should take the initiative to grab a new prompt from the pile. Let this activity grow organically; some prompts will receive thirty seconds of attention while others might take five minutes. We find it helps to instruct students to simply interpret the prompts as they wish rather than ask for clarification from the writer, since the prompts are generated anonymously. Also, know your group; if the group needs instruction on treating everyone's ideas with respect, be sure to do so at the start of this or any activity that involves sharing writing.

Floating comments

Often, in traditional "sit in a circle and talk" reflection periods, we notice students "reading the room" before making a comment. This practice reflects a normal and expected level of concern that one's ideas are welcome and in synch with the flow of the conversation, but from time to time we are interested in "shaking up" the group dynamic. A simple strategy like a group free association can help accomplish this goal while still building group cohesion, listening skills, and confidence.

Procedure: At the end of the lesson or activity, ask each participant to find a comfortable spot on the floor to lie down. Lead participants in a short relaxation exercise by asking them to tense and then relax muscles in their feet, calves, thighs, pelvis, core, chest/back, arms, and head in order, allowing a feeling of relaxation to fill them from toe to head as they move through the body. When everyone is relaxed, ask the group to focus on their breathing. After relaxing, ask participants to, as they feel inspired, allow a response to the day's work to escape their lips upon an exhale. If two people speak simultaneously, that is fine. Ask the group to listen and let their own comments flow naturally in response to what they hear and feel from themselves and the group.

Variation: Place limits or prompts on the responses that connect to your learning objectives. For instance:

> *"Share one word that describes how the main character felt."*

> *"Share the most important image you remember from today's work."*

> *"Share the question you most want to ask."*

Ingredient lists

A technique used by many devising groups, the ingredient list is a simple method to allow groups to reflect on the work they're doing over time. We use this tactic in longer units that involve making performance art or that involve other methods described in this book.

Materials: Large-format paper (or chalkboards that will not be erased), markers.

Procedure: At the start of a lesson or unit, place large sheets of paper on the walls around the room with markers or writing utensils easily accessible. Ask participants to be on the lookout for interesting ideas, images, or other work from their peers during the day's activities. These items will form the ingredients of a larger work or discussion. When a participant identifies something worthy of the list, they should take the initiative to go to the board or a sheet of paper and write the word, description, or drawing of the image on the list.

Reflection options:

- At the end of each day, at a break, or at the end of the unit, ask participants to review the ingredients list and comment on what trends they see. Let this moment jumpstart general discussion.
- Ask participants to create new performances exploring a lesson's central theme, using at least three elements from the ingredients list in some way.
- Have students create new composition assignments for peers (solo or in groups) using a set number of elements from the ingredients list.

Variation: Identify a single participant as the recorder of ingredients. This strategy helps draw in a reluctant or quiet learner, positioning him as a leader in the classroom while also encouraging others to engage with the "recorder" to point out ingredients that should be captured on the list.

Re-performing

Iterative processes create space for a non-verbal form of reflection that engages higher-order thinking skills of comparison, evaluation, and synthesis. We use this technique in longer units, often assigning participants to think about and "steal" elements from a peer's performance to incorporate into their work for the next session. Another tactic involves asking solo or paired participants to teach their performances to another individual or group, effectively swapping performances. The work of teaching another person to perform your piece can offer surprising insights into how and why you made certain choices in your work. Since the strategy of re-performing others' work involves a great deal of trust and respect, use this strategy with groups who are already comfortable with one another and who can be counted on to be respectful.

Procedure: After a round of presentations, allow participants ten minutes (or more, depending on the length and complexity of the work presented) to teach a partner their material. After another ten minutes of rehearsal time, ask participants to share the pieces they have learned.

Variations:

- Ask new performers to reinterpret the pieces taught to them in some way.
- Ask new performers to combine their original piece with one taught to them by their partner.
- Ask new performers to emphasize one element they love most about the piece they have learned as they perform it.
- Give new performers an extended period of time to reinterpret performances, asking them to expand them to twice their length in the intervening time.
- After exchanging performances ask participants to swap back to their original pieces, keeping the elements from their peer's interpretation of their performance.

Reflection questions:

"What surprised you about your performance piece when you saw another person do it?"

"What new interpretations emerged as you saw the same piece with a new performer?"

"How did it feel to see another person present your material?"

Tips for sharing performance art

Simultaneous sharing of performance art provides an easy method to help participants focus on process over product, especially for lessons that are not primarily focused on creation of performance art for its own sake. By either getting into a circle and performing as a group, performing in small groups, or having half the class perform while the other half watches, you can lessen performance anxiety and center the group's focus on using performance to think and learn about a concept. Simultaneous performance can also be a good strategy for sharing initial drafts of performance that will go through revision (see discussion of iterative processes above).

When choosing to make performance a central focus through individual sharing, set clear parameters for the sharing. For example, you might help participants take on the "mantle of the artist" by asking them to decide where they would like observers to sit, reminding them that they may use any space in the room as they wish, and encouraging them to make clear choices about how the performance will begin and end. Before performances, let the group know how post-performance reflection will work. If the group will be discussing questions about each other's work, try posing questions beforehand to enrich the viewing experience. If the group has just gotten to know one another, a few tips for being a good observer can also support engaged spectatorship. At a bare minimum, remind the group to focus on observing those who are sharing rather than on planning one's own performance.

Follow up all performance art activities with thorough reflective discussion to help students unpack the ideas they've explored. Often, students will make new discoveries about a topic, about their own opinions, or about their deeply held beliefs while making performance art. Giving voice to these discoveries deepens the rewards of the process for participants and leaders alike.

Performance art for teaching and learning: sample lesson plans

In the following section, we offer two lesson plans that showcase performance art techniques as teaching and learning methods. Each technique works for multiple age groups, and extensions are also possible. When using performance art in lesson planning, your options are vast, so articulate a clear idea of learning objectives to help guide your work. While the activities and structures described in this chapter can be combined in nearly infinite ways to build lesson plans, these examples combine concepts and techniques in ways that we find especially useful.

Composition for complex concepts—sample lesson: "US" and "Them"

The following sample lesson is a response to a news event our college students wanted to discuss in class. In 2013, Nina Davuluri became the first Miss America of Indian-American heritage. Sadly, social media almost immediately erupted in a flurry of racist comments about Davuluri's fitness to be crowned Miss America. As the story evolved, these tweets persisted alongside other comments celebrating diversity as a founding virtue of the nation, sparking debate in our classes over the notion of American-ness. In response, we designed a lesson that allowed students to use several free-association techniques to explore concepts of belonging and community alongside ideas of nation and nationalism. We have used compositional methods with success with middle- and high school-aged students as well. Don't be shy about giving a group a complex task, but do feel free to scale the difficulty of the assignment up or down depending on group size, maturity level, and experience working together. We find a list of ten to fifteen elements is ideal to give students productive ingredients for a collage-style performance art piece, but the format of presentations can vary widely to increase or decrease the complexity of the task. For instance, instead of requesting that students generate a three-part performance, we might require a simpler, one-minute performance on a theme in order to simplify the task.

Goal: To reflect on the current state of US attitudes toward citizenship and outsider status.

Objectives:

- Students will brainstorm about issues related to US attitudes toward belonging and foreignness through word association.
- Students will develop comfort in using their bodies to make art and begin responding to each other's ideas spontaneously through a "complete the image" activity.
- Students will synthesize an artistic response to the issue of insider/outsider status through creation of a performance composition.
- Students will reflect together on the work they've done using a five-word response technique.

Materials: Composition instructions (one copy per group, see below for a handout).

Procedure—Brainstorm/free-associate: Lying in a circle, call out words that spring to mind based on the word "America" (instructor can prompt to explore other areas).

Complete the image: The group stands in a circle. A volunteer moves into the circle to use his or her body to create a picture of "America." Another individual enters to "complete the image." The first person leaves, and the cycle continues, allowing physical free association. Internal reflection should be allowed so that class members have a chance to interpret the images created. Tip to increase the rewards of this activity: Ask observers to interpret freely using the prompt "*What do you see?*" rather than having the participant tell the group what he or she is trying to communicate.

Composition assignment: Groups of four are given composition instructions (see below). Explain that the groups should attempt a non-narrative performance art piece that allows free exploration of these ideas. If necessary, tell participants to think about the assignment as creating a "performance collage." Each group has twenty minutes to complete a composition.

Share compositions with the large group.

Short reflection: Five-word responses on board from each student.

Composition instructions handout

America: Inside and Outside
Create a composition for performance using the following guidelines:
The piece should be made of three distinct sections. Each transition from one section to the next should be clearly marked in some way (a pause, a repeated movement, a word, a blackout).

Section 1. America: Inside.

Section 2. America: Outside.

Section 3. America: Inside and Out.

The following is the only text you can use. Feel free to repeat single phrases or perform them out of order. Anything goes.

O beautiful for spacious skies,
For amber waves of grain,
For purple mountain majesties
Above the fruited plain!
America! America!

You must incorporate at least ten of the following twelve items at least once. They may be repeated. You can use them all.

1 A sustained moment where everybody is looking down.
2 One moment of great contrast (examples would be dark to light, loud to soft, stillness to great movement).
3 Use your body to create music (examples could be percussive sounds, singing, whistling).
4 Twenty consecutive seconds of silence.
5 Repeat a movement eight times in a row.
6 A surprise.
7 Movement in unison.
8 Fifteen consecutive seconds of laughter.
9 Everyone running in a circle.
10 Arm wrestling.
11 Change of light in the room.
12 Lift one person into the air.

Decide where you want the audience to be and how you will begin and end your performance.

Anything is possible. Try something new. The composition is completely open to your interpretation. It's okay for it to be funny, serious, or anything in between. You cannot be wrong. Keep your performances to around three minutes.

Reflection: Share and discuss.

Performance art for poetry: "The Jabberwocky"

The following lesson plan was inspired by both Laura Garner Salazar's work on performance art as a tool for exploring poetry and Sarah Taylor's approach to collaborative performance of nonsense poems like Lewis Carroll's famous "The Jabberwocky." Using an iterative procedure, students collaborate on a creative interpretation of Lewis Carroll's poem through sound and movement. Opportunities for reflection are integrated into the activity at multiple points throughout the lesson.

The lesson uses two engagement activities: first, students practice vocal skills with a warm-up and relaxation exercise. This engagement primes the group to explore the onomatopoeia heavily featured in the poem, mining Carroll's words for emotional content and inspiration for the imagination. Second, students collectively improvise a forest soundscape. This engagement, a variation on the visualization procedures found elsewhere in the book, helps the group imagine a setting for the rest of the improvisation while also scaffolding the main activity of collaborative improvisation with sound and movement.

This lesson can be adapted for learners of all ages and may be extended or shortened depending on learning objectives and available time and materials. See the listed extensions for ideas.

Goal: To engage with performance art techniques and bring a classic poem to life.

Objectives:

- Students will learn a simple vocal warm-up.
- Students will use their bodies and voices to create a soundscape.
- Students will collaborate to analyze a poem for information about mood, setting, and action.
- Students will provide verbal feedback on one another's work.
- Students will improvise performance art approaches to bringing "The Jabberwocky" to life.
- Students will reflect together on their aesthetic choices.

Materials: Copies of the poem, cut into stanzas.

Procedure—Vocal warm-up: Lead the participants through your favorite relaxation and vocal warm-up. We like the following, adapted from Kristin Linklater's work, which focuses on relaxing the body to free the voice and imagination:

> Ask participants to find a comfortable place to stand, relaxed, with feet shoulder-width apart. Remind them to not lock the knees. Ask participants to tense their muscles as tight as they can, starting at the feet. Label that feeling "tension." Encourage them to then release their muscles, imagining any stored tension seeping into the floor like electricity going to ground. Label that feeling "relaxation." Take participants through this process from feet to calves to thighs to pelvis to abdomen to chest to arms to neck (caution participants to tense gently with the neck) to face to scalp, keeping the feeling of relaxation in each body part as you go. After this exercise, ask participants to hum. After they develop proficiency with humming, ask them to open the mouth, allowing an "aaaah" sound out. Let the "aaaah" sound resonate deep in the pelvis. Next, ask them to raise the sound to the belly, then to the chest, then the throat, then the lips, then the nose, then the forehead, then out the top of the skull. Play with this process as an "elevator of sound." Repeat as necessary.

Soundscape—An eerie forest: Instruct students to find a comfortable spot in the room and close their eyes for visualization. Describe the forest space to the students using evocative language. Ask each student to think of a sound that might happen in that eerie forest (they must be able to make this sound with their voices). As you travel through the room, let students know you will tap them on the shoulder as a cue to begin making their chosen sound. Continue this process until all students create their sounds. Once the soundscape is established, ask students to explore volume and tempo, bringing the forest soundscape to a crescendo before calling for the group to freeze and open their eyes. Reflect together on sounds everyone heard.

Instructional presentation: reading "The Jabberwocky": Divide the class into five groups, giving each one a stanza of the poem (reserve the sixth stanza for the upcoming large-group activity). One at a time, have each group read their stanzas aloud in order.

Group poetry interpretation: Ask each group to use their voices and bodies to make a soundscape to fit the stanza they have been assigned. Instruct the group to recite the poem, adding in repetition, other sounds, and atmospheric noises to create a soundscape that feels right to them.

Share stanzas, discuss responses: In order, each group shares their interpretations. Ask group members to begin their soundscapes in order at your cue, and conduct the performances accordingly. After soundscapes have been shared, ask participants to respond to each other's work. Questions to include: *"What surprised you?"* and *"What ideas did you like best?"* Make sure each group gets feedback.

Groups refine stanzas and add movement: Return to small groups and refine soundscape choices based on feedback. Encourage groups to add at least one physical movement for each member of the group. Let the group know that literal and/or figurative choices are acceptable; they should bring the poem to life in whatever way feels best. Share choices and discuss responses again.

Introduce last stanza: At the end of the sound and movement reflection, introduce the poem's final stanza. Give each group a copy of the stanza, and ask them to strategize a way to bring the entire group together to "become" the Jabberwocky and enact the final encounter and death scene. Brainstorm in groups, then explore several options. Explore several ideas before settling on a single approach.

With the leader as conductor, perform the entire piece, including the final stanza.

Reflection: Conduct reflection using the five-word responses activity (see above).

Extensions and adaptations: Make this lesson part of a longer unit by adding on additional days for participants to construct nonsense poems. Start with free-writing exercises to generate poems and then choose poems to bring to life. Incorporate an aleatory procedure by having students place their poems in a hat and draw another student's work to enact.

Alternatively, choose additional nonsense poems to create a multi-day unit on performance poetry. Good sources include Kurt Schwitters' *Ursonate* (1922) and Edward Lear's "The Jumblies" (1895). *Ursonate* makes an excellent candidate for musical accompaniment, while "The Jumblies" offers additional opportunity for character work and improvisation.

Performance art with different age groups

Early childhood

With very young learners, performance art methods may be a natural extension of playtime. Performance art can become a vehicle for free association and experimentation that young children regularly engage in on their own. Younger populations, with their lower exposure to more traditional performance methods and their developmental focus on non-linear, repetitive, and imaginary play, are often adept at performance art.

With early childhood learners, performance art methods drawn from dance can be especially useful to explore abstract concepts.

Key techniques:

- Iterative procedures offer opportunities for young learners to discover new ideas slowly, through multiple attempts at a challenge.
- Young learners also respond well to the game-like structure of aleatory processes.

Early elementary

Early elementary learners are ready for greater challenges. Performance art techniques that use game-based aleatory procedures can be helpful to explore cause and effect, develop teamwork and problem-solving skills, and enhance traditional techniques for developing content-area knowledge. Performance art can also be an extension of writing workshop time, allowing students to explore the meaning of words in their bodies or use the poetry techniques discussed earlier in the chapter to bring poetry to life. As early elementary learners begin working to create new writing both collaboratively and on their own to meet learning standards, consider using performance art both as a pre-writing tool to generate story, abstract ideas, or material to which learners may respond in writing, or as a reflective tool through which to explore what they have created in writing workshops.

Key techniques:

- Aleatory procedures
- Iterative processes
- Starting with movement.

Upper elementary

Performance art tactics can be a basis for exploration of new concepts for older elementary students, but they can also provide quick methods for creating new characters, new poetry, or other creative work. Older elementary students will also exhibit greater competencies in working within multi-step processes like compositions.

Key techniques:

- Composition
- Performance art for reflection
- Contact improv.

Middle school

Middle school learners are more capable of adapting performance art techniques to create performances, as in the Jabberwocky lesson. This age group can benefit from the free interpretive space that performance art allows, though it is always a good idea to go over the need for open-mindedness and positive feedback in lessons involving the sharing of original work. Small-group performance work can help shy students overcome fear of sharing original creations, while still retaining the benefits of performance art tactics for this age group.

Key techniques:

- Starting with movement
- Iterative processes
- Aleatory procedures.

High school

High school students may benefit from discussion of performance art as a genre in order to build aesthetic and critical vocabulary that helps students articulate their response to one another's ideas. Relational art modes that focus on creating new social spaces through art can also be linked with exploration of social and political issues, connecting to service learning and community-based engagements.

Key techniques:

- Composition
- Relational strategies
- Performance art for reflection.

References

Ambady, Nalini and Michael L. Slepian. 2012. "Fluid movement and creativity." *Journal of Experimental Psychology: General* 141(4): 625–9. Accessed July 14, 2014. DOI: 10.1037/a0027395.

Bogart, Anne and Tina Landau. 2005. *The Viewpoints Book: A practical guide to viewpoints and composition.* Theatre Communications Group.

Bryan-Wilson, Julia. 2003. "Remembering Yoko Ono's Cut Piece." *Oxford Art Journal* 26(1): 99–123.

Etchells, Tim. 2002. *Certain Fragments: Texts and writings on performance.* Routledge.

Friswell, Richard. 2010. "Surrealist art form, exquisite corpse, still fascinates artists and collectors." *Artes Magazine*, June 22. Accessed July 14, 2014. www.

artesmagazine.com/2010/06/surrealist-art-form-exquisite-corpse-still-fascinates-artists-and-collectors/.

Graham, Scott and Steven Hogget. 2009. *The Frantic Assembly Book of Devising Theatre*. Routledge.

Harris, Mary Emma. 2013. "John Cage at Black Mountain College: A preliminary thinking." *Black Mountain Studies Journal* Volume 4 (Spring). Accessed July 14, 2013. www.blackmountainstudiesjournal.org/wp/?page_id=1276.

Mee, Erin B. 2002. "Shattered and fucked up and full of wreckage: the words and works of Charles L. Mee." *TDR* 46. 3 (Autumn): 82–104.

Rainer, Yvonne. 2009. "Trio A: genealogy, documentation, notation." *Dance Research Journal* 41.2 (Winter): 12–18.

Salazar, Laura Gardner. 1999. *Making Performance Art*. New Plays Books.

5 Assessment
Tools for effective and reflective practice

In this chapter we turn our attention to assessment, considering how teachers and facilitators evaluate drama-based learning and educational programs. We review definitions of assessment; discuss various skills and knowledge that participants might acquire, develop, or practice through drama-based learning; and describe approaches by which facilitators could generate assessment tools. We also articulate the unique qualities of assessment in arts learning, explaining key concepts and vocabulary. Finally, we outline strategies for lesson planning, highlighting how assessment influences instruction, and provide a variety of assessment resources you can adapt for your unique learning environments. Throughout the chapter, we offer sample assessment tools and practical examples to help you refine your assessment needs through practical examples and lesson plans. At the end of the chapter, you will find several important resources, including an Assessment Planning Guide, a Drama Skills and Knowledge Database, and a Drama Assessment Database.

While we have broken down assessment into specific categories and organized this chapter's progression in an order we find useful for planning lessons and residencies, we also encourage readers to adapt resources, tools, and techniques to best suit specific populations, goals or teaching styles. As an artist or educator, you will have to sift through different interpretations of assessment and determine a working definition and approach that best suits your needs. Also, keep in mind that assessment is a circular process. All components influence others throughout planning, teaching, evaluating, and reflecting on a lesson, unit, or residency. Take these resources as a point of departure to expand your knowledge and determine the processes and methods that work best for you.

Assessment as a starting point

Assessment, in its most basic sense, is the act of evaluating someone or something. However, assessment related to teaching and learning is a more complex concept. For education, assessment directly relates to evaluation. Sometimes these terms are used interchangeably (assessment *is* evaluation), and sometimes these terms are used in connection with one another (assessment *helps with* evaluation; assessment *informs* evaluation). In an effort to understand the many and varied ways assessment works in relation to schools, several assessment-focused, national-level organizations offer definitions that you may find useful. For example, the United Kingdom's Assessment Reform Group suggests that assessment is "the process of seeking and interpreting evidence for use by learners and their teachers to decide where the learners are in their learning, where they need to go and how best to get there" ("Assessment" 2002). The National Center for Research on Evaluation, Standards, and Student Testing (CRESST) of University of California Los Angeles defines assessment as "the process of gathering, describing, or quantifying information about performance" ("Assessment Glossary" n.d.). As these definitions highlight, assessment frequently involves articulating goals, collecting data or information, analyzing this information to determine how and what students can or should learn, and making choices about how to teach.

Assessment is also a notorious thorn in educators' sides. At times, it feels overwhelmingly time-consuming, and even leaves educators feeling frustrated and exasperated. It might even inspire fear. A small example: once, upon completing a rather grueling production-oriented residency about which we, a group of arts teachers, felt very positive and proud, we conducted a series of well-designed interview assessments with our students. We were disappointed to discover that while we, the teachers, had learned a great deal about producing theatre with our fourth and fifth grade students, those same students were only slightly better at production skills and even less enthused about drama after the residency. While disappointed, we quickly realized how much we had learned from this assessment data and made adjustments to future plans in the hopes of designing a learning experience that was more meaningful for our students. As this example demonstrates, assessment does not always have to produce positive results like increases in test scores, increased levels of empathy, or stronger awareness of the body in space to provide important knowledge to teachers and teaching artists. Assessment produces important and useful data for evaluating teacher and teaching artist instruction, student learning, and programmatic success. Furthermore, assessment need neither be complicated nor burdensome. Assessment is not required to follow the standardized testing models that dominate the US educational landscape at present. There are many alternative assessment models that capture a wider, richer picture of learning and teaching. In fact, assessment, when designed thoughtfully and rigorously, can be fun, illuminating, and empowering for both teachers and learners.

Assessment is also one of the key components of formal education in the contemporary US. Even though assessment is seemingly ubiquitous in education, with teachers, parents, students, and policymakers in constant debate over testing, alternative evaluation models, and accountability, it takes many different forms and occurs for a variety of reasons. A few guiding principles to keep in mind when thinking about assessment:

- Assessment often drives instruction (how a person teaches) and influences which activities a teacher chooses, how he sequences them, and how much time he spends on different tasks with learners.
- Generating assessment data forms the basis of testing, assignments, and schedules, and often directly impacts budgets and time allotment in classrooms and beyond.
- Assessment takes many forms: formal, informal, holistic, standards-based, diagnostic, performance-based, and more. (We will discuss these different formats in greater detail later in the chapter.)
- Assessment helps define education-related values as we ask ourselves: *"What skills are important to teach and learn? How do we know students have learned these skills? Why do they matter to a particular classroom, community, or country? What happens if students fail to learn skills? Who is responsible or accountable for teaching?"*
- Assessment frequently connects with concepts like performance, achievement, growth, accountability, testing, learning outcomes, differentiation, standardization, standards alignment, and other education catchphrases.

Types of assessment

When you think of assessment, what comes to mind? Tests, surveys, rubrics, portfolios, observations, interviews, performances, and journal entries are all assessment. Indeed, the types of assessment you might incorporate into your teaching or drama-based learning programs are seemingly endless. However, there are a few central categories that help you begin to narrow your approach. We will talk about each of these categories in more detail throughout the chapter.

Broadly, assessment includes three components:

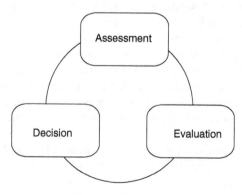

Figure 5.1

- Assessment: The actual tool, method or technique you administer to evaluate learning.
- Evaluation: The process of examining and interpreting data or information from the assessment tool or technique.
- Decision: Making choices about programs, teaching, instruction, or programming based on data.

As the figure demonstrates, these components work in circular fashion; all components inform one another. For example, a teaching artist might be hired for a residency in which she dramatizes folktales with a third grade class. Knowing very little about her student participants, she partners with her cooperating teacher and decides to conduct a diagnostic assessment to determine what students know about the skills involved in improvisation. For assessment, she and her cooperating teacher administer a survey a week before the residency begins. The survey asks participants to indicate their level of agreement with statements like, *"I feel comfortable acting out characters with my body," "I know what improvisation is,"* and *"I understand the difference between acting out a story and reading out loud."* Afterwards, the teacher and teaching artist review and evaluate the surveys, determining that students need additional instruction regarding differences between dramatization and reading aloud. They decide to adjust their residency plan, adding additional improvisation exercises that help students distinguish between reading aloud and dramatization. This example is one model for how the three components of assessment work together and help support high quality teaching and learning in drama.

Traditional/objective assessment

Traditional assessments emphasize mastery of discrete (individually separate and distinct) skills and knowledge in isolation from other subjects. They are largely product-oriented and generally evaluate learning at the end of a lesson, unit, or residency. Traditional/objective assessments usually assess students in isolation (for instance, one child taking a test by themselves without help from others), though data from traditional assessments may be used to make observations about larger groups of learners. Traditional assessments tend to be efficient and convenient; machines can quickly score traditional assessments like bubble-in tests, and teachers can easily evaluate student mastery of the tested items. Results from traditional assessments can also be evaluated through objective (without personal judgment) and quantitative methods including systematic, empirical methods that produce numerical data analyzed through mathematical analysis techniques like statistics (see Muijs 2010). Over time, these traditional assessments result in large amounts of data, helping educational policymakers and statisticians draw conclusions about learning amongst large groups of students. Examples of traditional assessment include multiple choice, true/false, fill-in-the-blank, and matching test questions. Traditional assessments probably feel very familiar to someone educated in US public schools. As we also pointed out in Chapter 1, traditional assessments have limitations. Namely, they capture a very specific, sometimes narrow, picture of learning.

Authentic assessment

Authentic assessments (sometimes also called holistic, alternative, process-oriented or performance-based assessment) evaluate a student's performance on intellectual tasks related to the curricula being taught. These kinds of assessments generally require learners to combine various skills and knowledge and then apply both to a relevant and realistic context. Given this focus on relevancy, authentic assessments provide learners with meaningful tasks, context, and content in regards to curricula, and help students cultivate vocabularies to talk about their own work. For example, during a math lesson that integrates technical theatre curricula, students might be asked to design a set to scale. Here, learners apply knowledge and skill in a real-world scenario that directly applies to the content being studied. Since authentic assessment is oriented toward practicality, teachers may also present students with opportunities to explain their ideas, partner with other learners to collaborate, or innovate based on loosely designed assignment parameters. However, authentic assessment typically takes more time to explain, complete, and evaluate. It can also be more expensive, requiring more resources to simulate real-world situations and problems for students. Authentic assessment also partly relies on subjective evaluation (teachers' use of personal judgment) and often produces qualitative data (generally, data that is not quantified with numbers or statistics, including descriptions, feelings, impressions, observations, interpretations, and interviews). Examples of authentic assessments include portfolios, performances, projects, and sharings. Rubrics (evaluation guides with specific criteria), task assessments (evaluations by both student and teacher) and contracts (agreements between teachers and learners regarding learning tasks) are also important components in conducting authentic assessment. Despite some inherent challenges, authentic assessment is a valuable way of assessing drama-based work and personal growth in students.

Standardized assessment

A form of traditional/objective assessment, standardized assessment is one of the more popular and controversial forms of assessment in contemporary US public education. Standardized assessments are concerned with consistency. They are generally wide-scale and administered to a large group of students using the same format, time limit, and question style. Standardized assessments set out to evaluate a large number of students in as uniform fashion as possible. For example, as a public school student in the US, you may have taken a state-mandated End-of-Course or End-of-Grade test that other students across your state also took. Often, data from these tests determine whether or not schools meet their desired learning and teaching goals for the year and affect individual students' promotion from one grade level to another. Currently, there are few standardized assessments for drama-based learning and teaching integrated into K-12 curricula in the US. However, many certified Theatre Arts teachers take the Educational Testing Service's *Praxis* standardized assessment in Theatre as part of their licensure requirements.

Programmatic and personal assessment

While the prior three categories fall explicitly under traditional models of assessment for learning and teaching, many of the techniques described in both traditional and authentic assessment models apply to programmatic and personal assessment as well. Programmatic assessment is a hybrid authentic/traditional approach to assessment that looks specifically at programs. For example, a theatre company's Education Director might want to learn more about her programs' effectiveness through assessment. She might conduct surveys, evaluate testing data, or review interviews with school participants and/or teaching artists. Similarly, a classroom teacher might want to conduct a personal assessment of praxis in regards to drama-based pedagogy. She might take an authentic approach, journaling each day about her experiences. While we primarily focus on learning-based assessment, you can also adapt many of these methods to support programmatic and personal assessment as well.

Overall, we prefer and prioritize authentic assessment for drama-based learning throughout this book. Nonetheless, we recognize the ever-increasing focus on traditional, standardized approaches to assessment despite our belief that traditional/objective assessments, in isolation, capture an extremely limited view of what learners learn and what teachers teach.

The 5Ws of designing assessment

Designing assessment can be simplified into easy-to-manage components by thinking of it as a method for gathering information. As you gather information about your programs and/or teaching through assessment, keep in mind the general information-gathering guidelines of Figure 5.2 on the next page.

Much like assessment itself, the 5Ws of assessment are also non-hierarchical and non-linear in theory and practice. For instance, the "who" of assessment will not uniformly take priority over "when" or "why" when designing a residency. Likewise, teachers might determine *when* assessment takes place before determining exactly *why* it will occur.

Who • will design, administer, complete, interpret, and evaluate assessments?	**Where** • will we assess?	**Why** • are we assessing?
What • information do we want to know? • format will we use?	**How** • will we assess?	**When** • will we assess?

Figure 5.2

Why do we assess?

In order to best meet the assessment needs of your organization or classroom, you need to determine the audience and purpose for your assessment. Making assessment more manageable requires teachers to think through, first and foremost, why they assess. For example, you will likely want to assess student learning, but you might also seek out programmatic assessment, assessment of teaching artists' skill or knowledge, assessment of your own teaching's effectiveness, or assessment of new program initiatives. Institutions, schools, and organizations define assessment differently and approach assessment in their programs from different perspectives and for different reasons. You may be deeply invested in assessment, hoping to demonstrate that your programs help students learn, or you may be required to assess, taking time out of your residency or lesson to complete rubrics, administer tests, or give surveys that you then pass on to a supervisor. For example, a teacher might assess a series of drama-based activities in order to demonstrate how they connect to a school-wide curriculum and help move forward school-wide curricular achievement goals. In contrast, a teaching artist might be interested in residency participants' growth in the areas of creativity, ensemble, or performance skills. In another example, an education director might obtain assessment data in order to prepare grant documentation or refine programs to better meet the needs of school partners. Some additional examples:

- In order to justify funding for this program, we need hard data to show that this residency helped students improve their ability to use descriptive language in English Language Arts.
- We need to assess creative skills in order to complete required grant documentation.
- We are mainly interested in assessing our teaching artists' experiences working with classroom teachers.

- We want to make sure both students and parents feel like they became better artists and had fun during our summer camp programming.
- We are piloting a new residency format, and we want to determine if teachers feel that it is more closely aligned to the curriculum they are already teaching.

We encourage you to approach these decisions with the understanding that *assessment is valuable and important*. A few possible outcomes from effective assessments include:

- understanding what kinds of skills participants possess before, after, or during a lesson;
- measuring growth or an increase in ability in regards to specific skills;
- giving learners feedback on their work;
- determining areas of strength and areas for improvement within a population of learners;
- demonstrating how your programs impact participants for purposes of program documentation;
- learning about most effective practices for a given lesson or activity;
- evaluating whether or not you have met stated and/or required goals and/or objectives in a specific curriculum.

What do you want to know?

Once you have determined, in broad terms, why you will assess, you will next need to determine both what kinds of learning, teaching, or other information you hope to learn through assessment and what method(s) or formats you will use to assess. Let us first consider a fundamental question when beginning to think about assessment: *What do you want to know?*

Determining what you want to know usually begins with an idea, brainstorming session, or general conversation about what you want to do in a lesson, unit, or residency. You may have fully developed these ideas or they may simply be initial thoughts you hope to expand through additional planning and research. For example, a teacher may decide to integrate drama-based methods into her upcoming literacy unit or a teaching artist may be contracted to conduct a drama-based residency about a topic related to character education. During this early planning, thinking what you want to know through assessment will help generate specific, relevant, and detailed residency/lesson plans and focus your choice of activities.

Determining what kind of information you hope to glean through assessment first requires a working understanding of the relationship between knowledge (what an individual knows), skills (what an individual can do), abilities (what an individual should be able to do), and competencies (the satisfactory combination of skills, knowledge, and ability) associated with learning with, by, and through drama.

Knowledge is intangible information a person knows about a particular subject. Examples of knowledge include knowing the criteria for effective communication, memorizing a mathematical equation, or describing the fundamentals of a descriptive essay. Simply stated, knowledge is all the information that swirls in our brains.

Skills are tangible acts that demonstrate knowledge. A learner might have memorized the beginning, middle and end of a scene for a sharing as part of knowledge, but they demonstrate their knowledge through the skill of enacting the scene in the correct sequence when called upon to do so. Skills can be practiced, but they may also seem inborn (see abilities). For example, we have all encountered natural athletes, artists, writers, and politicians, but we have also seen individuals become better at a discipline through practice.

Abilities are what learners should be able to do. Sometimes abilities are viewed as inborn or naturally occurring within an individual. For example, a student may be highly gifted in drama or have difficulty with reading. Other times, abilities are developmentally determined. For example, the cognitive abilities of a five-year-old in regards to problem-solving are different to those of a sixteen-year-old. Abilities might relate to a person's physiology, life experiences, or cultural heritage. Abilities also relate to all areas of learning, from cognition to emotion to creativity. However, keep in mind that abilities are not necessarily fixed. Like skills and knowledge, they can be developed and practiced (see also Chapter 1). For example, a beginning dancer may not possess the ability to master a complicated set of choreography, but as they develop dance competencies (skills + knowledge), their ability also increases. Part of assessment involves evaluating learners' abilities just as much as assessing skills, knowledge, and competencies.

Finally, *competencies* are behaviors that demonstrate mastery of specific combinations of skills and knowledge groups based on a specific curriculum or course of study. Competencies are also contingent on a learner's ability. For example, a student may understand that engaging their entire body, adjusting vocal quality and volume, and inferring character traits help them dramatize a character during an improvisation activity. However, in practice, they may stand stiffly or only repeat what the character has said in the folktale they are dramatizing. In this case, the student has not developed a competency in dramatization, even though they possess a great deal of knowledge on the subject. When designing assessment, you will determine if you are interested in assessing skills, knowledge, abilities, and/or competencies.

Determining the kinds of skills and knowledge you want to evaluate with regard to drama education assessment directly relates to your educational philosophy, programmatic goals, and institutional values. We will highlight several diverse skill categories and knowledge groups associated with both drama-based learning and arts learning as a whole. In order to capture the diversity of drama-based learning and teaching, we have synthesized our categories from a range of resources about learning including:

- Cognitive skills related to the Common Core and National Core Arts Standards
- Affective/social and emotional/self-system skills
- Creative skills
- Psychomotor/manual/sensorimotor skills
- Current trends in education including 21st Century Skills.

While we articulate these distinct categories based on trends and research in the field of educational and arts-based assessment and discuss each category in depth for purposes of designing assessment for drama-based learning, they are not the only groups of skills from which you can draw. For additional reading:

Table 5.1

Knowledge and Skill Groups	
Cognitive	• Bloom's Taxonomy of Learning • Marzano's Taxonomy • Krathwol and Anderson's Taxonomy for Learning, Teaching, and Assessing
Affective, and Social and Emotional Learning	• Krathwol and Anderson's Affective Domain Taxonomies • Daniel Goleman • Maurice Elias • Joseph E. Zins • Mark T. Greenburg • Linda Fredericks

Creativity	• E. Paul Torrance
	• Mihaly Csikszentmihalyi
	• Robert Epstein
	• Howard Gardner
	• Frank Williams (Williams' Taxonomy of Creative Thinking)
	• Self-assessments:
	  ○ Hocevar (Creative Behavior Inventory)
	  ○ Kaufman and Baer (Creativity Domain Questionnaire)

Aesthetics	• Maxine Greene • Philip Taylor • Ken Gale
Psychomotor/manual/sensorimotor	• Harrow's Taxonomy • Simpson's Taxonomy

Details of the relevant works of these authors can be found in the references for Chapter 5.

Additionally, you will notice a great deal of overlap between each knowledge group and skill set. This overlap highlights important and meaningful connections between different types of learning possible through drama methods, which we include in subsequent discussion throughout this chapter and in Chapter 1.

National Standards, the Common Core and Core Arts: defining a curriculum

Valuable information regarding knowledge and skills in drama-based learning can be found in state-mandated or state-supported arts curricula (the specific tasks, learning goals, and subjects that should be taught). We will go into greater depth regarding how to integrate state learning standards into your teaching and lesson planning later in the chapter, but keep in mind that these documents often provide important contextualizing information about what leaders in particular arts-learning disciplines such as drama have determined students should learn in order to develop competencies.

For almost twenty years, arts educators have looked to the National Standards for the Arts in music, visual arts, dance, and theatre arts. A consortium of arts educators, researchers, and policymakers came together between 1992–1994 to create National Arts Standards as a response to the 1994 "Goals 2000: Educate America Act," one of the first nationwide education policy initiatives in the US. As both a comprehensive national curriculum and an advocacy tool, these national standards were organized around grade level clusters (K-4, 5–8, 9–12) and indicated what students should do and know in the arts. Practically all states with arts education programs in their public schools adopted or adapted these standards for their arts curricula.

Although arts education has maintained a national model for arts standards for decades, in 2010 the role of state-mandated curricula for practically all subjects shifted to a national model with the introduction of Common Core State Standards, or the Common Core (see www.corestandards.org). As a national initiative funded and supported by politicians and business leaders, the Common Core has been adopted or adapted by many states in the US. The Common Core is a logical outgrowth of federal legislation and other initiatives that have increasingly pushed for high standards, accountability, and assessment in public K-12 education, including the 1965 Elementary and Secondary Education Act enacted under President Johnson, President Clinton's aforementioned "Goals 2000," President George W. Bush's 2001 "No Child Left Behind legislation", and President Barack Obama's 2010 "Blueprint for Reform in No Child Left Behind" and "Race to the Top" competition.

The Common Core offers a set of standards for all K-12 learners in the US in the hope of providing curricular consistency in education across and beyond state lines. However, debate about these national standards continues to occur as school districts, parents, researchers, teachers, and policy makers examine and refine the Common Core's development and implementation. Still, at the time of this book's publication in late 2014, forty-six states have adopted versions of the Common Core for their public K-12 curricula. At least for now, the Common Core is here to stay. While the Common Core does not include arts-related learning standards, great efforts have been made to demonstrate natural connections between arts learning and the Common Core. One of the leading organizations in this effort is the National Coalition for Core Arts Standards (NCCAS). The NCCAS, a national coalition of arts learning organizations, set out to revise the 1994 National Arts Standards, taking into account the Common Core, 21st Century Skills, and the evolving educational landscape. These educators, policymakers, and researchers in arts education (music, dance, visual art, and theatre arts) created the National Core Arts Standards (NCAS) (2014; http://nationalartsstandards.org). These extensive revisions were finished in 2014 and over forty states now reference these standards to define what learners in K-12 education should know and do in the arts. More are expected to follow. Both the Core Arts standards and the Common Core (or other state-adopted learning standards) are invaluable resources for determining what states value in regards to arts learning and for providing important contextualizing information about how drama skills and knowledge might be understood.

21st Century Skills

Twenty-first Century Skills (skills that focus on preparing learners for success in work and life in an increasingly global and market-focused twenty-first century society) are increasingly touted in discussions of value regarding arts education. For example, national organizations like The Partnership for 21st Century Skills (P21), one of the leading voices for 21st-century skills in K-12 education and creator of the Framework for 21st Century Skills, cites the value of the arts in areas of Critical Thinking, Collaboration, Creativity, and Communication (what P21 calls "the 4Cs") in supporting learners' with the development of 21st Century Skills. According to P21 literature, the 4Cs help learners develop new competencies in areas of learning like "global awareness" and "financial, economic, business, and entrepreneurial literacy" ("Framework" 2011: 2). Likewise, recent books like Tony Wagner's *Creating Innovators: the making of young people who will change the world* (2012) considers how skills in creativity help educators prepare learners to cultivate skills in entrepreneurship and innovation, leading to competencies in "global knowledge economy" and helping the US rise into global leadership positions in the face of outsourcing, automation, and the need to engage with knowledge in new, more complex ways (2012: 142). Arts organizations have made connections between the arts and 21st Century Skills, with articles and reports like The Kennedy Center's ArtsEdge program's "Raising 'Art Smart' Students in the 21st Century" (Saraniero n.d.) and Americans for the Arts' "The Role of the Arts in Strengthening and Inspiring the 21st Century Global Community" (2009) to name only a few. Other arts education organizations have responded by further highlighting connections between the arts and 21st Century Skills. P21's "Framework for 21st Century Learning":

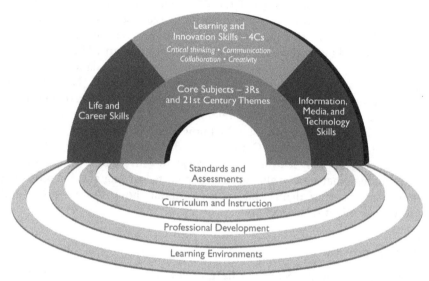

P21 Framework for 21st Century Learning
Partnership for 21st Century Skills © 2009
www.p21.org/framework

Figure 5.3

Creativity

Another important knowledge area often touted in arts-based learning is the development of creative skills. Many scholars and thinkers, from Sir Ken Robinson to Mihaly Csikszentmihalyi, speak about the importance of creative skills, and we touched on drama-based learning as a method for cultivating creativity in Chapter 1. Although creativity might be thought of as an inherent or inborn trait, creativity is made up of different competencies, both knowledge learners can acquire and skills they can practice. Scholars from psychology, education, and other related fields have devoted decades of research to examining the nature of creativity, designing measures to assess creative competencies, and considering how cultures have defined creativity through history. While still debated even today, scholars in the field of creativity studies have offered up the following two-part definition of creativity: originality and effectiveness (Runco and Jaeger 2012: 96). Within this definition, the notion of creativity relies on an individual's ability to put into practice new, novel, or innovative ideas. Contrary to some popular beliefs, this definition suggests that being creative is not simply dreaming big or imagining alternatives; a learner must also effectively give life to or put into practice their novel ideas (creative knowledge + creative skills = creative competencies). More importantly, creativity can be practiced. While some learners might have greater competencies in creativity (much like some students are more competent writers, readers, athletes, or peacemakers), these skills can be developed, honed, and refined.

With this focus on both originality and effectiveness, drama-based learning is an ideal pedagogical approach for developing creative skills. In fact, most activities in classrooms help learners or participants develop creativity. After all, students are constantly engaged in the process of generating new ideas, combining and synthesizing concepts, and effectively completing assignments. However, these connections to creative skills and knowledge are infrequently highlighted for learners. One way to emphasize the development of creative skills is simply to talk about creativity and point out how students practice it on a regular basis. For example, imagine a teaching artist decides to utilize a character worksheet to help third-grade participants create roles from a recent folktale the class read during a Drama/ English Language Arts residency that hopes to dramatize literature from the curriculum. When starting the activity, the teaching artist might point out:

> *"When you make connections between what you know about this character from the folktale and what you need to know to create a character for our drama sharing, you're practicing your creative skills. Being creative is an important skill for learning because it helps us think of new, unexpected ideas and see how they work with what we already know. As you're thinking about your character, come up with as many ideas as possible. We'll see which ones seem to fit your character the best later on."*

This example demonstrates both components (originality and effectiveness) included in creativity and makes clear for students the ways in which creative thinking connects to education and how they can practice creativity within this assignment.

Social and Emotional Learning (SEL)

Drama methods also present opportunities for learners to develop skills in Social and Emotional Learning (SEL). SEL is also known as emotional intelligence, self-science, emotional literacy, and affective education, among other terms. We address SEL and drama-based learning in greater detail in both Chapter 1 and Chapter 6, but it bears repeating that learning through drama supports the development of SEL skills. Psychologists and education researchers like Daniel Goleman (2012; see also Chapter 1), Maurice Elias (Elias and Arnold 2006), Joseph E. Zins (2004), Mark T. Greenberg (Greenberg *et al.* 2003), Linda Fredericks (2003) and many others have dedicated much of their careers to the study of SEL. As a result of this research, the Collaborative for Academic, Social, and Emotional Learning

(CASEL), the leading organization devoted to the study of emotional and social learning (see www.casel.org), has generated five "core competencies" for social and emotional learning ("Social" 2013):

- Self-awareness
- Self-management
- Social awareness
- Responsible decision-making
- Relationship skills.

Drama-based learning presents opportunities to develop and practice many SEL skill sets. For example, during the aforementioned third-grade folktale residency, as well as in several of our sample lesson plans throughout this book, students develop self-awareness while embodying and sharing characters. They practice social awareness and relationship skills when making artistic decisions with peers, and they engage in responsible decision-making and practice self-management as they refine their folktales through the collaborative rehearsal process and subsequent reflective discussions where they evaluate their group work.

While connections between drama and SEL might be clear to teachers or teaching artists, formal implementation and evaluation of SEL skills often fall by the wayside, given the emphasis on national learning standards and other objective assessment measures. In order to effectively assess SEL skills, drama facilitators should articulate specific SEL objectives during planning, discuss these skills with participants, and integrate assessment strategies to evaluate SEL learning. Some sample assessments of SEL learning might include selecting a sample of students who then, each day of a residency, self-monitor one aspect of SEL (for example, self-management) through a rating scale. At the same time, the facilitator also monitors self-management through the same rating scale. At the end of a residency, the facilitator notes any changes. Alternatively, students may keep SEL journals, writing each day about one SEL skill (for instance, decision-making) during a drama lesson. Afterwards, the teacher codes and evaluates student journal responses.

Aesthetic literacy

Drama-based learning also helps students cultivate aesthetic skills. Aesthetics, the category of knowledge related to perceptions of beauty and taste, also include skills that can be practiced and refined. Aesthetic skills can be discretely creative, cognitive, socio-emotional, or psychomotor-oriented, but they can also synthesize the four areas. Aesthetic literacy includes a variety of skills. A few examples:

- Developing vocabulary for speaking about aesthetic qualities of life (symmetry, form, shape, line, tone, texture, color, composition, presentation, flow/movement).
- Articulating and justifying artistic and aesthetic preferences.
- Evaluating performances or other aesthetic products.
- Determining the cultural, historical, or other contextual meaning integrated into or framing an aesthetic object or experience.

Aesthetic skills can also be assessed. A facilitator might ask students to respond to aesthetic qualities of performance or articulate their aesthetic choices in regards to a drama activity.

As this discussion demonstrates, determining what to assess is a complex but invigorating process. Many different types of learning occur through drama, and assessment helps teachers and students understand that learning more completely.

When will you assess?

In additional to determining what you will assess, you will also want to consider when you will administer the assessment within the lesson or residency. Practically all assessments fall into the following three categories related to time of assessment.

Diagnostic

Diagnostic assessments (or pre-assessments) help determine participants' prior knowledge *before* a lesson plan or residency. Diagnostic assessments help teachers know what students or participants already know about a topic, and they provide data to make instruction more relevant and specific. Sometimes no diagnostic assessment is necessary, particularly if a teacher knows the competencies and experiences of a particular group quite well. However, diagnostic assessments may reveal unexpected information about a group while also helping to incite interest about an upcoming unit or residency. Examples of diagnostic assessments include pre-tests, interest inventories, self-assessments, performance tasks, and anticipation guides.

Formative

Formative assessments help monitor learning *during* a lesson or residency. Formative assessments typically take place during a lesson and help teachers monitor student learning as it happens. Formative assessments tend to be informal. They also provide data to help modify instruction to better meet participants' needs within the lesson or unit. Examples of formative assessments include process journals, popcorn, certain types of graphic organizers, entrance and exit slips, and splashes or brainstorms.

Summative

Summative assessments help evaluate learning after a residency or lesson is over. Summative assessments usually measure cumulative knowledge and help teachers determine if students mastered longer-range learning objectives. Examples of summative assessments include end-of-unit tests, contracts, portfolios, and presentations.

Who will assess?

Once you decide the main goals and purposes of your assessment, you will also want to give some thought to who will design, administer, complete, interpret, and evaluate assessments and also make a plan about who will decide next steps based on assessment data. The "who" of assessment can take many different forms. Here are a few examples you may encounter:

- A theatre company education director designs a series of surveys that teaching artists administer at the end of a camp program. The teaching artists return the completed surveys to the education director and the education director analyzes the responses, generates a report, and shares data with teaching artists. The teaching artists develop new teaching techniques.

- A seventh-grade teacher designs a pre-test/post-test assessment examining students' ability to distinguish fact, opinion, and reasoned judgment as part of a drama-based lesson in a Social Studies unit. She administers the tests to her students before and after the residency, reviews the results, assigns grades to students, and reviews the data. She determines that the lesson integrating drama into the Social Studies unit was an effective method to help students distinguish fact, opinion, and reasoned judgment. She makes notes on effective components of the lesson outline and plans to teach it again in the future with a few modifications.

- A teaching artist attends a professional development workshop on reflective practice. He decides to keep a journal during an upcoming teaching residency, based on a series of prompts offered in the session. Each day of the two-week residency, he journals a one-page response. At the end of the residency, he reviews his entries, determining areas of strength and weakness. He decides to give additional attention to his planning in order to feel more confident at the start of a residency.

Each of these examples demonstrates how diverse the "who" of assessment can be. However you decide to assign assessment responsibilities, carving out time during planning to articulate these details will help ensure that assessment occurs in a timely and useful fashion. A few questions to help guide your planning:

- Will you want learner evaluations (what the participants feel they have learned), expert evaluations (what the artist/teachers think participants have learned), or both?
- Will you collaborate with fellow teachers and/or teaching artists to administer, complete and/or evaluate assessments?
- Who has final say when interpreting assessment data?
- Who makes final decisions about programmatic or curricular changes based on assessments?
- Who else needs to see these assessments?

The following is a simple assessment design from the example of the folktale residency.

Design: A teaching artist and teacher collaborate to create a rubric outlining criteria to evaluate students' improvisation skills during a series of games. They decide to randomly select a group of ten students.

Administer/complete: While the teaching artist leads the activities, the teacher fills out rubrics for the ten-student sample.

Interpret: The teacher and teaching artist tabulate scores for each component of the rubric.

Evaluate: The teacher and teaching artist review the data and determine that students need more practice in listening to peers during the improvisation activities.

Decide: Together, the teaching artist and teacher decide to add two additional listening games to the next day's lesson plan.

How to assess: methods, techniques, and tools

After determining the who, when, and why of assessment, you will likely turn to the "how" in order to determine assessment formats or methods. After you have determined the type of assessment you will use (authentic, traditional, standardized, programmatic), why you want to assess and what you hope to learn, who will participate, and when you will complete the assessments (diagnostic, formative, summative), you will next need to determine appropriate and effective assessment methods. From tests to portfolios, assessment tools take many different forms. Choosing a method of assessment requires you to consider the unique qualities and potential value of drama-based techniques and skills in regards to learning.

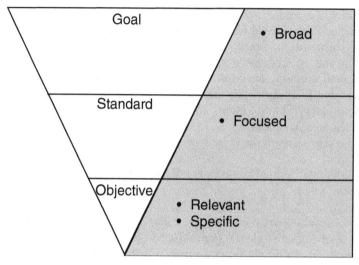

Figure 5.4

Goals, standards, and objectives

When planning both assessment and lesson plans (discussed in greater detail in Chapter 1), you will consider what you want to accomplish by articulating goals, standards, and/or objectives (see also Chapters 2, 3, and 4 for concrete examples of lesson plans). These terms, pervasive in contemporary education settings, all relate to learning outcomes (what teachers expect students to accomplish through a lesson, unit, or residency). However, these terms can be a bit confusing since they overlap a great deal and are sometimes used interchangeably. Understanding general differences between each of these categories not only helps artists and teachers assess learning in drama-based programs, but also helps to plan effective and focused drama-based learning opportunities for students. While we draw on recent US educational trends regarding curriculum in public education, namely the Common Core, similar principles apply to any curriculum you choose to use for planning lessons or residencies. Also, although we start our discussion about lesson planning and assessment with a discussion of goals, objectives, and standards, we have found that many teachers and artists, particularly those with experience, first develop broad goals, follow with planning lessons and assessments, and finally align their lessons to standards and/or objectives at the end of planning. Referencing standards and generating objectives at the end of planning acts as a check, helping teachers to ensure their plans are focused and aligned with larger curricular goals. Feel free to adapt these techniques to a format that most suits your planning needs and preferences.

Goals

Both lesson-planning and assessment require you to set goals. In education, goals are broad, general statements that a teacher or teaching artist references when planning a lesson. Goals are typically general in nature and provide a broad sense of where you want to go, what you want to do, and what you value most in the lesson. You can also refer back to your goals throughout the lesson as a basic temperature-taking measure to evaluate the residency's progress. Often, goal-setting starts with an informal brainstorming conversation around three simple questions:

- *What do we know?*
- *What do we want to know?*
- *What do we want participants to learn or do?*

To return to the earlier example, the teaching artist and cooperating teacher collaborating on a residency dramatizing folktales likely met several weeks prior to the start of their residency to plan their work together. Their goal-setting conversations likely occurred during initial planning meetings and might have sounded something like the following dialogue:

Teaching artist: *I'm excited to work with you and your students on this folktale unit. In order to prepare, I thought we could brainstorm some goals for the residency.*

Teacher: *Great, me too. I know my students are doing a great job distinguishing the folktale genre from other genres of literature, which is one of our learning standards this quarter, but I'm not sure they connect folktales to the experience of passing down stories through generations in their families. I think acting out the stories might help them connect to standards related to personal heritage that are also included in our folktale unit.*

Teaching artist: *I see. Maybe we should set a goal related to students adapting folktales to include information from their family memories and cultural traditions?*

Teacher: *I think that would work well.*

They articulate a goal:

Goal one: Students will adapt folktales, integrating cultural and family history into their dramatizations.

While this sample dialogue is an abbreviated version of a typical conversation that often occurs when planning a drama lesson, it demonstrates how you might quickly articulate goals based on the three criteria listed above. In these early stages, feel comfortable brainstorming a wide variety of different potential goals for your residency or lesson. You will have opportunities to narrow and refine further along in planning.

After this brainstorming period and depending on the time you have available for planning, you may want to let these ideas incubate for a while or you may need to start immediately refining your goals. Either way, we recommend narrowing goals for a residency into a short, manageable list. A few additional guiding questions to help you refine goals:

- What are your curricular priorities in this classroom/school/school district/organization?
- How do you typically measure learning or growth?
- What markers do you look for when determining learning success?
- Who will see assessment data? What will they hope to see?
- How do you see drama contributing to your larger programmatic/curricular goals?
- In your mind, how do you envision this residency from start to finish? What do you expect to observe in the classroom?
- At the end of this lesson, how will participants have changed or what will they know that they did not know before?

We typically write goals in student-centered language and include elements from all disciplines addressed in the residency. Some examples:
Develop one over-arching goal for an entire residency.

- During the residency, students will develop skills in dramatic improvisation and critical literacy by analyzing and creating improvised dramatizations from folktales.

Develop one goal for each lesson plan involved in a unit.

- Lesson one: Students will read and analyze folktales, identifying character traits of Rabbit, Frog, and Coyote and relating them to personal histories.
- Lesson two: Students will synthesize character traits from the text with their interpretations and impressions of Rabbit, Frog, and Coyote to create characterizations.
- Lesson three: Students will embody characters, bringing to life their versions of Rabbit, Frog, or Coyote during process-oriented improvisational activities.
- Lesson four: Students will rehearse and refine their folktale dramatizations.

Develop daily or weekly goals.

- Week one: Students will read folktales, synthesize character traits from the text, and begin to develop characters that combine personal history with the folktale narrative.

• Week two: Students will dramatize characters during improvisational games, then develop improvised dramatizations of their chosen folktales.

Standards

Increasingly, goal-setting with regard to learning also requires you to consider learning standards. Standards (sometimes called benchmarks) are statements that help define what learners should be able to know and do at each level of their education. Generally, standards are created for wide-scale use and may be mandated by government agencies like Departments of Public Instruction in individual states in order to create a norm for educational practices and provide curricular consistency across the board. In most contemporary US public schools, state-regulated learning standards define school curricula, and, increasingly, these state standards are adapted from national initiatives like the aforementioned Common Core and the NCAS. For example, a National Core Arts Standard for third grade (nationalartsstandards.org):

> NCAS Theatre 1.1.3.a: Learners will create roles, imagined worlds, and improvised stories in a drama/theatre work.

To determine specific standards for your lessons, before planning details of your residency you might utilize a state's Standard Course of Study, Curriculum Guides, or other sanctioned learning standards for alternative educational philosophies and approaches (Montessori, Waldorf/Steiner, International Baccalaureate, Sudbury, and Open Schools curricula are a few examples) to determine if your lesson is on the right track regarding desired learning outcomes. Conversely, you may want to plan the residency, then return to curricular standards and objectives to help you refine and revise the lesson. The choice is yours. However, because of the diversity of standards available and the rapidity with which they change, we have not included standards in our lesson plan examples in Chapters 2, 3 and 4. Please refer to the standards commonly used in your own teaching situation and insert them where necessary.

Objectives

Much like goals and standards, objectives are specific statements about desired learning outcomes. However, objectives differ from both standards and goals in their specificity and relevancy for a particular lesson. For example, a teaching artist might choose the NCAS standard listed above for a residency standard. They would then generate more specific and relevant objectives that demonstrate how the lesson will achieve this standard. Usually, objectives, like goals, are written in student-centered language and include a verb to demonstrate how and what a student will learn. For example:

Objective one: Participants will create roles and infer character traits by completing a character worksheet based on folktales and personal heritage.

Objective two: Participants will embody their character by dramatizing their character during process-oriented improvisation games.

In this sample objective, the teaching artist explains what participants will do (create roles; infer character traits) and how they will do it (completing character worksheets; embodying characters). Lessons or residencies will likely have numerous standards and objectives. Typically we like to include an objective for each activity in order to demonstrate how each component of a lesson supports overall lesson goals and/or standards. See sample lessons throughout this book for examples of goals and objectives in practice.

Choosing an assessment methodology

Once you have articulated goals (and likely objectives and standards as well) and determined the 5Ws of assessment, you next need to select an assessment method. By this point, you have very likely developed a strong sense of your assessment design. You understand what knowledge you hope to learn through assessment, have determined who will be responsible for each phase of assessment, decided when the assessment will occur, and articulated what you will do with assessment data. You will next decide on a design for your assessment. Instead of describing all possible assessment methods, we describe here a few options we find most useful for the drama-based teaching and learning methods established in this book, and include a larger appendix of potential assessment strategies at the end of the chapter. You can also look back to the sections on types of assessment earlier in this chapter. We have selected a few tools and methods we like to adapt for assessments. All of these examples are highly adaptable to a variety of populations and for a variety of different assessment models. We include additional practical examples of each of them at the end of the chapter.

Rubrics

Rubrics are invaluable tools for assessing drama-based learning and teaching. In its most basic sense, a rubric is a framework or matrix used for evaluating learning. Rubrics help teachers and facilitators quickly evaluate learning, and they provide students with clear criteria for reference when preparing an assignment. They are also highly adaptable and can be easily modified for diagnostic, formative, summative, authentic or traditional assessments.

Rubrics contain four parts: a task, a scale, a breakdown of skills, and descriptions of skills (Stevens and Levi 2011). Here is a sample rubric based on skills related to the aforementioned drama-based folktale residency:

Table 5.2

Sample Folk Tale Improvisation Rubric—Third Grade

Student Name:

	1	2	3	4
Vocal Expression	Student rarely expresses themselves verbally during improvisation activities.	Student infrequently uses their voice, rarely changing volume, pitch, or quality.	Student frequently uses their voice, regularly changing volume, pitch, and quality.	Student demonstrates advanced proficiency in adjusting volume, pitch, and vocal quality.
Character	Student demonstrates little understanding of character. They may appear distracted or uninterested throughout the activity.	Student demonstrates basic understanding of character. They present somewhat believable ideas.	Student demonstrates clear understanding of character. They present believable ideas about characters.	Student demonstrates advanced understanding of character. They present very believable ideas about characters.
Collaboration	Student does not work successfully with others. They may initiate arguments, choose to work alone, or refuse to contribute ideas.	Student works somewhat successfully with others. They may dominate conversation or offer few contributions, but they make an effort to collaborate with peers and listen to ideas.	Student works successfully with others. They share leadership and take responsibility within the activity. They generally collaborate well with peers and effectively contribute ideas.	Student works very successfully with others. They expertly share leadership and take responsibility. They are patient with others, sharing ideas in a respectful, thoughtful manner.
Imagination	Student does not independently generate material that adds to or enhances the work.	Student occasionally generates new material within the activity, usually with assistance from a teacher or peer.	Student regularly generates new material within the activity and only minimally relies on assistance.	Student always independently generates detailed material that adds to or enhances the work.
Embodiment	Student limits their movement during the improvisation activity. They may stand stiffly or refuse to move.	Occasionally, student incorporates movement. They infrequently commit their entire body. Their physical interpretation may lack detail and nuance.	Student regularly incorporates movement into their character work. They inconsistently commit their entire body, including the face.	Student always incorporates movement into their character work. They consistently commit their entire body, including face.

Reflection

Reflection is the act of looking at one's own learning or teaching. Various strategies for reflection can also be adapted for assessment. Reflection-based assessments are generally authentic in nature and help learners and teachers develop strategies for metacognition (a learner's awareness of their ability to evaluate, control, modify, and manipulate their learning and thinking processes). Reflection creates space in learning for both teachers/facilitators and students to think about the process of learning. Reflection can be a sustained activity, completed over time in a journal or reflection log. It can also be an informal assessment tool, helping teachers and students generate quick data about their work. Reflection can be oriented in a variety of different ways. Learners can reflect on their experiences, emotions, and thought processes. Reflection can occur before, after, or during a lesson or unit. Individual reflections can also be put into conversation. For example, a teacher and student might compare experiences by writing back and forth in a dialogical assessment journal, or students working on a drama residency might reflect each day and compare notes about their experiences.

Portfolio assessment

Portfolio assessment is a systematic collection of student work and related materials that demonstrate learning over time. Portfolios allow for authentic assessment since they demonstrate what students can do in addition to what they know. For example, a student may successfully complete an objective quiz by listing qualities of embodying a character, thus demonstrating what they know. However, in a portfolio they can combine the quiz with a video of themselves embodying a character, demonstrating what they both know and can do. Portfolios may include work samples like writing, artwork, recordings of performances or monologues, or interviews. They also frequently include student reflection and self-evaluation about the learning process. For example, the aforementioned student might also include with her video and quiz a series of journal entries about the process of creating a character. Portfolio assessments can be process-oriented, product-oriented, or a combination of both. However, portfolios require diligence and planning and can be time-consuming. Also, they must be designed well in advance of a program or residency, and they must be regularly monitored to ensure participants or teachers keep them up-to-date.

When designing a portfolio assessment, keep in mind a few key concepts:

- Decide whether or not you want to focus on process, product or a combination of both.
- Select a focus or theme ("Production Skills" or "Characterization Techniques in Drama").

- Decide which work samples should be included in the portfolio (portfolios should be systematic; all work samples should be chosen deliberately). Seek out a diverse combination of work samples that reflect students' knowledge, skills, and personal response to their work.
- Determine and prepare a scoring guide for your portfolio. Typically, we use a rubric.
- Make portfolio work an integral component of a unit or residency. Explain to students the portfolio's purpose as well as how you will evaluate it. Allot time for participants to put together their materials. You might even show samples of successful portfolios created by previous students.

Ensuring quality assessment

No matter which strategy you choose, keep in mind a few guiding principles when planning assessment. First and foremost, an assessment method should connect to both teaching and learning. For example, a teacher may present a large amount of information in a lecture-style presentation. She then administers a quiz on the content. If students fare poorly on the exam, the teacher may need to question both how students are learning this information (passive listening, note-taking, memorization) and how she teaches the information (lecturing with limited interaction amongst class participants). She might determine that other strategies for both teaching and learning can better help students learn and help her become a better teacher. In addition to designing assessments relevant to teaching and learning, keep in mind four additional principles to help guide your assessment design. These four principles ensure useful and meaningful data that helps you effectively evaluate your programs and make informed decisions about teaching and learning:

Validity

Your assessments must be valid. In basic terms, a valid assessment evaluates what it was intended to evaluate. For example, if a teaching artist hopes to evaluate whether or not students can distinguish between dramatizing folktales and reading them aloud at the end of a residency, she will design a valid assessment of that objective. A valid assessment might be a Venn diagram, a compare and contrast visual graphic organizer (see the figure overleaf) that students fill out either during the residency (formative) or after it ends.

By filling out the diagram, students demonstrate their knowledge of distinctions between reading aloud and dramatization by articulating similarities and differences between the two. An invalid assessment might be a survey question that asks students to rank the following statement; *"I know the difference between dramatization and reading aloud."* In the case

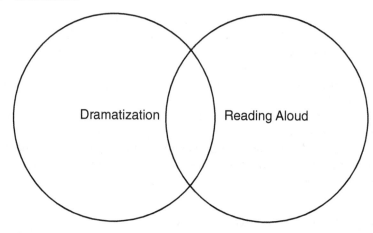

Figure 5.4

of this survey question, the data produced only shows what participants think they know, but does not require them to demonstrate their knowledge of the subject. When designing assessments, make sure they assess what you want to assess.

Reliability

Assessments must also be reliable. A reliable assessment produces consistent and reasonably predictable outcomes. Reliability becomes a particularly challenging task when assessing learning in drama that may have a subjective dimension, which is often the case with assessing emotional literacy, aesthetic choices, or creativity learning. For example, a group of third-grade teachers come together to evaluate the final folktale dramatizations presented at the drama residency's conclusion. One teacher who values polish and refinement in final products will assess the students' presentations very differently from the teacher who values the students' willingness to collaborate with peers. In this case, the teachers came together ahead of time and created a rubric based on specific skills outlined during planning, which each teacher uses when watching the performance to help protect the assessment's reliability.

Feasibility

You must also generate feasible assessments. Feasible assessments must be effectively completed with the resources and time available. For instance, the teacher and teaching artist propose an assessment model for their third-grade folktale residency:

> *"Each day, every child who participates in the residency will enter a video booth and record their reflections. Afterwards, the teacher and*

teaching artist will watch each video, code student responses, then analyze the coded responses to generate data."

While this assessment would produce rich data for both formative and summative assessment purposes, the time commitment required to view hundreds of hours of video would make it infeasible. To make this assessment feasible, the teacher and teaching artist might generate a sample of ten randomly chosen students (two from each class) and conduct a video interview every other day, then code and evaluate the sample.

Fairness

Finally, your assessments must be fair. Fair assessments give every participant an opportunity to demonstrate their learning and present an honest picture of learning as it actually happens. Returning to the previous example, here are a few unfair assessments the teaching artist and teacher might develop, along with suggestions regarding how to make them fairer:

- *The teacher and teaching artists select ten random students for interviews, but none of the students has practiced one-on-one on-camera interview skills. Many students become extremely nervous during the filmed one-on-one session, failing to respond or responding with, "Umm, I don't know."* This example is an unfair assessment because it calls on the students to utilize skills they have neither developed nor practiced. In order to make the assessment fairer, the teachers should give all students a chance to practice interview skills prior to the assessment.
- *The teachers select ten students for interviews, and two students have limited English proficiency (LEP) and are currently enrolled in English Language Learning (ELL) classes.* This is an unfair assessment. If the teacher and teaching artist only ask the interview questions in English, the students with limited English proficiency cannot demonstrate their learning in drama as well as their English-proficient peers. To make the assessment fairer, the teachers could provide accommodations for the ELL students. They might ask the students questions in their native languages or give the ELL students a copy of the questions to review ahead of time.
- *The teacher or teaching artist choose ten high-achieving students in third grade for the interview sample in the hopes of generating richer interview material.* This selection process leads to an unfair assessment because selecting only one kind of learner for assessment purposes biases the data, producing neither an accurate nor honest snapshot of the diversity of student learning during the residency.

In order to produce fair assessments that give every participant an equal chance to demonstrate their learning, remember to take into account both the nature of the assessment and the diversity of participants as regards age, gender, race, socioeconomics, ability, sociolinguistics, and cultural heritage.

Evaluating assessment

You have concluded a lesson or residency and a pile of journals and rubrics sit before you. What do you do with all this information? We conclude this chapter with a few suggestions for evaluating and interpreting assessment data and information and practical tips for evaluating assessments. Regardless of the methodology you select for evaluating data, keep a few principles in mind:

- Work to avoid bias in interpreting the students' responses.
- Trust your interpretation of material.
- Record your observations fairly and honestly, working to represent a diverse section of student responses (even if a few make you cringe with embarrassment).

Look at data holistically

At first, piles of numbers and journal entries can be overwhelming. Consider taking a step back from your data to look at the larger picture. For instance, read over journal entries several times. Give yourself breaks in between data analysis sessions. Look for trends, aberrations, and surprises. Continue to take notes and review them. You might also consider bringing in some additional collaborators to help sort through data with you. In total, if at all possible, give yourself time to process this new knowledge. Some guiding questions:

- What is your gut reaction to this information?
- What do you think students learned?
- What do you think students still need to learn?
- What do students value?
- What surprises you about this information?
- What ideas does this information confirm?

Look at data quantitatively

After taking a broad, holistic look at assessment information, you may want to assign numeric value to data in order to help generate statistical information about your assessments. Quantitative data interpretation most closely relates to traditional assessments, but can be adapted to authentic assessments as well. For example, a teaching artist might assign numeric values to pre- and post-residency performance rubrics on a sample of students. The teaching artist assigns a numeric value (one being "Low

Competency" and five being "High Competency") to each scored component and compares the numerical difference between the pre- and post-residency assessments to determine if there was any student growth. Depending on your comfort level with statistical approaches to data interpretation, quantitative data assessment can produce a great deal of interesting data that can also be represented through graphic means like charts and graphs. Quantitative data analysis also helps teachers and other evaluators maintain a bit more objectivity in regards to data interpretation.

Look at data qualitatively

You may also want to look at data with a more qualitative approach in mind, looking at more factors than just numbers. For example, you may use student narratives in journals or your own reflections on student learning. There are rigorous methods for evaluating qualitative assessments that involve coding (a process by which a facilitator analyzes and sorts qualitative data in order to make more specific observations about the subject of inquiry). We encourage you to investigate different methodologies, including ethnographic research models, to help you generate and evaluate educational assessment data qualitatively.

Look at data from multiple perspectives

You might also consider a hybrid approach to data interpretation that combines different categories of quantitative, qualitative, and holistic data analysis to capture as broad a picture as possible of learning and teaching.

Finally, make a decision

Once you have effectively evaluated data, decide what you want to do with this new knowledge. Perhaps you will adjust your teaching style, making the classroom more interactive. Maybe you will decide that a residency was more successful than you initially believed, and make plans to repeat it. You might decide that students need additional support in different knowledge groups or you might notice that your assessment tool was not the best fit for your programs, and set out to refine it. Assessment helps empower your decision-making and professionalism, and it enables you to make informed, data-supported decisions about learning and teaching.

Lesson planning

We close this chapter with a brief overview of lesson planning. In planning drama programs, you will likely want to create a lesson plan to help you ensure that all components of your lesson or residency (goals, activities and assessments) work together. Keep in mind that lesson planning is a very personal endeavor. Your unique set of circumstances helps contextualize your approach to lesson or residency. For example, a school administrator might dictate a lesson plan format that must be used by all teachers. Also, different teachers may have different styles of planning in general. One teacher may prefer a highly detailed lesson plan with an instructional script that helps the teacher know exactly what to say. Another teacher may prefer a more flexible lesson plan that provides a general overview of a day, week, or month-long unit, but that leaves room to adapt within the given circumstances of a particular classroom. Thus we have included a list of components you may want to include in your lesson plan.

When planning a lesson, keep in mind that a lesson plan is only a roadmap for your work. While rigorous, detailed, and thoughtful lesson planning helps guide your instruction and assessment, teachers and artists should also leave room both to adapt to unique environments and to evolve in regard to philosophical, aesthetic, and pedagogical values. In the actual day-to-day work of teaching drama, lesson plans often change based on both experiences in the moment and assessment data acquired by the facilitator. Changing course in the middle of a lesson, finding flow during a particular activity, or even losing track of your lesson plan during a moment of engaged learning all happen from time to time. For a very basic lesson plan, we recommend you include:

- A goal (*What should we accomplish?*)
- Procedure (*How will we accomplish it?*)
- Assessment (*How do we know we accomplished it?*).

Other information you may want to include:

Subject area: A segment or segments of knowledge addressed in the lesson ("English Language Arts and Improvisational Drama").

Time for activities: A general breakdown of how long you expect each lesson component to take. Noting time on your lesson plan helps you stay on track and conclude the lesson with time for reflection. We frequently include times when designing a new lesson or working within a tight schedule.

Age/grade level: Ages of participants most suited to the lesson. This can be a range ("ages 5–7").

Number of participants: Number of participants for which the lesson will work best ("15–30 participants").

Topic: A general overview of the lesson ("Dramatizing folktales: personal heritage and storytelling").

Objectives: Relevant and specific goals for the lesson.

Standards: Wide-scale learning goals included in the lesson.

Essential questions: Questions with which participants will engage in the lesson (*"How can we adapt folktales to reflect our personal heritage?"*)

Materials: Items you will need to complete the lesson ("Markers, large chart paper, scarves").

Anticipatory Set/Hook/Focus/Engagement: An attention-grabbing device or activity to excite participants about the lesson or unit (As a class, brainstorm a list of characters and their character traits in the story).

Warm-up/Starter: Similar to an Anticipatory Set, a Warm-up also prepares learners for activities for the lesson. The Warm-up can relate to any skill or knowledge group, from the physical to the cognitive.

Mechanics/Procedure/Method: Activities you will include in the lesson.

Direct instruction: Information the teacher or facilitator will present to students. Examples of direct instruction include short lectures, instructions for an activity, a slideshow of pictures with teacher discussion, or teacher-modeled skills.

Guided practice: Activities that students complete independently or in small student groups that the teacher supervises from a distance. (Students work in groups on sequencing a folktale and the teaching artist circulates to answer questions, offer feedback, and steer group learning.)

Independent practice: Activities that students complete without teacher input or guidance. Teacher will review the work after it is mostly complete. (A group of students write short dialogue based on a moment from their folktale for homework.)

Closure: An activity that wraps up a lesson or unit. Students will organize, review, or synthesize knowledge. (As a class, each group shares their folktale scene's sequence, pointing out central concepts presented in the lesson. Other groups ask questions of the presenting group.)

Checking for understanding: Formative or summative assessments that help teachers and students assess whether or not students understand major concepts included in a lesson. (The teacher maintains a "Question Box" on the board. As students have questions during group work, the teacher records the question in the Question Box. At the end of the lesson, the teacher reviews the questions, asking groups to discuss and come to consensus on an answer.)

Back-up Activity/Extensions/Variations: Activities to extend learning should any component of the lesson run short or fall flat, or if a learner or group finishes before others (If time permits, students will storyboard their folktale sequence).

A sample lesson plan

Here is a sample drama lesson plan that includes many of the elements described above.

Subject—Bullying: Little Bunny Foo Foo revisited.

Age level: Pre-Kindergarten.

Time: 30–40 minutes.

Goal: Using process-oriented and linear drama techniques, learners will draw inferences about the fictional nursery rhyme "Little Bunny Foo Foo."

Objectives:

- Students will independently observe and dramatize characteristics of bunnies and mice.
- Students will apply choral speaking and dramatic movement (finger plays, etc.) to recite "Little Bunny Foo Foo."
- Students will engage in discussion with and actively listen to "Bunny" to hear why he has decided to bop mice on the head.
- Students will work independently and as a group to develop solutions for the Bunny's problem.
- Students will dramatize their solutions by enacting the story with a new ending.

Materials: Bunny costume piece (ears and nose), letter from Good Fairy, pictures of bunnies and field mice, markers, paper.

Procedure:

Focus: After reviewing the class attention-grabber, the leader will share pictures of bunnies and field mice and discuss how those kinds of animals move. The group will practice moving as bunnies and field mice (with leader sidecoaching).

Teacher-stated objective in student-appropriate language: *"Today we are going to explore what happens in a story of Bunnies and Field Mice who do not get along. We will act out the story, trying to understand different views from the Bunnies and Mice in the story. We may even have a special letter from someone."*

Lesson input: The leader will teach the children's poem "Little Bunny Foo Foo" to the students, adding in a finger play component. The group will repeat the poem several times. The teacher will then explain that the Good Fairy from "Little Bunny Foo Foo" has sent a letter to the group. The teacher will open the letter and read it to the group:

> *Dear Friends,*
> *Hello. I am the Good Fairy. I am very worried about Little Bunny Foo Foo. I have talked to him, but he keeps bopping the field mice on the head. I'm not sure why he keeps doing this because he is usually such a good friend. I think there is more to the story! Can you get to the bottom of this?*
>
> *Your Magic Friend,*
> *The Good Fairy.*

The leader will explain that Bunny Foo Foo is coming to visit the class. She says although Bunny Foo Foo is coming for a visit, the Bunny is just an imaginary character. The teacher then models and contrasts going in and out-of-role for participants: *"When I have on these ears and this nose, I am playing Bunny. When I take off these ears and nose, I am back to myself. Can we all agree on that?"*

After reviewing the in-role transition, the leader will then review the "Little Bunny Foo Foo" narrative and the Good Fairy letter, brainstorming questions to ask Bunny. Next the leader exits the room (or simply turns around) for a moment to don the rabbit ears and nose, then re-enters the room in-role.

Guided activity: The leader/Bunny re-enters and engages with students, discussing her problem with bopping field mice. She will take participants' questions, eventually getting around to the fact that sometimes the birds make fun of her because she can only hop.

> *"They make me feel like I'm not very important because I can't get up into the trees and because I only eat vegetables. They dared me to pick on someone smaller than me to prove I was really as special as them. I guess I bop field mice to feel big and tough. I don't know why I think bopping field mice will make me feel better because it doesn't. I just feel*

like a bully. I don't like scaring the field mice, and they've never done anything bad to me. I feel really bad."

Bunny then asks the group for help on what to do. The group will break into smaller groups or partners (the leader can stay in-role or step out-of-role to facilitate discussions) and brainstorm ideas, then come back together to decide on a solution.

The group then dramatizes the story with the new ending devised by the group, using narrative pantomime and/or improvisation. The leader casts three group roles (a group of Little Bunny Foo Foos, a group of Field Mice, and a group of Good Fairies). If necessary/possible, repeat the dramatization several times, giving each group a chance to play each role. End with applause.

Checking for understanding: Participants break into smaller groups or partners and talk about the drama:

"Why was Bunny mean to the field mice?"

"Have you ever felt like Bunny? Have you ever felt like a field mouse?"

Backup activity: Recite the poem once more, moving like bunnies and field mice.

Assessment:

Formative: The teacher will evaluate student responses to sidecoaching and other prompts in the drama. She will also informally note whether or not students generate independent responses when asked to identify questions for Little Bunny Foo Foo.

Summative—Anecdotal assessment and rubric: During or after the lesson, the classroom teacher or teacher's assistant records data on a sample of participants using a performance rubric assessing independent expression and creative movement and an anecdotal assessment form that includes teacher observation of student work and any quotes from the participants in reaction to the lesson.

Conclusion

Assessment is a combination of planning, teaching, evaluating, and reflecting. It need not be a thorn in your side, an afterthought, or a frustrating item on your to-do list. Effectively implementing assessment not only improves instruction in drama-based learning and teaching, but also empowers teachers and artists to make thoughtful, well-informed choices about how

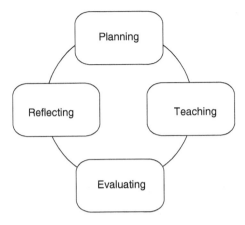

Figure 5.5

drama-based methods might be most effectively integrated into teaching and learning. After reading this chapter, we hope you feel more equipped to generate assessment models that capture diverse, honest pictures of learning and to make changes to the ways in which you teach based on assessment data. We end the chapter with a few practical tools for assessment planning and implementation.

Skills and knowledge reference guides

In order to help you quickly and easily determine skills and knowledge groups for planning and assessment purposes, we have included a reference guide that includes sample drama-based activities. We have categorized skills and knowledge groups into four main categories (cognitive, affective/social/emotional, creative, and psychomotor/sensorimotor/manual), but many overlap multiple categories. Use this reference guide to help you generate goals and/or objectives or to help you brainstorm, evaluate, or review lesson plans and assessments.

Table 5.3

	Cognitive Skills	
Analyzing	Elaborating	Reflecting
Applying	Evaluating	Remembering
Choosing	Focusing	Responding
Combining	Generating	Reviewing
Communicating	Inferring	Sequencing
Connecting	Interpreting	Summarizing
Critiquing	Planning	Synthesizing
Describing	Predicting	Understanding
Devising	Preparing	
Discovering	Refining	

Table 5.4

Creative Skills	
Broadening	Hypothesizing
Challenging	Identifying solutions to problems
Combining ideas	Imagining
Composing	Inventing
Considering new ideas	Justifying
Creating	Problem-solving
Designing	Restructuring
Evaluating	Seeking
Experimenting	Surrounding
Forming conceptual understandings	Suspending assumptions
Generating	Transferring knowledge

Table 5.5

SEL (Social and Emotional Learning)/Affective Skills
Adjusting/modifying behavior
Advocating for self and others
Articulating beliefs and values
Collaborating
Directing attention
Disagreeing and agreeing
Helping/Aiding/Assisting self and others
Identifying, describing, and expressing feelings
Managing conflict
Managing impulses
Negotiating
Participating
Persevering
Practicing self-acceptance and self-discipline
Recognizing and responding to social cues from others
Seeking and giving information and feedback
Sharing

Table 5.6

Sensorimotor/Psychomotor/Manual Skills	
Building/Constructing	Manipulating the body
Choreographing	Moving
Communicating without words	Naturalizing
Controlling the body	Performing
Demonstrating	Practicing
Displaying	Reacting
Embodying	Sensing
Imitating/Mimicking	

Assessment Database

Table 5.7

Drama Assessments Database

	Diagnostic Assessments
Pre-test	Test given prior to a unit or lesson to assess participants' knowledge or skills. Pre-tests are usually combined with a post-test.
Interest inventory	A survey that assesses participants' interests and preferences.
Self-assessments	A survey in which participants evaluate their skills, knowledge and performance. Can also be administered as a summative assessment.
Performance tasks	An assignment (or task) that directly relates to skills/knowledge being learned (e.g. planning a performance, writing a scene, designing a set).
KWL chart	Graphic organizer that documents what participants (K)now, (W)ant to know, and have (L)earned
Group/individual brainstorming activities	A creative exercise completed in groups or individually that helps generate ideas. Consider structured brainstorming by presenting problems or focused questions, setting time limits, and encouraging participants to take different perspectives on issues.
Anticipation Guides	A technique that helps incite interest and activate knowledge. Present participants with a series of questions or statements about an upcoming topic. Participants may respond or agree/disagree.
Formative Assessments	
Process journals	Participants regularly journal about a process. Journaling should be structured; include prompts.
Popcorn	An embodied learning exercise that generates ideas in the moment. See Chapter 3 for additional details.

Table 5.7 continued

	Drama Assessments Database
Entrance and exit slips	Short writing assignments that participants complete at the beginning of a lesson (Entrance Slip) or at the end (Exit Slip). Generally these deal with a question, belief, or opinion related to the lesson topic. Prompts might include: Entrance: What will we work on today? What questions do you have starting the lesson? How do you feel about our work so far? Exit: What did we do? Why did we do it? What did you learn? How can you apply it? What questions do you still have?
Splashes	A structured brainstorming activity in which participants generate a "splash" of ideas related to a concept in order to develop a schema. Generally, splashes are written, but they can be drawn or embodied as well.
Anonymous quiz	A quiz anonymously completed by participants. Afterwards, mix up the quizzes and have participants grade the quiz. As a group, evaluate questions or concepts that the group appears to have mastered and those that need more time/instruction.
Points of Confusion	A document (whole-group or individual) on which participants record questions or confusing ideas. Encourage participants to add to the document at any point during a lesson.
Running Records	A document upon which a teacher or facilitator records information about a participant at regular intervals over time. A running record can be as simple as a checklist or as complex as narrative observation about a participant.
Self-report (Vote with hands, vote with feet)	An embodied approach to assessing learning in the moment. Participants vote with their hands or feet: "Show how ready you are with your hands, with one being 'not ready at all' and five being 'completely ready'." "Walk to the side of the room that best expresses your opinion on this subject. The left side of the room is 'strongly agree'. The right side of the room is 'strongly disagree'. The middle is neutral."

Table 5.7 continued

Drama Assessments Database

Summative Assessments

End-of-unit tests	Objective tests administered at the end of the lesson to determine mastery of specific knowledge groups or skills.
Contracts	An agreement collaboratively generated between participants and leaders. The agreement includes learning tasks participants will complete, evidence participants will show/demonstrate, and criteria upon which participants will be evaluated.
Portfolios	A collection of student work that demonstrates learning over time. Work samples might include images, writing samples, video, interviews, or artwork.
Presentations	Oral or video presentations in which students prepare and share knowledge. Participants may need additional instruction in effective presentation skills.
Performances	An assessment whereby participants synthesize information and create a new creative interpretation. Performances typically reimagine narratives and demonstrate participants' aesthetic ideas as well as their interpretation of several components that make the dramatic form.
Capstone projects	A rigorous and comprehensive summative assessment that evaluates a participant's learning over time. Typically, capstone projects culminate a longer learning project (for example, the end of a school year or program of study).

Assessment Planning Guide

Table 5.8

Assessment Planning Guide		
Why:	What information will you gather through assessment?	
What (content):	Type: Authentic/Traditional/Hybrid Goal: Standards/Objectives: Knowledge: Skills: Competencies:	
What (format):	Design:	
Who will:	Design:	
	Administer:	
	Complete:	
	Interpret and evaluate:	
	Decide:	
When:	Diagnostic (before) Formative (during) Summative (after)	Details:
Where:	Where will assessments occur?	
	Materials needed:	
Review:	Is your assessment:	Reliable?
		Valid?
		Fair?
		Feasible?
Final Notes:		

References

Anderson, Lorin W. and David R. Krathwohl (eds). 2000. *A Taxonomy for Learning, Teaching, and Assessing: A Revision of Bloom's Taxonomy of Educational Objectives*. Complete Edition. Pearson.

Anderson, Lorin W., and David R. Krathwohl (eds). 2001. *A Taxonomy for Learning, Teaching, and Assessing: A Revision of Bloom's Taxonomy of Educational Objectives*. Longman.

"Assessment for Learning: 10 Principles." 2002. Assessment Research Group.

"Assessment Glossary." N.d. National Center for Research on Evaluation, Standards, & Students Testing. Accessed 10 Aug 2014. http://www.cse.ucla.edu/products/glossary.php

Elias, Maurice J., and Harriett Arnold. 2006. *The Educator's Guide to Emotional Intelligence and Academic Achievement: Social-Emotional Learning in the Classroom*. Corwin Press.

Epstein, Robert. 1996. *Cognition, Creativity, and Behavior: Selected Essays*. Praeger.

"Framework for 21st Century Learning." 2011. Partnership for 21st Century Skills. Accessed 10 Aug 2014. http://www.p21.org/storage/documents/1._p21_framework_2-pager.pdf

Fredericks, Linda. 2003. "Making the Case for Social and Emotional Learning and Service-Learning." ECS Issue Brief. *Education Commission of the States (NJ1)*. http://eric.ed.gov/?id=ED505359.

Gale, Richard. 2005. "Aesthetic Literacy and the 'living of Lyrical Moments.'" *Journal of Cognitive Affective Learning* 2 (1): 1–9.

Gardner, John. 2006. *Assessment and Learning*. SAGE.

Goleman, Daniel. 2012. *Emotional Intelligence: 10th Anniversary Edition*. Random House Publishing Group.

Greenberg, Mark T., Roger Weissberg, Mary Utne O'Brien, *et al.* 2003. "Enhancing school-based prevention and youth development through coordinated social, emotional, and academic learning." *American Psychologist* 58 (6–7): 466.

Greene, Maxine. 1977. "Imagination and Aesthetic Literacy." *Art Education* 30 (6): 14–20.

——1991. "Aesthetic Literacy." *Aesthetics and Arts Education*, 149–61.

——2011. "Releasing the Imagination." *NJ (Drama Australia Journal)* 34: 62.

Harrow, Anita J. 1972. *A Taxonomy of the Psychomotor Domain: A Guide for Developing Behavioral Objectives*. D. McKay Co.

Hocevar, Dennis. 1981. "Measurement of Creativity: Review and Critique." *Journal of Personality Assessment* 45 (5): 450–64.

Kaufman, James C., Jason C. Cole, and John Baer. 2009. "The Construct of Creativity: Structural Model for Self-Reported Creativity Ratings." *The Journal of Creative Behavior* 43 (2): 119–34.

Marzano, Robert J., and John S. Kendall. 2007. *The New Taxonomy of Educational Objectives*. Corwin Press.

Muijs, Daniel. 2010. *Doing Quantitative Research in Education with SPSS*. SAGE Publications.

"National Core Arts Standards." 2014. Accessed 10 Aug 2014. www.nationalartsstandards.org.

"The Role of the Arts in Strengthening and Inspiring the 21st Century Global Community." 2009. Americans for the Arts. Accessed 10 August 2014. www.

americansforthearts.org/by-program/reports-and-data/legislation-policy/
national-arts-policy-roundtable/2009-the-role-of-the-arts-in-strengthening-and-
inspiring-the-21st-century-global-community.

Runco, Mark A., and Garrett J. Jaeger. 2012. "The Standard Definition of
Creativity." *Creativity Research Journal* 24 (1): 92–6. doi:10.1080/10400419.20
12.650092.

Saraniero, Patti. N.d. "Raising 'Art Smart' Students in the 21st Century." The
Kennedy Center ArtsEdge. Accessed 10 August 2014. https://artsedge.kennedy-
center.org/families/at-school/all-for-arts-education/raising-smart-art-students

Simpson, Elizabeth. 1971. "Educational Objectives in the Psychomotor Domain."
*Behavioral Objectives in Curriculum Development: Selected Readings and
Bibliography*, 60.

"Social and Emotional Learning Core Competencies." 2013. Accessed 10 August
2014. http://www.casel.org/social-and-emotional-learning/core-competencies.

Stevens, Dannelle D., and Antonia J. Levi. 2011. *Introduction to Rubrics: An
Assessment Tool to Save Grading Time, Convey Effective Feedback, and Promote
Student Learning*. Stylus Publishing, LLC.

Torrance, E. Paul. 1962. "Guiding Creative Talent." http://psycnet.apa.org/
psycinfo/2008-13285-000/.

——1965. "Rewarding Creative Behavior; Experiments in Classroom Creativity."
http://eric.ed.gov/?id=ED027652.

——1988. "The Nature of Creativity as Manifest in Its Testing." *The Nature of
Creativity*, 43–75.

Wagner, Tony. 2012. *Creating Innovators: The Making of Young People Who Will
Change the World*. Simon and Schuster.

Williams, Frank E. 1969. "Models for Encouraging Creativity in the Classroom by
Integrating Cognitive-Affective Behaviors." *Educational Technology* 9 (12):
7–13.

——1980. *Creativity Assessment Packet: (CAP)*. DOK Publishers.

Zins, Joseph E. 2004. *Building Academic Success on Social and Emotional Learning:
What Does the Research Say?* Teachers College Press.

6 New landscapes

Advocacy for drama-based learning programs and partnerships

Thus far we have discussed techniques for implementing and assessing drama-based methods for learning. Although acquiring different skills for incorporating and assessing drama and performance-based techniques in both teaching and learning is valuable, knowledge of these skills is only part of the equation for successful arts-based learning and teaching. As a teacher, artist, or community leader interested in incorporating the arts into education settings, you will increasingly be called upon to advocate for your programs and justify why learning with, by, and through drama is valuable and, more importantly, worth time, money, and resources. In this chapter, we will cover strategies and techniques to help you advocate for your programs.

Why is advocacy important?

This chapter on advocacy responds to the changing landscape of United States education, K-12 and beyond, in the late 2000s and early 2010s. The 2001 educational reform legislation now known as "No Child Left Behind" brought about sweeping reforms in public-sector education that focused national attention on accountability, assessment, and quantitative measures of learning's efficacy. In response, schools have incorporated elaborate and time-consuming accountability measures, mostly in the form of standards-based tests that measure every student's growth according to government-mandated learning standards in math and reading. Between 2008 and 2010, school districts also incorporated similar testing protocols for science. School districts that fail to meet important benchmarks or achieve Adequate Yearly Progress (AYP) must give their students the option to change schools. If a school repeatedly fails to make AYP, they face potential state takeover, or, in extreme cases, shutting down due to low enrollments as families depart for more (supposedly) successful schools.

This focus on tested learning has diminished time for non-tested subjects, including drama. In a 2007 report about the first five years of NCLB, the Center for Education Policy (CEP) reported that since 2002, 84 percent of school districts reported that they had changed their curriculum "somewhat" or "to a great extent" to put greater emphasis on tested content at the elementary level ("Choices" 2007: 2). The report also indicated that 44 percent of school districts cut time in other subjects, like the arts, to make room for additional instruction in tested subjects like English Language Arts ("Choices" 2007: 1). Moreover, schools at risk of failing to achieve NCLB benchmarks *further* cut time for additional subjects to focus instruction on the high-needs tested subjects. These realities prompted the CEP, along with countless arts education organizations, to publicly advocate for "adequate emphasis" on non-tested subjects like the arts as a part of a well-balanced curriculum ("Choices" 2007: 2).

While NCLB legislation changes the US educational landscape, other new initiatives like charter schools (both non- and for-profit schools funded with public monies but run independently from school districts) and school vouchers (portable public money that can be applied to a family's choice of public or private school) also threaten public school budgets and siphon off students from traditional school districts, leading to lower school enrollments, rapidly changing demographics, and shrinking public districts due to school shuttering based on low enrollments. For example, in 2013 Chicago Public Schools approved the largest school closure in the district's history, eliminating forty-nine elementary schools due to budget crises and low enrollments (Ahmed-Ullah, Chase, and Secter 2013). There are similar stories across the United States, with many districts, particularly those that serve urban students, low-income students, and students of color, struggling to meet increasingly stringent accountability standards and to adapt to new paradigms for public education. The stakes are high for teachers, administrators, and school districts. Time is at a premium, and resources are often scarce. Teachers of history, civics, character education, health education, community education, the arts, and all other non-tested subjects must compete for dwindling time and money.

At the same time, teachers in the US and abroad must also adapt practices to meet the changing demographics of learners. For example, in 2012 the US Center for Public Education pointed out that persons of color will make up the majority of school-age children by 2023, the majority of working-age Americans by 2039, and the majority of all Americans by 2042 ("The United States" 2012). Schools not only need to be prepared to teach a diverse population of students, but also need to prepare those students to interact effectively with a diverse group of people in their communities and at work.

In response to these developments, the landscape of arts-based learning is also changing and becoming more diverse. As a teacher or artist interested in drama for teaching and learning, you will likely encounter opportunities to work alongside arts organizations in a variety of capacities in partnerships, in co-teaching situations, or as an independent teaching artist. Some examples of innovative partnerships include:

- teachers contracting with arts organizations or teaching artists for residencies at schools;

- artists working as teaching artists or artists in residence in schools or through employment with arts organizations;
- teachers hosting a performance or drama-based workshop in their school;
- teachers and their students traveling to a performance or performance workshop;
- teachers participating in drama-based professional development with the goal of incorporating drama into their classrooms;
- community groups (after-school programs, religious groups, or charities) contracting with arts organizations for performances, workshops, or other artist residencies;
- theatre companies leading tuition-based and/or subsidized arts classes or camps either on-site or at satellite locations.

Given the rapidly changing landscape in regards to how arts learning happens in the 2000s, including recent neuroscience findings and research in brain-based learning, advocacy becomes even more important in helping make clear the unique ways in which drama-based learning and teaching occur in schools and communities. Thus, in this twenty-first century education landscape, advocacy becomes one of the most important skill sets needed by arts educators. But what does it mean to advocate?

In simplest terms, advocacy is the act of supporting a cause. However, the practicalities of advocacy may be challenging or confusing. In addition to identifying and effectively describing a cause you believe in, you must also know who to talk to, where to look for resources, how to speak about your programs, and how to clearly and succinctly explain why your work in the arts should be valued and supported.

Sometimes, advocacy is very straightforward. You might be called to discuss with a community leader or school administrator what you hope to accomplish with drama, how you will measure success, and why your program's particular approach to learning is unique and valuable in the context of a larger institutional understanding about the arts. At other times, advocacy might be more ambiguous. You may be extended support for drama programs, then left to prove their worth as you go along or at the end of the partnership. For example, you might be asked to direct a performance for parents or contribute to an overall push to increase test scores in English Language Arts without a clear sense of how or when to evaluate your program's effectiveness. Advocacy might also produce challenges for you as an artist or arts educator. You may have to explain to parents, funders, or administration why a residency's culminating performance is rough around the edges or otherwise not in keeping with administrative expectations. Sometimes, advocacy even means preemptively divining expectations from the subtle clues of a myriad of individuals during the planning stages of an arts-based residency, then carefully navigating the complex negotiations present when differing opinions emerge. For example, you, as a fourth-grade classroom teacher, might decide to incorporate linear drama techniques into your literacy lesson. Your Reading Facilitator might hear about this plan during a weekly planning meeting and ask you to share your student-generated scenes with the entire fourth grade. Suddenly, a process-oriented lesson becomes a product-oriented performance. Now you must explain why a performance might not best fit with your plans (or, on the other hand, why you would be open to producing student performances, but not necessarily in the context of your literacy unit). No matter the situation, teachers and artists interested in drama-based learning will perpetually advocate for themselves and their programs.

As the aforementioned examples demonstrate, advocacy is both a science and an art. In this chapter, we'll explore the nuances of both in order to help prepare you to advocate for drama-based learning and teaching. While advocacy takes many forms, two important unifying factors will help guide you, no matter the situation:

- Know your worth
- Know your audience.

Know your worth

In both arts and education fields, practitioners and teachers must regularly explain their program's worth. Worth, in basic terms, relates to value: whether or not a program, a lesson, or a performance is deserving of time, attention, resources, and money. An important component of advocacy involves knowing and articulating worth in meaningful terms for invested participants including learners, teaching artists, administrators, and funders. However, articulating worth can be a challenging prospect. As teachers and artists, we define our work's worth in a variety of ways, and often more diversely than many other fields. Therefore developing skills in how we speak about worth and how we might use different vocabulary and rhetoric (or argumentative techniques) for different situations is important when advocating for programs.

When undertaking goal-setting in regards to advocacy, consider the customer service adage: under-promise and over-deliver. At the very least, you should *only* promise what you know you and your students can accomplish during a lesson/residency, and address other desired outcomes with honesty. For example, a cooperating teacher may ask a teaching artist to produce a performance for parents and administration in order to demonstrate their two-week residency's curricular worth. While a production might be possible, the teaching artist might need to talk with the teacher about typical production timelines, the resources that might be necessary to produce a performance complete with costumes and sets, and the challenges associated with focusing on a product over process during a concentrated residency. Then the teaching artist might propose some alternatives: maybe parents and administrators could be invited into an open house where they observe students at work, or perhaps the students might create a less formal "gallery crawl" in which they establish stations throughout the hallway, demonstrating an example or activity and discussing their work with visitors. These performance alternatives take the pressure of production off the residency, but provide an alternative product to help cooperating partners demonstrate the program's worth to important community members.

In order to think about how teachers and artists talk about worth, we have borrowed from some of the more widely known theories about taxonomies of learning set forth by education scholars Lorin Anderson, David Krathwohl, and Benjamin Bloom (theories closely related to "Bloom's taxonomy", see Anderson and Krathwohl 2000), as well as Robert Marzano and John Kendall (*A New Taxonomy of Educational Objectives* [2007] or the "New Taxonomy"). Connecting to these larger theories of educational objectives and evaluation provides vocabulary that extends across and beyond disciplines, but keep in mind that these are simply one set of ideas about how educators might organize the complex processes of learning and teaching and should be viewed with a critical eye.

Affective or self-system worth

As artists and arts advocates, we often define our work's worth in *affective* terms. Qualities of learning such as David Krathwohl's *affect* (1974), Marzano's Self-System of Learning (2007), Social and Emotional Learning (SEL), Emotional Intelligence, and other similar concepts (see Chapters 1 and 5) usually connect with the emotional and personal aspects of learning. Terms like emotional growth, energy, creativity, self-development, ensemble-building, and character education all fall under the umbrella of affect or self-systems (Krathwohl, Bloom and Masia 1964; Marzano and Kendall 2007). Affective worth is an important component of advocacy for arts-based learning through drama and performance. For example, a teacher might say a residency transformed participants' creativity or that a student production was magical. Teachers and artists might also mark success by noting the space's positive energy or observing that a particular lesson feels alive with excitement. We might also sense that our participants cared more deeply for one another, cooperated more effectively, or engaged in fewer fights after their work in drama.

These kinds of emotional responses are invaluable to our work, but they also require some critical awareness in regards to advocacy, especially when working within the increasingly standards-oriented and accountability-focused landscape of twenty-first century education. First, affective worth is notoriously difficult to document, especially if teachers or artists try to apply the same kind of quantitative measures we typically associate with the standards-based testing that has become so ubiquitous. As you might expect, this difficulty in documenting affective worth also means that it easily comes under scrutiny because teachers and others cannot always prove its existence in explicit, tangible, and quantifiable terms. For example, a teacher who employs an affective approach when articulating a drama residency's worth to a curriculum-focused school principal may find herself frustrated. While the teacher has been fundamentally changed by her students' creative and emotional growth, the administrator wants to know, "*Yes, of course, but how does this drama work improve our test scores?*"

You may rightly ask, "*But why do we need to quantify our emotions? Doesn't the feeling alone mean something important has happened?*" These questions are the source of much heated discussion and debate. Unfortunately, and perhaps sadly, given the trend in US education, the need for accountability in regards to learning standards in many instances trumps the need to understand the affective dimension of the arts. We would be remiss to suggest that articulating the affective worth of your drama residencies would consistently be enough for advocacy, as much as we wish that were the case. Still, the affective qualities of arts education are very important and should be included in any type of advocacy.

Techniques for demonstrating affective worth

While you may need more than affect-based advocacy, here are a few techniques you can use to more effectively document your work in order to produce tools for advocacy.

Acknowledge both that affective worth exists and that it has limits

An important part of engaging with affective advocacy is acknowledging both its existence and its limitations. Often times, the emotional dimension of drama-based learning has a strong influence on our impression of our work. However, much of this affective value often fails to translate for those not present during the lesson or residency. A hypothetical scenario: a middle-school English teacher and a teaching artist come together to generate a drama-based curriculum unit about bullying. The student participants mature during their time together, and both the teacher and the teaching artist notice the group working more cohesively and being more tolerant of one another. After the residency, the teacher must report on the learning outcomes in a grant report. In order to make the affective dimension of the program's value compelling in this narrative report, the teacher has to step back from the emotional dimension of the work even as she advocates for its importance. For instance, instead of reporting, "*The students were transformed through this experience!*" the teacher might instead write, "*I believe that transformation occurred in my classroom in regards to how students treat one another and respect diverse ideas. I know we cannot easily quantify this kind of change in a way that shows growth on test scores, but I still feel it is valuable to observe and document as an indicator of this work's value to our students."* In this example, the teacher's language both acknowledges the program's affective worth and acknowledges the limitations of documenting affective worth in regards to test scores or other learning outcomes. This example demonstrates the teacher's critical distance from her own and her students' emotional experiences, but also gives credence to the real and important affective growth in her students.

Approaching affective growth with a critical eye also shows a willingness to think critically about how affect works within the larger climate of education. While many educators, administrators, and other education leaders recognize the larger issues associated with testing-heavy assessments, they, as members of larger institutions, are bound by these expectations. Acknowledging these constraints and requirements while still maintaining the value of affect-oriented learning will help you form allies with school partners.

Honestly and rigorously document affective growth

Make an effort to document affective learning during your drama residency or drama lesson. With the ever-limited time for arts learning, documenting affective learning can fall by the wayside. This is not unexpected, especially since classrooms and learning environments are increasingly oriented toward objective, standards-based assessment. Given these expectations, teachers are infrequently trained in techniques for documenting affective learning, and even if they possess competencies in these areas of assessment, they may not have time to integrate them into the classroom. However, documentation is important. Some of the problems that come up in critiques of affective worth arise from a lack of documentation (*"Trust me! If you had been there, you would have felt it too!"*) or inconsistently generated documentation (*"Oh, this is just the best quote about the students' residency. I left out the other ones. They weren't as good."*). Instead, treat documentation of affective learning with the same rigor that you might use for curricular/cognitive learning. Here are a couple of suggested documentation strategies.

Multimedia documentation: Assign a few students to take pictures, record video, or conduct two-minute interviews before, during, or after the work each day with a focus on an affective quality of learning. Sample prompts might include:

- *"Record/observe/ask about how our class collaborates on generating material for our tableaux."*
- *"Record/observe/ask about how other students feel about their creativity during our residency."*

Post these images or videos on a class blog or in another central location during each session of the residency. As the teacher or artist, record what you see each day in your notes:

- How do their responses change each day?
- How do the students talk about their work with peers? Their creative growth? Their self-development?

Journaling: Start and/or end each session with a series of prompts related to affect and/or self-systems of learning. Select a sample group (five to seven randomly-chosen students) and make notes about these students' responses based on related affective categories.

No matter how you choose to document your participants' affective growth, keep in mind a couple of principles (also, review Chapter 5 for additional details about each of these elements):

- Work to avoid bias in interpreting the students' responses.
- Trust your interpretation of material.
- Record your observations fairly and honestly, working to represent a diverse section of student responses.

For example, after a production-oriented drama residency in which students participated in a musical, we interviewed a sample of students about the process as part of our documentation. When asking the students to comment on changes in their creativity after the process, more than one student responded, *"Well, I don't think it really changed much. I mean, actually I learned how much work it takes to make something, so I think I was more creative before this residency because I didn't realize all the practical parts."* While my colleagues and I were somewhat mortified that we had failed to nurture some of our brightest students' creativity, these responses helped us to reflect honestly on our residency and engage in frank conversations about the goals of our arts residencies and the nature of creativity with young people. Offering a wide representation of students' responses to affective learning during and after drama lessons and residencies supports your credibility, but also demonstrates that you think reasonably and level-headedly about the potential outcomes of arts learning, good, bad, and indifferent.

A final word on communicating affective worth in regards to advocacy: many teachers or artists will likely connect their work with the large-scale, transformational dimension of the arts' affective value. These feelings often lead us to grow, to explore, and to share experiences with others in ways that other forms of learning might not. In some cases, we believe the arts helped us become who we are by breaking us out of our shells. In even more extreme cases, the arts saved our lives, giving us an outlet for expression when we could not otherwise find one. The arts tell our stories, give life to our histories and heritages, and allow us room to explore gray areas in the human experience. They are powerful. No matter how one connects with the arts, there are a lot of emotions tied up in their value to us as individuals and as a society. Therefore, we often believe that the arts have the ability to transcend ordinary life and give us a glimpse into new possibilities, new ways of thinking, and new ways of interpreting the world. This is the stuff that motivates us to keep pursuing our work in drama.

However, this affect-oriented rhetoric becomes tricky when we talk about the worth of arts education. Our passion for the arts, as well as our affective affinity for drama-based learning, sometimes leads us, as artists and arts supporters, to suggest that drama and/or other arts-based learning can do it all—stop bullying, teach everyone to love reading or math, eliminate obesity, or occasionally, save the world. While these goals are great motivators, they may not always be achievable. Even though emotions may strongly influence our belief that arts help people learn, drama cannot and will not solve all learning or community concerns. In truth, no single intervention can meet all learners' needs or solve the world's problems. People learn in different ways, come from different backgrounds and cultural heritages, and care about different kinds of knowledge and experiences. Some students love drama. Others will hate it. Some will be indifferent, viewing it as one of many different learning tools they encounter each day. Likewise, artists and teachers will have different and diverse affinities for drama-based learning and teaching. If we promise to change the world with arts education, and we fail to meet that goal, we shall find ourselves in a difficult place, likely being perceived as out of touch with reality. All this is to say that thinking about worth relies first and foremost on being realistic about potential learning outcomes, including how drama may, *or may not*, change the world.

Cognitive and curricular worth

Given the relationship between drama/performance and education articulated throughout this book, we must also consider how we talk about our programs' cognitive and curricular worth. More broadly, we must articulate how our drama programs help students learn. Cognitive worth refers to the many and varied ways in which arts learning helps participants improve their thinking. The first chapter of this book deals explicitly with the cognitive dimensions of arts-based learning from brain-based perspectives, and Chapter 5 considers how a teacher or teaching artist might design and assess rigorous arts learning experiences. We encourage you to reference these chapters, along with the many scholars, books, and studies mentioned throughout this book when you speak about how the arts help people learn.

Curricular worth closely connects to cognitive worth. As mentioned in the assessment chapter, understanding curriculum, or the course of study within a given learning institution, is not only valuable in planning meaningful residencies, but also in effectively advocating for your programs. Our chapter on assessment goes into greater detail about standards, objectives, and goal-setting, but when thinking about advocacy, remember to articulate realistic outcomes. Will an entire fourth grade class experience 10 percent growth in their reading scores after a two-week drama residency? Unlikely. Will some fourth graders show greater competencies with using descriptive language after a two-week residency that specifically targets use of descriptive language in writing? Perhaps. Once, we were asked to lead an hour-long drama session with teenagers with the goal of making them less competitive and more cooperative when working with each other. We agreed, but explained that a one-hour session might not provide enough time. Still, the teachers welcomed us. A few weeks after the sessions, we contacted the cooperating teachers. We were not surprised when they remarked that our methods were interesting but the students were still not working together effectively. Our partnership ended shortly thereafter. In retrospect, we should have been more explicit in discussing the goals of the residency. Take our experience as a cautionary tale; keep in mind how much change a short-term drama-based learning experience might realistically contribute to students' learning when you think about advocating for your program's curricular worth.

One easy strategy to help demonstrate your program's curricular worth is to ask questions early and often when collaborating with schools or other programming partners. These questions about the educational dimension of drama-based learning and teaching also help you assess your program's curricular worth, articulate its value to you and your partners, and reflect on programs throughout the process. Some questions you might consider:

- What are the large-scale learning goals of the organization with whom you plan to work?
- What are the specific learning objectives of your residency?
- What do you and/or your cooperating partners hope to accomplish through your residency or lesson?
- Do natural connections exist between all curricula involved in a lesson/ residency? If so, what are they? If not, how can you find common ground?
- How does this program/lesson complement the larger curricula?
- How might this drama-based lesson or residency extend or enhance current curricular programs?
- How might drama-based lessons/residencies challenge or detract from current curricular programs?
- How will students/participants prepare for the lesson/residency? How will they extend their learning after the lesson is over?
- What curricular guides can you reference or draw on when planning your programs?

- Where do overlaps exist between state standards, curriculum guides, and your programs?

Once you have established a dialogue, the process of reflection will become a more natural, integral component of the entire process. Also, you will naturally arrive at some larger objectives or desired outcomes:

- As these program/lesson objectives emerge from your discussions, examine them with a critical eye: Are they realistic and attainable?
- Can you reasonably accomplish them in the time you have?

Also ask questions during the process:

- Are the lessons proceeding as everyone expected?
- Do the students seem to be investing to the degree you expected?
- Are the original goals still realistic and achievable?
- What new concerns have arisen?

Finally, ask questions after the sessions conclude. Start with broad questions and move to more specific questions related to curricular worth:

- What worked? What would you change?
- Did the residency meet your expectations? If not, why? If so, why?
- Did you meet your goals and objectives? How do you know?
- What is your evidence of student learning/success?
- How could you modify activities to make the lesson more successful or to meet the needs of different populations?

In addition, remember to build in space for participants and partners to ask questions of you. In addition to seeking out broad feedback (*"What questions do you have for me?"*), look for specific topics about which new partners might have questions or concerns or may not even know to ask. Some examples you might ask yourself or your collaborators:

- What questions do you have about the curricular connections we are making between Drama and English Language Arts curricula (or any chosen subject) with this residency?
- How can I support your classroom procedures and routines?
- Do you have questions about my presentation style or how I like to work with students?
- How do you and your students work best? Can the room be loud and energetic?
- What questions do you have about the drama side of our work? Can I clarify any of my activities for you?

Overall, be rigorous and detailed in thinking and planning in order to demonstrate both respect and knowledge for your programs and the programs of partnering institutions in regards to curricular worth. Demonstrate that you understand and appreciate the curriculum and have carefully considered both the strengths and potential weaknesses of drama-based learning in connection with these larger programmatic and curricular goals. Clearly and effectively communicating details about your work and its curricular value helps you advocate for your programs.

In addition to asking questions, also set achievable goals based on matched expectations with advocacy in mind. While we discuss goal-setting in regards to assessment in greater detail in Chapter 5, reasonable goal-setting also relates to advocacy. Goals ensure effective evaluation and assessment of your programs and help you advocate on behalf of your program's curricular and cognitive worth. Some of these achievable goals will arise during the planning phase, but sometimes expectations can be mismatched. Often, one party feels uncomfortable saying, *"I don't know if we can accomplish that goal"* because they either feel out of their depth with the content or because they are hoping to form a strong and successful partnership. They do not want to disappoint their partners, just as we didn't when planning our short high school residency on cooperation. However, matching expectations is one of the most important components of curricular advocacy.

Be honest, if not conservative, when you discuss what your program or lesson might do for students. For instance, your co-teachers might express some reservations about a process-based drama lesson because they are anxious about their students' ability to navigate the freedom present in the open structure. Instead of simply insisting, *"Oh, they'll be fine! They're going to learn and grow so much from this experience,"* consider discussing at length what kinds of learning outcomes might come about from this freedom, how you all might mark student learning in this process, or how you might hybridize the lesson to make them feel more comfortable. Also, speak openly about the limitations of these styles of drama residencies, acknowledging that "off-task" students are a real possibility in this kind of format or that each student will self-determine their experience within the lesson, leading to engagement looking quite different from typical classroom behavior. Then discuss the potential positives and negatives of these kinds of learning experiences. For example, you might explain how passive participation in a process-oriented drama allows English Language Learners (ELL) a comfortable role within the lesson, or that process-oriented drama allows students to self-select their learning focus in the context of the drama, and thus opens up room for a diversity of opinions.

Also, remind collaborators about the larger goals of drama in collaborative language that all members can understand. In response to this conversation about concerns with a process-oriented drama, you and your colleagues may establish some basic temperature-taking measures to assess if the lesson is proceeding as hoped, and make a plan for adjusting the lesson if chaos reigns. By realistically evaluating collaborators' concerns, you demonstrate that you have reasonable and achievable goals in mind and appreciate the structures and rhythms of classrooms and how foreign this kind of creative learning can initially feel for both students and teachers.

Finally, consult research and advocacy groups. You are not alone when it comes to curricular advocacy for arts education. Many organizations already commit a large amount of time and money to research, publications, and other resources that help demonstrate how one might learn through the arts. These organizations might provide you with an article, some data or statistics, or even some sample lesson plans that have been tested and evaluated in a previous partnership. These organizations want you to succeed, and most maintain free or inexpensive literature documenting their studies. In essence, they exist to help you articulate your program's curricular worth. Some organizations you might look to for resources include:

- American Alliance for Theatre and Education
- Americans for the Arts
- Arts Education Partnership
- The Arts-in-Education Consortium
- ARTSEDGE: the Kennedy Center's Arts Education Partnership
- ASSITEJ
- Association of Teaching Artists
- Center for Arts Education
- Educational Theatre Association
- Inclusive Arts Network
- Ingenuity
- Institute for Education and the Arts
- International Drama in Education Research Institute
- International Theatre for Young Audiences Research Network
- Lincoln Center Institute
- National Education Association
- National Education Taskforce
- National Endowment for the Arts
- Partners in Arts Integration Research
- Southeast Center for Education in the Arts
- TYA-USA
- Theatre Communications Group (TCG).

Monetary worth

When talking about worth in regards to the arts, a conversation about money must also occur. Money pays our salaries, makes new initiatives possible, and grows our programs for new learners and audiences. However, for many reasons many of us feel uncomfortable talking about money. First, we often avoid conversations about money because many of us think of our work as service-oriented. After all, we probably did not choose careers as teachers and artists to become wealthy. Instead, we may look at artistic work as fulfilling a higher, altruistic purpose. Perhaps we want to prepare young citizens for the world, create art that makes a difference in people's lives, build communities, or use art to address social justice issues. These values echo the affective worth of both arts and education, and they function as powerful motivators for many of us. However, this service-oriented mindset also leads many of us to feel as if talking about money in relation to these higher ideals somehow taints the value of our work.

The realities of public and private not-for-profit (also called non-profit) funding models, the most common tax designations for arts education programs, further discourage frank conversations about compensation and money in general. First, not-for-profit values can lead to tensions between what organizations do (serve people and better society) and what they need in order to maintain and grow programs (money, resources, and labor). These types of public and not-for-profit organizations are assigned a tax status in which they are not permitted to earn a profit for owners. For example, teachers in public school receive their pay from public money, e.g. taxes, administered through state and local governments. Artists likely operate within a not-for-profit model when developing and marketing programming. They might work at the behest of grants provided by government agencies or foundations or from other not-for-profit or public institutions like schools. This not-for-profit status often translates into a system of values that minimizes profit and highlights the societal value provided by workers. While not-for-profit and public entities undoubtedly provide important services to our society, not-for-profit employees are often uncomfortable talking about compensation because it seems to call into question their altruistic motivations. Furthermore, working in a not-for-profit often means employees are shielded from the intricacies of money as it relates to their work. Instead of seeking out investment funding, securing paying clients, managing books and expense reports, or completing many of the other money-related tasks that are integral to for-profit businesses, not-for-profit and government models often entrust these responsibilities to government officials, managing directors, arts administrators, development teams, and board members. Employees are sometimes even excluded from conversations about the nitty-gritty details of compensation and programmatic monetary worth.

Finally, conversations about money are difficult because artists and teachers work in historically undercompensated professions. While readers will likely agree that teachers and artists should make more money, the reality opposes this view (Apple 2013; Hassel 2002; Salamon and Geller 2007; Salamon 2012). In the United States, and many other countries, teachers and theatre artists are generally not highly compensated for their work relative to other professions ("Labor" 2013). This reality results from a variety of factors, including the historical connection between lower wages for women's professions, the predominance of women in both arts education and education fields, larger views of the arts as extraneous to the essential functioning of society, or biases regarding the training or education necessary for these professions. While these dynamics have shifted over the past hundred years toward increasing professionalization of the arts and education in the US, many of us still consider ourselves quite lucky to make money *at all* when choosing arts education as a profession.

These dynamics become even more complicated when we consider the ways in which identities (such as gender, class, racial and cultural heritage, sexual orientation, or ability) factor into discussions of financial and monetary worth. For example, studies have shown that, as compared to men, women more frequently experience negative consequences when they attempt to negotiate salaries (Bowles, Babcock, and Lai 2007). Accordingly, women may feel justly uncomfortable when it comes to discussing money, from compensation to budgets.

All of these factors translate into difficulty when it comes to talking about money at a time when arts funding is increasingly complicated and increasingly stretched. A discussion of contemporary arts funding in the United States both demonstrates the complex nature of arts education funding and contextualizes discussions of monetary worth in regards to advocacy for drama-based learning and teaching. The National Endowment for the Arts' 2012 Report, "How the United States Funds the Arts," states that, on average, government funds (state, local, or federal) account for less than 7 percent of an arts organization's budget. The rest of budget comes from earned income (about 40 percent from ticket sales, admission prices, or concession profits) followed by individual, foundational, and corporate giving and monies from the organization's endowment. As this data shows, arts education programs, which frequently set out to work in schools and other non-profit institutions, often do not earn a lot of their income from sources like ticket sales or admission prices. For example, a drama residency does not charge parents an admission to attend their child's sharing. For many arts educators, passing the hat or selling tickets may feel like a crass gesture, and it may not even be permitted by the complicated financial policies of school districts or community partners. As a result of these realities, arts education entities rely heavily on grants and government support that limit the possibilities for individual fundraising, or they use the producing arm of their organization (for example, ticketed professional theatre for youth productions) to underwrite some expenses for education initiatives.

Teachers similarly encounter challenges when funding their programs and professional development in drama-based learning. Frequently, teachers supervise, fundraise, manage, and administer funds for their arts programs. Often these tasks are additional volunteer-based responsibilities on top of their usual day-to-day duties. Teachers must also seek out professional development through regional and national organizations, often paying out-of-pocket for these opportunities. They must navigate complicated financial policies, working alongside financial administrators at the school and district level to ensure funds are properly managed. Funding these kinds of programs requires a great deal of additional (and frequently uncompensated) labor. Again, affective worth provides motivation for many teachers who take on these additional responsibilities by forging relationships with community partners, writing grant applications, and working beyond contractual obligation; they do it because they love it. However, they are rarely paid.

Given the complicated and challenging relationship between money and arts education, including drama-based learning and teaching, it is important to both think about *and* talk about the monetary worth of your work, your programs, and your involvement. Speaking about money (compensation and beyond) is not crass; it is necessary. Advocating for the monetary worth of your labor and your programs demonstrates that you are a professional with a strong sense of self-worth and a clear understanding of why and how your work benefits others. Speaking level-headedly about money also demonstrates that you understand the complex systems that contribute to value in the arts in a society, from affective value to the very tangible need to be compensated for your time and effort, and that you plan to navigate all of them in pursuit of successful programs that benefit your target populations.

Speaking about monetary worth also helps you know when to say "Yes" and when to say "No." As artists and educators, we are taught to come from a place of "Yes:" How can we make these programs work? How can I help every child learn? How can I meet your expectations? Coming from a place of "Yes" is a valuable skill that helps you cultivate connections, resources, and allies for your programs; however, you must balance the desire for successful programs with a desire to protect yourself and your programs' financial health (and, in many cases, your sanity). Unfortunately, given the affective value of arts in our society, many organizations will encourage you to work for severely depressed wages, for experience, or even solely for the love of the arts or personal satisfaction (Scott 2014). For example, an up-and-coming theatre company may recruit groups of unpaid interns to support their productions, providing college credit to these student volunteers. However, these under- and un-compensated opportunities can undermine advocacy of programs and may even be illegal. As you likely know, despite their affective value to society, arts education opportunities are not solely created with love or passion. Although love and passion are certainly important components of our work, arts education residencies and lessons require resources, skill, and time. In fact, they often require a great deal of all three. You demonstrate your worth in regards to these areas when you talk about how much each is worth in financial and monetary terms.

As you develop arts programming for your school or community, ask yourself the following questions about monetary worth. They will help you to articulate both the cost and the value of your programs, which will not only be useful for formal documentation like grants and foundation reports, but also help you develop a sense of your programs' financial worth.

Material resources

You will likely need resources to successfully complete your lesson or residency. Paper, markers, costumes, materials for sets, and a budget for copies should all be considered when thinking about the monetary worth:

- What resources will your programs need to be successful?
- Who will provide resources?
- What will schools donate (e.g. paper, markers, and scissors)? What will be purchased? What can be donated (e.g. reams of paper from an office supply store) or recycled?
- Who will buy materials? Who will supervise and document donations?
- By what date do you need materials?
- What kinds of documentation are required for bookkeeping (purchase orders, purchase cards, reimbursement, tax forms)?
- Will you need other forms of consumables, like snacks?

Space

Take into account where your work will take place. Buildings, from rehearsal studios to school multi-purpose rooms, require maintenance, lights, and support staff in order to be used. You should consider how much your programs cost in regards to the physical space in which they occur:

- What spaces will you use? If someone is donating space, what is the value of this donated space?
- If you must rent space (rehearsal spaces, theatres), who will pay? If you work in donated space, how do you document the donating organization's contribution?
- Will additional personnel (support staff, technical support, custodial support) need compensation for maintaining the space?
- How can you maximize the effectiveness of time in rented or donated space?
- Will you need to purchase or rent additional equipment (stage lights, heaters)?
- What kinds of documentation are required for bookkeeping regarding space rentals?
- Will you need to travel for any reason? If so, who will pay for gas, bus rentals, or public transportation vouchers?

People

People are your most precious and expensive resources. The issue of personnel presents one of the most significant challenges in effectively planning to advocate for the monetary worth of the people with whom you work. You may ask, *"How much is an hour of a teacher or artist's time worth?"* or *"How can we possibly afford to pay people to do this work?"* Some very simple data may help you speak about compensation for your work and the work of partnering organizations or artists. A 2011 National Opinion Research Center (NORC) report entitled "Teaching Artists and the Future of Education" states that teaching artists are, on average, paid $40 per hour of work (Rabkin *et al.* 2011: 9). When planning your budgets, you should make plans to compensate artists within this range, based on the cost of living in your community and adjusted for inflation from 2011 to the present. Similarly, as a teacher, unpaid intern, or other professionally oriented volunteer, you should speak openly about the time you choose to donate, at an approximate rate of $40/hour, if you are not monetarily compensated for your work. Remember to count planning, assessment, and documentation in these figures. Any budgets you create should include the cost, whether donated or compensated, of labor. Demonstrating how much money your programs require and how much work you and your partners donate helps you advocate for your programs' monetary value. For example, compensating a teaching artist for a two-week drama residency (let us assume two hours of contact with students per day for five days) equals $800. Add in two hours for planning, one hour for documentation, and two hours for assessment, and your artist residency now costs at least $1000 before purchasing any resources or factoring in any additional costs for donated time by partnering teachers for planning, grant writing, documentation, or assessment. As this example demonstrates, taking into account the value of people rapidly increases the cost of partnerships. Some questions to consider when evaluating the monetary worth of people involved in your programs:

- Who will be involved in your programs?
- What are reasonable targets for each hour of work? What can you accomplish in the time you have? What could you do with more time? What can be condensed or eliminated if you end up with less time?
- How many hours will planning require? How many actual contact hours will you or artists have with participants? How many hours will you need for concluding the residency or lesson, including time to document, evaluate, and report on the program?
- How much will you pay artists and yourself? How are you determining this rate?
- Who will compensate you and your partners for their time?

- If you are relying on volunteer support, how will you document the monetary value of their labor contribution?
- Do you have all appropriate insurance to cover your work and any travel?
- Have you taken into account all support staff (administrators who must stay on-site during after-hours programs, bus drivers, technical staff) that will also be impacted by the residency?

While you may initially worry about articulating these expenses for fear of losing partners or institutional support because of cost, explaining how much it costs to hire personnel for your programs helps you demonstrate their monetary worth and supports professionalization of the field as a whole. In all, talking about money demonstrates your professionalism, your willingness to broach difficult subjects, and your commitment to providing excellent value to your partners and students. Talking about money also helps current and future generations of artists and arts educators by making clear that the arts are work and deserve to be considered with the same level of respect and financial support that we extend to other kinds of labor.

A final note on worth

No matter which dimension of worth you hope to communicate (affective, curricular/cognitive, monetary/financial, or some other dimension not discussed in this chapter), trust your professional competencies. Remember: whether a teacher, teaching artist, or community facilitator, when it comes to advocacy, you can and should project competence and confidence. Trust your gut. If something feels off in a planning session, ask questions. If you make mistakes, quickly and succinctly apologize and move forward to correct the problem. Reflect on your work with rigor and honesty, provide materials in a timely fashion, and speak truthfully about challenges. Speak openly with partners about ways to improve in future lessons, and document successes. Each of these elements will help you demonstrate your worth and help you form meaningful, long lasting, and mutually beneficial partnerships that enable participants to learn through drama and performance.

Know your audience

While understanding and articulating your worth is a vital component in advocating for your programs, you must also know your audience and adapt to meet the needs of all partners involved in your programs. For example, knowing an audience from a teacher's perspective might require refining language and articulating goals in order to communicate with parents, colleagues, or administrators about your interest in arts-based learning and how it connects to larger classroom learning objectives. Education directors might need to acquire hard data and measured outcomes of programming in order to advocate for programs with granting institutions, foundations, and community partners. Theatre companies with an educational wing might advocate for their programs through slick press materials, a branded identity, and a well-maintained relationship with the production wing of the company that helps both areas succeed. Independent theatre makers and teaching artists might advocate for themselves by engaging in professional development that helps them effectively run their small business, network with colleagues and potential partners, and market themselves to potential partners and clients. Individuals and organizations should consider audiences they hope to reach and adjust advocacy strategies in order to form successful and professional partnerships.

Knowing your audience involves several skills and strategies. We'll focus on strategies for communication and practical tips for working with different groups involved in a partnership or residency.

Practical tips for knowing your audience

Be professional

As mentioned previously, demonstrating professionalism is one of the hallmarks of knowing your audience and advocating for your programs. Articulate (say) and demonstrate (show) your professional competencies. Feel comfortable communicating expectations and concerns. Ask questions. Likewise, acknowledge areas of strength and weakness, particularly with arts partners. Most classroom teachers have not had extensive training in the arts and teaching artists are not well-versed in classroom management strategies or teaching math or science. Consider your partnership to be a learning opportunity for all participants, including the artists and teachers. Trust all parties involved. Respect their professional competencies, even if they feel very unorthodox to you. Similarly, articulate and demonstrate a deep and vested interest in the partnership, and show willingness to adapt to the group and to the desired learning outcomes.

Observe and adjust to fit within the culture of your partnering educator or community group.

Be flexible, arrive to planning meetings with several different approaches in mind for a single lesson, and maintain an open mind.

An example to illustrate knowing audiences: a teaching artist is hired to work with a team of second-grade teachers. In any given school, a group of second-grade classrooms will likely have vastly different cultures based on the teacher and students. One teacher may be soft-spoken, with the general tone of their classroom being quiet and calm. Another teacher may be loud and outgoing, and their classroom may be very tightly organized. Still another teacher may have a more free and open classroom, with the room constantly in motion and more clutter than other classrooms. Each of these environments possesses attributes and challenges that will impact the residency. As a collaborator, the artist must navigate these differences and find a way for programs to succeed in all of these classroom settings. This challenge requires the teaching artist to communicate with partnering teachers, learn about their classroom and their students, and adapt activities for their environment. Similarly, teachers will also adapt to different personalities in their classrooms and amongst their partnering colleagues. Sometimes, you will immediately gel with a partner, working together almost effortlessly. Other times, your styles will be somewhat mismatched, and you will have to find middle ground together. Occasionally you may find yourself working alongside someone who has fundamentally different values and philosophies from you, and collaboration is strained. Part of being professional rests with finding the value of each unique learning environment in which you work and making your programs complement these different cultural dynamics.

Be mindful of time

We cannot overstate the value of keeping track of time when developing partnerships. Arrive early to all meetings, teach lessons according to a schedule, and provide any documentation or materials to all invested parties by an agreed-upon deadline. This element is particularly important for artists working with schools and community groups. In most instances, schools are impressively organized institutions, with all parts, including trips to the bathroom, lunch, and transitions between subjects, functioning together as a well-oiled machine. Your presence will be a shift in the normal routine, and thus much preparation and juggling of different schedules has taken place to accommodate your partnership or residency. Showing up late, even by a few minutes, can radically alter the day's agenda in a school. Give yourself ample time to find parking, navigate a school office, use the restroom, and double-check materials well before the scheduled meeting time. On a similar note, confirm the meeting agenda with all participants at least twenty-four hours ahead of the meeting time. It is not uncommon for participants of a residency to plan a follow-up meeting, at which point one member of the group develops a conflict or worse, and forgets about the meeting, necessitating a new round of schedule-juggling. Save yourself the additional time and effort by sending a confirmation. Finally, plan your contributions to the meeting to be succinct but informative. Generally, everyone is happy when a meeting runs smoothly and ends a bit early. You will likely find partnerships more successful if everyone respects each other's time.

Be visible, available, and authentic

Knowing your audience requires you to maintain visibility and make yourself available to other partners, professional associates, and collaborators. Visibility may take many forms. As an artist or education director, you might maintain a program website and regularly update your social media feeds with news about your work. As a teacher, you may maintain a class blog or share some of your students' work on the morning announcements. You might also attend press events like a local arts organization fundraiser, or present your work at local or national conferences. In addition to visibility, you must also be available. In practical terms, being available may mean answering emails and phone calls promptly. It may also mean meeting deadlines ahead of schedule. Being available also means arriving at meetings prepared for the discussion at hand.

Being visible and available also requires you to maintain authenticity. Many of us have encountered someone who seems "fake" or superficial. They may talk more than they listen or they may perform instead of genuinely interacting with people. Faking it may be a coping mechanism. For instance, an education director may be nervous, so they fall back on acting skills, putting on a false air of confidence. A little faking can help anyone get through some initial nervousness, but constantly interacting on a superficial level not only makes others uncomfortable, it also indicates a strong sense of disregard for the unique needs of partners and colleagues. Strive to be honest and genuine in your interactions with others. If you dislike an idea, respectfully express your thoughts on the matter. Similarly, if you like something, demonstrate your genuine enthusiasm. Partners and colleagues will appreciate knowing where they stand, and you will feel more settled. In addition to helping you make more meaningful relationships, personal authenticity will also help you navigate potential conflicts or disagreements. Instead of trying to please everyone all the time, being realistic and honest helps you maintain an ethical and moral compass, allowing you to step back and express yourself with honesty and integrity.

Availability and visibility also requires you to toot your horn and others' horns. You are your own best advocate, so speak with confidence, excitement, and a healthy dose of humor and humility about your work. Cite your achievements, discuss plans for the future, and brainstorm with partners. In a similar vein, share exciting work completed by your colleagues. Genuinely congratulate people on jobs well done, and thank professional acquaintances for their help and support. By speaking about your competencies and achievements along with celebrating those of others, you demonstrate both enthusiasm and professionalism. You also establish yourself as a partner or colleague who might serve as an ally, and you will likely foster supportive, mutually beneficial working relationships.

Being visible and available requires practice. For many of us, being authentic, engaged, enthusiastic, and responsive requires courage, energy, and a heightened sense of awareness regarding those around us and ourselves. This is no easy combination of skills to sustain over time. However, by practicing authentic, engaged interaction, you can make the skills easier and more ingrained. For example, rehearse your lessons before teaching them the first time, practice a speech you will give to funders or to conference participants, and take opportunities to push yourself beyond comfort zones. Practice saying, *"You're welcome"* without additional caveats like, *"Oh well, it was nothing!"* Likewise, rehearse saying, *"I'm sorry"* without excuses. Apply for a grant you think may be out of your league or submit an article about your work. Reflect on your experiences in a journal, taking note of both successes and areas for improvement.

Find allies

Advocacy requires other people. In order to create successful programming, you should ask, *"Who are the members of this community who share values about arts learning?"* These people are your allies. Allies might be supportive administrators, teachers, or community members. Allies might be peers in other arts organizations or fellow artists who work in the same or different disciplines. Allies do not need to be people with whom you will necessarily work directly, but many will be co-workers, colleagues, and professional acquaintances. Allies might help you advocate for your programs, their objectives, and their value to the learning communities. Teachers may seek out artists with consonant values about education who demonstrate a clear respect for the parameters in which they work and with whom they connect regarding different curricular areas upon which they intend to collaborate. Artists can look for teachers who are open to their ideas and/or arts-based skills and knowledge, who prioritize time for planning and teaching, and who express interest in the type of art they create. Additionally, anyone interested in arts education should seek out allies from the scores of school administrators, parents, and community leaders who understand your work and want to help you succeed.

Document, document, document

Documenting your work helps your audience to see what you do. Document as much of your work as possible. Take pictures, record video, and even consider maintaining a current and content-heavy web and social media presence. Maintain records of participants and partners, and keep track of data (numbers of students served, numbers of performances, or audience members) you can use to communicate your program's impact on your community. Maintain an archive of all materials generated in the course of your work, as well as sample participant work (with appropriate permissions if you will share this work with others).

Communicating with your audiences

Communication is one of the most important components of interacting with audiences for purposes of advocacy. Whether in print materials, conversations during planning meetings, formal presentations to potential funders, or in assessment documents, communication about your programs should use language and take forms your unique audiences and partners can understand.

Communicating with educators

Teachers can be tough audiences. Not only are they master communicators, managing and teaching in their classrooms with sophistication and competence, but they also work long hours for modest pay. Additionally, they are perpetually inundated with new literacy trainings, additional testing mandates, and a never-ending schedule of meetings. Their time is precious, and they are experts at discerning meaningful learning opportunities for themselves and others. Accordingly, they often and rightly approach extra responsibilities and new initiatives with a healthy dose of skepticism: is this partnership a smart and meaningful use of my time? How will this opportunity help my students or improve my teaching? Will we learn something new? As a teacher, you should ask yourself these questions in the face of new partnerships. As a partner, you must be sensitive to these realities. Whether you are a classroom teacher looking to partner with your grade-level team on a project, or an independent teaching artist forging a new partnership with a school, you must discuss how new initiatives in drama-based curricula will support learning goals and competing influences that already steer teachers' lesson plans. You must also convince them that a shift in a well-oiled schedule and set of procedures will produce a worthwhile learning experience for their students.

One of the most compelling ways to communicate with educators rests with the impact drama-based learning will have on their students: what will students learn or experience through this process that they would not otherwise learn or experience? Demonstrate that you have considered an educator's curriculum and understand their larger expectations in regards to testing, literacy programs, or administrative pushes. Does the district have a system-wide literacy program? If so, approach any first meetings with knowledge of these programs. You might also consider developing sample lesson plans that address some of the grade-level learning objectives pertinent to your proposed program. Above all, demonstrate a working understanding of the classroom and how you can support the learning goals already in place at the school.

Even though teachers can be tough audiences, they can also be very open to the diversity of potential learning outcomes that their students can experience via drama. Given their close relationship to their students, teachers are students' primary advocates in schools. Moreover they are often deeply invested not only in teaching curricula, but also in nurturing their students' personal, social, and moral development. Accordingly, they often dislike the mandates pressed upon them in regards to rigid testing requirements and look for opportunities for their students to have freedom to try new styles of learning and develop new competencies. If you, as an artist or teaching colleague, can communicate to teachers the affective worth of the arts to their students, you can more effectively cultivate a relationship with these important allies and, in some cases, staunchest supporters. In practical terms, find out what teachers feel their students miss out on in the current school experience (character education, creative writing, and understanding the human side of history are some examples we have heard in planning partnerships, but there are many others), and collaborate on a way to provide learning opportunities that are not otherwise available. You can help teachers make connections between drama-based learning and this desire to give their students a broad education with a variety of experiences. Instead of promising a sharp increase in reading test scores, you might suggest that your programming addresses character education objectives. You might discuss too how the programs support a district-wide writing-across-the-curriculum initiative, as well as give students an opportunity to explore creative writing and independent expression.

You might also enter conversations about drama-based learning by discussing pedagogical innovation: how and why do these less familiar methods work in their classrooms and why are they worth incorporating into the classroom? Teachers are masters of their routines, but they are also interested in new ways of teaching. Team-teaching with an artist can provide new methods for introducing material or reveal new strategies for engaging different kinds of learners.

Communicating with artists

Much like teachers, artists who work in education-related fields come from diverse backgrounds and have a range of experiences that inform their work with learners and teachers. However, in most cases artists do not receive the same training as licensed teachers or administrators, and they may not be familiar with the commonplace terms and procedures found in school environments. When communicating with artists, keep an eye out for blind spots when it comes to issues like classroom management, objectives-based assessment, differentiated instruction, and other topics specific to teaching. Similarly, look for connections between their art practice and its cognitive and curricular worth to learners involved in their programs, and point out natural connections between their programs and your teaching.

Also, respect your cooperating artist's professional competencies. They have very likely trained for years in their artistic discipline. For instance, the aforementioned NORC Teaching Artist Review reports that half of teaching artists hold master's degrees and two-thirds hold college degrees in an art form (Rabkin *et al.* 2011: 3). Likewise, the average teaching artist has twelve years of experience, entering into education fields later in their lives (the average age of a teaching artist is 45 years old). They are at their best when given the opportunity to demonstrate what they know and engage with participants in activities that directly relate to their extensive arts training. In order to facilitate these kinds of learning experiences, cooperating partners should approach arts partnerships with an open mind in regards to how an artist's work connects with different kinds of learning.

For example, several years ago we hosted a residency partnering a scenic designer and technical director with a group of fourth graders for a unit that combined math skills with scenic design. As teachers, we imagined that the group would learn about scale, practice drawing sets, and talk about how the artist incorporated math into basic construction techniques for the theatre. During planning, the artist expressed a much more ambitious plan. He wanted to lead classes through actual building techniques, complete with real wood, tape measures, nails, screwguns, and even a tablesaw managed by parent volunteers. Naturally, we felt anxious about our nine-year-old students' capabilities (let alone safety!) for actually measuring and assembling set components. However, we discussed these concerns with our partnering artist, and quickly realized that he had a great deal of experience in leading novices through basic construction skills, and advanced competencies in health and safety regulations. The residency proceeded according to the teaching artist's ideas and with a leap of faith from us. The result was a much more rich, hands-on, and skills-oriented residency in which students engaged in activities that moved beyond scale drawings on a page. Because we, as teachers, kept an open mind about our partnering artist's competencies, our students benefitted.

Communicating visually and electronically

One important way in which you communicate about your work occurs with marketing and visual media. Visual media, including videos, images, infographics, logos, and websites, all help you communicate with a broad section of groups who might be interested in your programs. Increasingly, public and not-for-profit entities are borrowing directly from for-profit enterprises in regards to visual communication. For example, practically all organizations, from schools to theatre companies, have a branded identity. Branding, a concept initially designed to help consumers recognize a product, is a method of developing a signature look, usually in concert with an artist like a graphic designer. Branding helps an organization unify press materials and other visual information in order to communicate quickly and efficiently with partners. You may want to create a branded identity for your programs that communicates key components of your work.

In addition to a consistent branded identity, you will also likely communicate electronically. For example, you may want to create a website that not only explains your programs, but that also includes sample lessons, pictures of residencies in action, student or parent testimonials, or a blog from teaching artists. Additionally, in an era where social media reigns, communicating visually on social media sites like Facebook or Instagram is another way to distinguish your programs and circulate information about your lessons.

A word of caution: it is absolutely vital that you confirm and follow privacy policies of any organization or individual with whom you work. Schools, along with many other community groups, have strict and legally binding policies regarding students' privacy. Do not post images of participants without express permission, and consider seeking legal advice to ensure that you are protecting the privacy of your participants.

Conclusion

Advocacy for drama-based learning is a complex and exciting component of any lesson, residency, or program. It combines assessment, advertising, communication and documentation. It is also both a skill and an art that requires practice and commitment. Advocacy helps you demonstrate how your programs help participants learn and/or teach through drama methods. To conclude, we offer a practical resource to help you with planning residencies and partnerships.

Arts partnership planning guide

Table 6.1

Arts Partnership Planning Guide
Partners *(Who is involved?)*:
Goal *(What will we accomplish?)*:
Timeline *(Where have we been? Where are we starting now? Where are we going?)*:
Desired Outcomes *(How will we know we have met our goals?)*:
Summary of Partnership *(What will we do?)*:

Table 6.1 continued

Assessment Methods *(How will we produce data and generate information?)*:

Funding *(What money do we have/need?)*:

Labor *(Who will work for pay or donate time?)*:

Resources *(What do we need?)*:

Responsibilities of each participant *(What will I do? What will you do? What will we do together?)*:

Questions:	Next Steps:

References

Ahmed-Ullah, Noreen, John Chase, and Bob Secter. 2013. "Chicago School Closings." *Chicago Tribune.* 23 May. Accessed 8 April 2014. http://articles.chicagotribune.com/2013-05-23/news/chi-chicago-school-closings-20130522_1_chicago-teachers-union-byrd-bennett-one-high-school-program.

Anderson, Lorin W., and David Krathwohl (eds). 2000. *A Taxonomy for Learning, Teaching, and Assessing: A revision of Bloom's Taxonomy of Educational Objectives.* Complete Edition. Pearson.

Apple, Michael W. 2013. *Teachers and Texts: A Political Economy of Class and Gender Relations in Education.* Routledge.

Bowles, Hannah Riley, Linda Babcock, and Lei Lai. 2007. "Social incentives for gender differences in the propensity to initiate negotiations: sometimes it does hurt to ask." *Organizational Behavior and Human Decision Processes* 103 (1): 84–103.

"Choices, Changes, and Challenges: Curriculum and Instruction in the NCLB Era." 2007. Center on Education Policy.

Hassel, Bryan C. 2002. "Better pay for better teaching: making teaching compensation pay off in the age of accountability." May. http://eric.ed.gov/?id=ED467050.

"How the United States Funds the Arts." 2012. 3rd edn. National Endowment for the Arts. Accessed 11 August 2014. http://arts.gov/sites/default/files/how-the-us-funds-the-arts.pdf

Krathwohl, David R., Benjamin S. Bloom, and Bertram B. Masia. 1964. "Taxonomy of Educational Objectives, Handbook II: Affective Domain." *Krathwohl's Taxonomy of Affective Domain*. David McKay Company.

"Labor Statistics – May". 2013. *May 2013 National Occupational Employment and Wage Estimates United States*. Bureau of Labor Statistics. Accessed 11 August 2014. http://www.bls.gov/oes/2013/may/oes_nat.htm.

Marzano, Robert J., and John S. Kendall. 2007. *The New Taxonomy of Educational Objectives*. Corwin Press.

Rabkin, Nick, Michael Reynolds, Eric Hedberg, and Justin Shelby. 2011. "Teaching artists and the future of education." NORC at the University of Chicago. Accessed 11 August 2014.www.norc.org

Salamon, Lester M. 2012. *The State of Nonprofit America*. Brookings Institution Press.

Salamon, Lester M., and Stephanie Lessans Geller. 2007. "The nonprofit workforce crisis: real or imagined?" *Listening Post Project*.

Scott, A.O. 2014. "The Paradox of Art as Work." *The New York Times*, 9 May. http://www.nytimes.com/2014/05/11/movies/the-paradox-of-art-as-work.html.

"The United States of education: The changing demographics of the United States and their schools." 2012. Center for Public Education. Accessed 11 August 2014. http://www.centerforpubliceducation.org/You-May-Also-Be-Interested-In-landing-page-level/Organizing-a-School-YMABI/The-United-States-of-education-The-changing-demographics-of-the-United.

Appendix A
Annotated bibliography

Note: We have listed both recent and historical sources. While the historical sources should be read in the context of the times when they were written, many of the activities are adaptable to contemporary practices.

For the most extensive annotated bibliography to date, see McCaslin, *Creative Drama in the Classroom and Beyond*. 8th edn, 2006, 415–46.

Bailey, Sally Dorothy. 1993. *Wings to Fly: Bringing theatre arts to students with special needs*. Rockville: Woodbine House.

A nuts and bolts handbook for special education and K-12 drama teachers, this text includes practical examples and discussion of the benefits of drama for students with special needs.

Baldwin, Patrice. 2008. *With Drama in Mind: Real learning in imagined worlds*. London: Continuum International Publishing Group.

Baldwin offers a thorough and authoritative rationale for teaching through drama, based on brain-based research. The book includes an essential toolkit of drama techniques and strategies.

Bernardi, Philip. 1992. *Improvisation Starters: A collection of 900 improvisation situations for the theater*. Cincinnati: Betterway Books.

This resource book features improvisation starters for character conflicts, physicality, solo improvisations, lines of dialogue, and reactions to the environment.

Boal, Augusto. 1985. *Theatre of the Oppressed*. Translated by Charles A. and Maria-Odila Leal McBride. New York: Theatre Communications Group.

This text lays out Boal's theoretical and historical argument for the necessity of Theatre of the Oppressed, providing some discussion of his early forum theatre work. A must-read for those with a serious interest in drama for social justice.

——1992. *Games for Actors and Non-Actors.* Translated by Adrian Jackson. New York: Routledge.

This essential guide to Boal's work features comprehensive descriptions of image work, forum theatre, and invisible theatre, along with games and activities that can be plugged into lesson plans or used as stand alone activities to increase awareness, build community, and facilitate dialogue among students.

——1995. *The Rainbow of Desire.* Translated by Adrian Jackson. New York: Routledge.

This guidebook lays out additional games and methods for empowering participants to see, understand, and transform the internalized oppressions that Boal referred to as "the cop in the head."

Bogart, Anne, and Tina Landau. 2004. *The Viewpoints Book: A practical guide to viewpoints and composition.* New York: Theatre Communications Group.

This guide discusses tips and tricks for composition work, along with dozens of theatre games and exercises you can use to interpret works of art and literature through performance or to create new performances together.

Bowles, Norma, and Daniel-Raymond Nadon (eds). 2013. *Staging Social Justice: Collaborating to create activist theatre.* Carbondale: Southern Illinois University Press.

This edited collection lays out the methodology of Fringe Benefits, a group that creates theatre for social justice education in schools throughout the US, Australia, Canada, and the UK. Though the collection focuses on devising theatrical performances for use in schools, rather than on drama as a teaching tool, the discussion of methods for measuring impact and practical advice on creating performance collaboratively will be of use to teachers.

Burke, Margaret R. 2013. *Gavin Bolton's Contextual Drama: The road less travelled.* Chicago: Intellect.

This book describes the methods of another important process-oriented drama practitioner. Bolton is directly inspired by Heathcote, but has made significant interventions into the field, creating a signature method now known as "contextual drama."

Cattanach, Ann. 1992. *Drama for People with Special Needs.* New York: Drama Book Publishers.

This text includes practical methods for using drama with special needs students, as well as sections on drama therapy and play therapy.

Cossa, Mario, Sally Ember, Lauren Glass, and Jennifer Russell. 1996. *Acting Out: The Workbook. A guide to the development and presentation of issue-oriented, audience interactive, improvisational theatre.* New York: Brunner-Routledge.

This practical guide to the development and presentation of issue-oriented, audience-interactive, improvisational theatre is for leaders who are already somewhat familiar with improvisational theatre and working with groups.

Duffy, Peter, and Elinor Vettraino (eds). 2010. *Youth and Theatre of the Oppressed.* New York: Palgrave Macmillan.

A collection of essays exploring contemporary TO work in educational settings, prisons, and communities around the world, this texts offers theoretical, practical, and historical perspectives on TO practices involving young people.

Etchells, Tim. 2002. *Certain Fragments: Texts and writings on performance.* New York: Routledge.

This book discusses Etchells's work with British performance group Forced Entertainment and details a wealth of short writing exercises you can adapt for your classroom.

Ganguly, Sanjoy. 2010. *Jana Sanskriti: Forum theatre and democracy in India.* London: Routledge.

A first-hand account of the development and growth of the Jana Sanskriti Center of Theatre of the Oppressed, founded in India in 1985, this book also includes discussion and analyses of Augusto Boal's practices.

Gerke, Pamela, and Helen Landalf. 1999. *Hooves and Horns, Fins and Feathers: Drama curriculum for kindergarten and first grade.* Hanover: Smith and Krauss.

A comprehensive guide for integrating drama in early childhood classrooms and connecting it to other areas of curriculum, this text includes detailed lesson plans.

Gómez-Peña, Guillermo, and Roberto Sifuentes. 2013. *Exercises for Rebel Artists: Radical performance pedagogy.* New York: Routledge.

This handbook describes acclaimed performance artist Guillermo Gómez-Peña's method for teaching performance art. A text focused on working with adults, the book includes a large collection of exercises and lesson plans you can adapt for other age groups.

Gonzalez, Jo Beth. 2006. *Temporary Stages: Departing from tradition in high school theatre education*. Portsmouth: Heinemann.

This text outlines the author's Critically Conscious Production-Oriented Classroom (CCPOC) approach to supporting drama-based learning with adolescents and young adults. Focus is on issues of diversity, privilege, and oppression, and the author generates practical examples from case studies.

——2013. *Temporary Stages II: Critically oriented drama education*. Chicago: Intellect.

An invaluable resource for theatre teachers (especially those who work with adolescents and young adults), this book extends the author's writing on CCPOC (described above).

Grady, Sharon. 2000. *Drama and Diversity: A pluralistic perspective of educational drama*. Portsmouth: Heinemann.

One of the first and most comprehensive texts on drama and diversity, including chapters on race and ethnicity, gender, sexual orientation, class and ability, Grady's book includes sample lesson plans and extensions.

Graham, Scott, and Steven Hogget. 2009. *The Frantic Assembly Book of Devising Theatre*. New York: Routledge.

One of our favorite books for exercises in physical theatre, as well as a number of fun and easy games to get your students up and moving, this text describes Frantic Assembly's collaborative process of creating new performances.

Heathcote, Dorothy, and Gavin Bolton. 1995. *Drama for Learning: Dorothy Heathcote's mantle of the expert approach to education*. Portsmouth: Heinemann.

A series of essays describing Dorothy Heathcote's "mantle of the expert" approach to drama, this text does not feature lesson plans, though activities could be extracted from the narrative.

Heddon, Deirdre, and Jane Milling. 2006. *Devising Performance: A critical history*. New York: Palgrave Macmillan.

For students with an interest in the history and working practices of Goat Island, Forced Entertainment, and others, this text provides a comprehensive history and analysis of collaboratively devised theatre since the 1950s.

King, Nancy. 1994. *Story Making and Drama: An approach to teaching language and literature at the secondary and postsecondary levels*. Portsmouth: Heinemann.

This manual of storytelling and story drama includes techniques and lesson plans using novels, plays, poetry, and autobiography.

Landy, Robert, and David T. Montgomery. 2012. *Theatre for Change: Education, social action and therapy*. New York: Palgrave Macmillan.

An overview of drama therapy, theatre education, and applied theatre tactics used in schools, community groups, prisons, and performance spaces for the creation of dialogue, change, and personal growth, this book offers an international perspective on applied theatre techniques and features interviews with contemporary practitioners.

Lazarus, Joan. 2012. *Signs of Change: New directions in theatre education*. Chicago: Intellect.

This accessible guide to theatre education practices in the United States includes interviews with 140 drama teachers.

Manley, Anita, and Cecily O'Neill. 1997. *Dreamseekers: Creative approaches to the African American heritage*. Portsmouth: Heinemann.

This text focuses on strategies for implementing drama using multicultural prose and poetry, including holistic lesson plans that explore significant themes and events in African American history for middle through high school.

Miller, Carole, and Juliana Saxton. 2004. *Into the Story: Language in action through drama*. Portsmouth: Heinemann.

A practical text with resources for structuring and implementing drama lessons based on picture books. This text also includes detailed lesson plans.

Oddey, Alison. 1994. *Devising Theatre: A practical and theoretical handbook*. New York: Routledge.

Both a history and a how-to manual, this text discusses some of the groups mentioned in chapter four, provides practical tips for collaborating to create new work together, and lists exercises you may find useful in putting together new lesson plans that involve students creating new performance together.

O'Neill, Cecily. 1995. *Drama Worlds: A framework for process drama*. Portsmouth: Heinemann.

A thorough examination of process drama, this handbook connects process drama to improvisation and theatre arts.

Prendergast, Monica and Juliana Saxton. 2010. *Applied Theatre: International case studies and challenges for practice*. Chicago: Intellect.

Though this collection also focuses on a variety of applied theatre areas outside traditional classrooms, Chapter 3, on Theatre in Education, should be of particular interest. Readers interested in ethical issues in the use of theatre for social justice will appreciate the diverse set of international case studies in applied theatre, from prison theatre to theatre in health education.

——2013. *Applied Drama: A facilitator's handbook for working in community.* Chicago: Intellect.

This book, a companion text to *Applied Theatre* (above), provides a wealth of techniques and practical tools for creating drama sessions with various community groups.

Rohd, Michael. 1998. *Theatre for Community, Conflict & Dialogue: The Hope Is Vital training manual.* Portsmouth: Heinemann.

Adapting aspects of Boal's forum theatre as well as Spolin's improvisation and theatre games to the task of creating dialogue about social issues with young people, Rohd's book is a practical handbook filled with games and exercises as well as a complete method for doing forum theatre with young people.

Rosenberg, Helane. 1987. *Creative Drama and Imagination: Transforming ideas into action.* New York: Holt, Rinehart and Winston.

A comprehensive study based on the Rutgers Imagination Method (RIM), focusing on the role of imagination in drama, this textbook contains many drama activities.

Salazar, Laura Gardner. 1999. *Making Performance Art.* Charlottesville: New Plays Inc.

A classic in the field, and one of the first texts to discuss the use of performance art as a teaching and learning tool, Salazar's book is out of print but may be available secondhand or in your university library. The book includes lesson plans and descriptions of performance art activities, and is focused largely on working with poetry and the use of performance art to explore social issues.

Saldaña, Johnny. 1995. *Drama of Color: Improvisation with multiethnic folklore.* Portsmouth: Heinemann.

This unique resource covers multiethnic folklore presented in detailed drama lessons that examine different perspectives and worldviews.

Salisbury Wills, Barbara. 1996. *Theatre Arts in the Elementary Classroom: Kindergarten through Grade Three.* 2nd edn. New Orleans: Anchorage.

——1996. *Theatre Arts in the Elementary Classroom: Grade Four through Grade Six*. 2nd edn. New Orleans: Anchorage.

These two collections of drama activities are intended to be used as a teacher's resource guide.

Siks, Geraldine. 1958. *Creative Dramatics: An art for children*. New York: Harper and Brothers.

One of the first drama books offering a comprehensive methodology for working with children in drama programs, this classic includes detailed examples and photographs.

Smith, J. Lea, and J. Daniel Herring. 2001. *Dramatic Literacy: Using drama and literature to teach middle-level content*. Portsmouth: Heinemann.

A manual for using age-appropriate literature as a starting point for creating drama lessons for literature, science, social studies, and ESL classrooms, this text includes lesson plans.

Spolin, Viola. 1963. *Improvisation for the Theatre: A handbook of technical and directing techniques*. Evanston: Northwestern University Press.

This classic book includes exercises and theatre games for introducing theatre concepts to all ages.

——2000. *The Theatre Game File*. Evanston: Northwestern University Press.

This unique work is a box of notecards with a variety of games to be used in the classroom.

Sternberg, Patricia, and Antonina Garcia. 1994. *Sociodrama: Who's in your shoes?* Westport: Preager.

This practical guide covers sociodrama as a method of fostering personal and social expression, understanding, role experimentation, and problem solving.

Taylor, Philip. 1998. *Redcoats and Patriots: Reflective practice in drama and social studies*. Portsmouth: Heinemann.

A narrative account of the author's attempt to integrate drama into his social studies classroom. Although it does not have lesson plans, plans and activities could be extracted from the text.

Wagner, Betty Jane. 1976. *Dorothy Heathcote: Drama as a learning medium*. Washington: National Education Association.

This classic describes Heathcote's influential techniques in drama in education and her use of "teacher-in-role."

Ward, Winifred. 1930. *Creative Dramatics for the Upper Grades and Junior High School*. New York: D. Appleton and Company.

One of the first texts that dealt explicitly with drama as a method for teaching and learning, this work primarily focuses on linear methods.

——1957. *Playmaking with Children*. New York: Appleton-Century Crofts.

This US classic focuses on the use of linear creative drama methods with children.

Warren, Kathleen. 1993. *Hooked on Drama: The theory and practice of drama in early childhood*. Waverley: Macquarie University.

This collection focuses on lesson plans using the "mantle of the expert" approach for preschool through first grade.

Way, Brian. 1967. *Development Through Drama*. Atlantic Highlands: Humanities.

This classic text takes a humanistic approach to drama with young people.

Weigler, Will. 2001. *Strategies for Playbuilding: Helping groups translate issues into theatre*. Portsmouth: Heinemann.

This step-by-step manual covers devising performance pieces and writing scripts with young people of middle and high school age.

Appendix B

For course instructors

This appendix is specifically for instructors who would like to use this textbook. It consists of a sample syllabus and course schedule, preceded by some tips on how to implement this syllabus.

How to use this syllabus and schedule

We give our students experience in drama-based teaching through laboratory workshops with K-5 students from the community. We work with up to twenty children per section of the course in these free drama labs, allocating places on a lottery system. Each college student is paired with one grade school student to observe that student's experience in drama, as well as be a resource for the child during drama labs. If your institution does not support this system, students can lead drama lessons for one another instead.

The final assignment changes every semester depending on the opportunities offered by the institution. Some semesters we assign the students to see the annual Theatre for Young Audiences Production, while other semesters we send them to lectures on diversity or neuroscience research, or to a hands-on drama workshop.

We put great emphasis on individual reflection and reflecting as a class because we feel this is where the most important learning takes place. When teaching prospective drama and performance facilitators we conduct meta-reflection at the end of each class to discuss the activities done in the class and the work of the students. This reflection focuses on suggestions for improvement in activity and lesson plan design and execution, as well as discussion of alternative applications for the same activities. To encourage reflection, we also assign most reading material to be completed after students have had one demonstration session with a technique (for instance, students read about linear drama after participating in a demonstration of a linear lesson plan).

Students sign up to lead starter activities and full lesson plans during the first week of class, after which all individual due dates are set. We strongly encourage you to organize assignments so that each student's workload is appropriately spread through the semester. For example:

- The first teams that are leading a lab should also be the first to do a starter.
- Once starters and labs are in place, allot time in class for students to note when their post-starter and post-lab reflections are due, as each student's due dates will differ depending on when they lead their activities.
- Make sure groups have ample time between their K-5 lab and their "Drama for Social Justice" lesson. This usually means that some students will do a social justice drama before they lead a lab.
- "Drama for Social Justice" lessons are done with the college students in the class and focus on applying techniques discussed in Chapter 3 for exploring issues of social justice with young adult populations.

Sample Syllabus

Introduction to the course

This course is meant for undergraduate students who intend to become professional educators, students who are interested in using drama in recreational settings, students who would like to work with education programs at professional theatres, and students who simply love improvisation, play, young people, and theatre.

The course will begin with an introduction to the history of drama in the United States and the different methodologies associated with drama as an educational tool. It will lay out the philosophy of this course, which is that creativity is a necessity in our lives, that embodied learning is essential, that our emotions determine our sense of well-being, and that contextual learning offers a way of trying on the world and helps us to find our place in the world in relationship to other people and cultures. The philosophy of the course draws heavily on current neurological, psychological, and sociological research.

Based on the above, the course embraces embodied learning, which means that it is highly practical. All drama and performance strategies and methods offered in the course will be practiced by the participants in the classroom with each other and the instructor. Students will lead activities, design, implement, and evaluate lesson plans (labs), and discuss the value and purpose of the methods offered, demonstrating metacognition. The students will also discover ways to assess drama in formal or informal assessment, which is not only mandatory in a school setting, but also required for measuring effect and applying for grants in non-educational situations.

Assumptions

This course focuses on inclusion and diversity in theory, practice, and pedagogy. We assume that you are open to exploring alternative ways of teaching and learning, and to challenging your own (pre)conceptions.

We assume that you took this course not only because of requirements, but because you believe that drama could enhance the school curriculum and/or offers different ways of teaching and learning in community work and recreational settings. We also assume that you see drama as an art form and indispensable in the education of young people.

We assume that you will take responsibility for your own learning, for creating and maintaining a respectful classroom environment, and for appreciating the cultural diversity of our society.

Goal

The goal for this course is that the students demonstrate metacognition (an awareness and understanding of your own thought processes) about the place and function of drama and performance in society.

Objectives

By the end of the course students will be able to:

- articulate the import of drama in education;
- connect drama to multiple forms of expressing and receiving experiences, ideas, and feelings;
- know the basic terms, skills, philosophies, and methodologies for leading drama sessions;
- articulate the difference and similarities between the drama methodologies offered in the course;
- connect the use of drama with current brain-based research;
- demonstrate ability to design, implement, and evaluate activities and lesson plans with sound objectives and goals;
- make connections between community-based and school-based drama in theory and practice.

These objectives can only be met if you are thoroughly prepared for each class, fully participate in all class activities, fulfill your assignments, and thoughtfully reflect on your personal progress.

Course organization

During the first three weeks you will be exposed to a variety of methodologies to prepare you for the design, implementation, and evaluation of the drama activities and sessions with your peers and lab participants. After the first three weeks one class per week will be devoted to labs designed by the students in pairs.

Assignments and grading

This course has some whole class assignments, some group assignments, and some individual assignments. It is the *student's responsibility* to keep track of due dates, presentations, and meetings with the instructor.

(1) Class participation and reflection journals

Class attendance, punctuality, and active *participation* in activities during regular classes and labs are required to support your peers and get the full benefits of the class demonstrations. At the end of each class you will write a one-page entry in your journal in which you will be asked to reflect on the class or lab experience of that day. Journals will be collected after each class.

Your journal

- Bring a blue book.
- Reflect on the work done (e.g. record an insight you had, something you learned, something that caught your interest).

(2) Readings/discussions

Assigned readings will be discussed in each class. Often you will be asked to identify major points in writing beforehand. You will be graded on participation in and contributions to the discussions, and on depth of observations in writing.

(3) Starters

During the first weeks you will lead a *starter activity* assigned by the instructor *or* a starter activity of your choice to be approved by the instructor. You will adapt this activity to an intended age group of your choice, identify the possible objectives of the activity, and explain briefly how this activity might fit into a broader lesson plan. A *detailed description*, including the above, will be handed in to the instructor. A *self-evaluation* is due one week after presentation.

Description

- Provide your name, name of the starter, and the date you conducted the activity.
- Identify the target age group for the activity.

- State the purpose of the activity.
- List the materials needed for the activity.
- Describe the procedure.
- Give some suggestions on how you might fit this activity into a broader lesson plan.

Note: Do not copy directly from the book. Use your imagination and present your own interpretation of this activity.

Self-evaluation

- Provide your name, name of the starter, and the date you conducted the activity.
  Answer ALL of the following questions (3–5 sentences each):
  - Did you present all information clearly?
  - Were your objectives clear?
  - Were your transitions smooth?
  - Did you ask appropriate and open-ended questions?
  - Did you monitor and sidecoach effectively?
  - Was your pacing appropriate for the activity?
  - What did you learn from the activity and what would you do differently if you could do it again with the same type of group?

(4) *Text report*

You will write a *text report* on a book from the resource list in your course book. Text reports are due two weeks before you lead your lab. Text reports will be discussed in class.

Format

- Name, date of text report, and date you will lead your lab.
- Provide full bibliographical information on the text (author, title, publisher, publication, date).
- Give a general overview of the content.
- Briefly summarize one chapter.
- Discuss the material from this chapter in regard to a population of your choice.
- Describe your personal reaction to the text (Do you agree/disagree with the writer's approach to drama? Why? Was it an insightful or significant work for you? Why? How is the text of value to you?).

A text report should be 2–3 pages, typed, double spaced.

(5) Lab session

For your *lab* you will, in pairs, design, implement, and evaluate a one-hour drama session. This session will be accompanied by a *detailed lesson plan*, including goals, objectives, procedures, and reflection questions. This lesson plan will be distributed and explained to the class during the class period prior to the lab. Lab leaders need to be prepared to justify their choices with sound ethical and pedagogical justifications. The lab will be evaluated in discussion and writing immediately after the lab class. An *extended self-evaluation* is due one week after presentation.

Note: Each pair should confer with their instructor during office hours one week prior to their lab and present a typed draft of their lesson plan.

Self-evaluation

- Provide your name, name of the story, and the date you conducted the drama.
  Answer ALL of the following questions:
  - How effective was the preparation process (division of labor, research, consensus/disagreement?)
  - Did you present all information clearly?
  - What were the variables that contributed to the participants' effective/ineffective work?
  - Were your objectives clear? Were they met?
  - Were your transitions smooth?
  - Did you ask appropriate and open-ended questions?
  - Did you monitor and sidecoach effectively?
  - Was your pacing appropriate for the activity?
  - What were some of the emotions you experienced as a leader during the session and what generated them? (Discuss both positive and negative feelings.)
  - How was your drama linked to inclusion and diversity in theory, practice, and/or pedagogy?
  - How effectively did the reflection time link the lesson's goals and objectives to the children's lives?
  - What did you learn from the activity, and what would you do differently if you could do it again with the same type of group?

(6) Lab observation

You will hand in one *lab observation* of a lab led by your peers. Lab observations are due one week after observation.

Guidelines

- Provide your name, the names of the leaders, the title and date of the lab you observed.

  Answer ALL of the following questions (3–5 sentences each):
  - Were the objectives clear?
  - Was all the material clearly presented?
  - Were the directions effective?
  - Was the main idea, conflict/tension of the drama clear?
  - Were the transitions smooth?
  - Did the leaders monitor and sidecoach effectively?
  - Was the pacing appropriate for this activity?
  - What were the variables that contributed to effective/ineffective work?
  - At what point in the drama do you think your "buddy" was focused or engaged? Unfocused or disengaged? Why?
  - How was this drama linked to inclusion and diversity in theory, practice, and/or pedagogy?
  - How effectively did the reflection time link the lesson's goals and objectives to the children's lives?
  - What would you do differently if you taught this lesson? (What could be added or deleted?)

(7) *Drama for Social Justice*

In the final weeks you will, in small groups, design, lead, and evaluate a 50-minute session that addresses issues of race, class, gender, sexual orientation, ableism, or another relevant topic to be discussed with your instructor. The lesson should be an original drama, and may include any of the drama strategies or methodologies learned in class. This activity will be accompanied by a *detailed lesson plan*, including goals, objectives, procedures and evaluation strategies, for all class members. Groups need to be prepared to justify their choices of activities in reflection, backed up by texts used. A *self-evaluation* is due one week after the presentation.

Self- evaluation

- Provide your name, topic/diversity addressed, and the date you conducted the drama.

  Answer ALL of the following questions (3-5 sentences each):
  - How effective was the preparation process (division of material, research, consensus/disagreement)?
  - What was effective/ineffective? Why? (Be specific!)
  - How was this drama linked to inclusion and diversity in theory, practice, and/or pedagogy?

     ○   What did you learn from the activity, and what would you do differently if you could do it again with the same type of group?

(8) Final in-class reflection paper

In a *final reflection paper* you will reflect on your own progress, incorporating previous reflections (*with references*), the readings (*with references*), and other learning experiences you had during this class.

Sample questions for final reflection may include:

- What have you learned in class and how and why have your attitudes about the role of drama in education and community work been changed or reinforced?
- What is the connection of drama with embodied learning and brain-based research and why is it important to be aware of this?
- Pick a topic and compare and contrast two different methodologies you learned in class to work with this topic. Include objectives, and reflection. Which method suits your teaching style best?
- What is the connection between community-based and school-based drama?
- How were you affected by our labs with the children and the progress (or lack thereof) you saw the children make?
- How could drama contribute to inclusion and diversity in theory, practice, and/or pedagogy?
- How do you intend to incorporate drama in your own teaching situation?

(9) Improvement as evidenced in portfolio

In accordance with the goal, objectives and philosophy of this course, your final grade will be partly based on how much *improvement* you've made over the semester with regard to:

- your metacognition of the place and function of drama and performance in society;
- your understanding of the connection between the theory and practical methods offered in the course;
- your ability to apply concepts and methods and demonstrate effective leadership skills.

For portfolio assessment you will hand in all your assignments in a *portfolio* on the day of class before the final reflection.

(10) TBA

This assignment is open and will be determined by the instructor of the class.

Sample Course Schedule

This schedule is based on sixteen students per class. The "labs" are drama lessons with elementary school children from the local community.

Week 1

Intro to course
Syllabus, assignments, calendar.
What is "drama"? Ice breakers, ensemble, concentration, trust activities.

Drama for all children; theories of teaching and learning
Linear, process, and hybrid drama.
A sample linear drama lesson.
Sign up for starters and lab dates with a partner.
  Assignments due:
• Textbook Chapter 1
• Background Information sheet.

Week 2

Getting Started on a Drama Lesson: The Basics
Storytelling/Storydrama.
  Assignments due:
• Two starters
• Textbook Chapter 2: "Linear Drama."

Process/Holistic/Educational drama
A process drama lesson.
  Assignments due:
• Two starters
• Text Chapter 2: "Taro Urashima" lessons.

Week 3

Hybrid Drama
  Assignments due:
• Two starters
• Text Chapter 2: "Process-oriented and hybrid methods."

Hybrid Drama continued
   Assignments due:
- Two starters
- Text Chapter 2.

Week 4

Drama for Social Justice
   Prep lab 1.
   Assignments due:
- Two starters
- Chapter 3 through "Forum Theatre."

LAB 1 (Instructor)

Week 5

Lab preparations
   Prep lab 2.
   Assignments due:
- Six starters
- Materials, ideas, and research for labs.

LAB 2 (Instructor)

Week 6

Drama for Social Justice
   Prep lab 3.
   Assignments due:
- Chapter 3
- Lesson plan lab 3.

LAB 3

Week 7

Performance Art
   Prep lab 4.
   Assignments due:
- Chapter 4 through "Using Performance Art"
- Lesson plan lab 4.

LAB 4

Week 8

Performance Art continued
    Prep lab 5.
    Assignments due:
- Chapter 4
- Lesson plan lab 5.

LAB 5

Week 9

Prep Drama for Social Justice Labs
    Prep lab 6.
    Assignments due:
- Chapter 5 through "Choosing an Assessment Methodology"
- Lesson plan lab 6
- Materials, ideas, research for dramas all groups.

LAB 6

Week 10

Drama for Social Justice Group 1
    Prep lab 7.
    Assignments due:
- Chapter 5
- Lesson plan lab 7.

LAB 7

Week 11

Drama for Social Justice Group 2
    Prep lab 8.
    Assignments due:
- Chapter 6 through "Know Your Audience"
- Lesson plan lab 8.

LAB 8

Week 12

Drama for Social Justice Group 3
    Prep lab 7.
    Assignments due:
- Chapter 6
- Lesson plan lab 9.

LAB 9

Week 13

Drama for Social Justice Group 4
　　Prep lab 10.
　　Assignments due:
• 　Lesson plan lab 10.

LAB 10

Week 14

Catch Up and Portfolio Prep
　　Assignments due:
• 　Appendices
• 　Portfolios.

Final Reflection.

Index

Page numbers in **bold** indicate tables and in *italics* indicate figures.